FRANKLIN D. ROOSEVELT AS GOVERNOR OF NEW YORK

NUMBER 585
COLUMBIA STUDIES IN THE SOCIAL SCIENCES
EDITED BY
THE FACULTY OF POLITICAL SCIENCE
OF COLUMBIA UNIVERSITY

FRANKLIN D. ROOSEVELT

AS

GOVERNOR

OF NEW YORK

By BERNARD BELLUSH

NEW YORK 1955

COLUMBIA UNIVERSITY PRESS

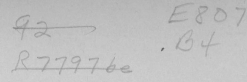

The Columbia Studies in the Social Sciences (formerly the Studies in History, Economics, and Public Law) is a series edited by the Faculty of Political Science of Columbia University and published by Columbia University Press for the purpose of making available scholarly studies produced within the Faculty.

For Jewel

ACKNOWLEDGMENTS

SINCE the start of my research I have had the benefit of the warm and friendly guidance of Allan Nevins. For fatherly advice I was always able to turn to my mentor, Harry J. Carman. Mr. Herman Kahn, Director of the Franklin D. Roosevelt Library at Hyde Park, gave me much of his time and made available the wholehearted cooperation of his able staff. Thanks go to the custodial and maintenance men and women of the Roosevelt Library and mansion, who made the many months spent at Hyde Park, away from my wife, livable and pleasant. Basil Rauch deserves much credit for his incisive and challenging comments. To the Baker Library at Dartmouth College— truly a scholar's haven—are due my heartfelt thanks for three wonderful summers spent in preparation of this final work. Richard B. Morris was more than patient and understanding in reading and commenting on the manuscript.

Thanks are due to Howard S. Cullman, Felix Frankfurter, Herbert H. Lehman, Henry Morgenthau, Jr., and Samuel Rosenman for permission to quote from their letters. Also, I am grateful to Random House for permission to quote from *Public Papers and Addresses of Franklin D. Roosevelt*, Volume I, and to Harper and Bros. for permission to quote from Eleanor Roosevelt, *This I Remember*.

Above all, to Frank Freidel I shall always be indebted, for he gave me the confidence and assurance needed at crucial periods, in addition to invaluable criticisms and suggestions. Jewel Bellush, with her interdisciplinary background in history and political science, was ever present to suggest, to counsel, and to threaten, in hope that this might be a competent work. Whatever shortcomings remain are mine alone.

BERNARD BELLUSH

The City College, New York
December, 1954

CONTENTS

INTRODUCTION

When I began this work, I hoped to analyze a few major contributions of a public servant during four tumultuous years as Governor of the Empire State. It was my early impression that Frankin D. Roosevelt was not a great Governor, not to be placed in the same category with his predecessor, Alfred E. Smith. I originally believed, as many do today, that Governor Roosevelt did not exhibit any unusual executive or administrative abilities, or possess a social or economic program which would have suggested the bold leadership of his presidential administrations. As late as January, 1932, the renowned journalist Walter Lippmann characterized Roosevelt as lacking a firm grasp of public affairs and being without strong convictions. He is, said Lippmann, "an amiable man with many philanthropic impulses, but he is not the dangerous enemy of anything . . . for F.D.R. is no crusader. He is no tribune of the people. He is no enemy of entrenched privilege. He is a pleasant man who, without any important qualifications for the office, would very much like to be President."[1]

After much labor in Franklin D. Roosevelt's personal files at Hyde Park, and in the official records of New York State, I have strengthened my original conclusion that Roosevelt did not make the same crusading impact on New York's social, economic, and political history that Al Smith made.

There are those historians who still contend that Roosevelt did not have a program when he became President of the United States, other than the reform program which he had inherited from Al Smith. As proof they cite some of Roosevelt's glittering generalities during the 1932 presidential race. Too often, American voters appear satisfied with candidates who speak in glowing and optimistic metaphors, a situation especially noticeable in 1932 when Roosevelt conveyed a feeling of greater assuredness and confidence in the future than did Herbert Hoover.

Despite campaign talk, which may at times serve as a superficial guide to the thoughts and objectives of a candidate, Roosevelt had already formulated the basis for a program when he campaigned for the presidency in 1932. Many of the New Deal seedlings which did not flower under Governor Smith blossomed forth during Franklin D. Roosevelt's two terms as Governor. His timing of decisive political acts, his lucid education of the public, his able handling of obstructionist Republican majorities in the State legislature and of a divisive and corrupt Tammany Hall in New York City showed unusual executive ability and political acumen. When comparing Roosevelt's legislative goals as Governor with his domestic program as President, one notes, more often than not, a striking, logical development.

Franklin D. Roosevelt viewed the governorship as the last steppingstone to the presidency. With the advent of the terrible depression late in 1929, Louis Howe and Roosevelt knew that their goal was close at hand. Both sought to avoid developments which might alienate important individuals or groups across the nation. Many were the occasions when Roosevelt, in contrast to other presidential hopefuls, liberal spokesmen, and his successor in Albany, abstained from public commitments on national and international controversies.

How then shall we judge Roosevelt's governorship? Shall we gauge his administration solely by comparing his executive and administrative achievements with those of his predecessors and successors? Or shall we view him in the light of his expectations and planning for higher office, using therefore a different measuring rod with which to judge his activities, or lack of them in certain instances?

To appreciate fully the role of Franklin D. Roosevelt as Governor, however, much must yet be written by political scientists, sociologists, psychologists, and others in the social sciences.

Equally as important is the great need for a comprehensive work on Alfred E. Smith as four-time Governor of New York State.

FRANKLIN D. ROOSEVELT AS GOVERNOR OF NEW YORK

I

A NEW GOVERNOR

THE SNOWSTORM in Albany had changed to gray rain and sleet by noon, that first day in January, 1929. A tall, handsome, composed but crippled forty-six-year-old New Yorker tediously plodded his way to the podium of the Assembly Chamber in the State Capitol Building. With his left hand on the Bible, which had been in his family for over 200 years, Franklin Delano Roosevelt took the oath of office as the forty-eighth Governor of the State of New York. Eight months later the all-encompassing stock market crash thrust Roosevelt before the eyes of the nation and enabled him, by 1933, to pursue on the national scene the objectives he had sought as Governor of the Empire State.

While exercising his enervated legs in sun-baked Georgia four months before his inauguration as New York's Chief Executive, Roosevelt had not harbored the slightest thought that he would soon be succeeding the beloved Al Smith as Governor. Despite his vigorous devotion to the fascinating game of practical politics, infantile paralysis in 1921 had all but ended Roosevelt's ardent participation in elective contests. Eight years later some people still doubted this man's ability to carry on his shoulders the burden of the greatest state in the Union. The fact that Roosevelt was selected by the people of New York in 1928 to sit in the Governor's chair, and again in 1930, was in part a tribute to those who refuse to be overwhelmed by physical setbacks, and to those with everlasting faith in the handicapped.[1]

By 1929, Franklin Roosevelt had garnered many lucrative years of political service. Behind him lay eighteen crowded years as

Democratic State legislator, Assistant Secretary of the Navy, vice-presidential nominee, and active party leader.

By entering the contest for the State Senatorship from the Republican-dominated Hyde Park area in 1910, Roosevelt clearly indicated that his major interests were politics and public service, not law. His energetic, unorthodox, yet successful campaign offered a preview of future contests in which he would confound his foes and force from them reluctant praise. His opposition to William F. Sheehan, Tammany's designee for selection by the State legislature as United States Senator in 1911, illustrated a fundamental distrust of boss rule, though practical politics would later decree his cooperation with these same party bosses. His progressivism at first was restricted to supporting woman suffrage, the direct election of United States Senators, and direct primaries. As he matured politically he pushed for the enactment of social welfare legislation. His opposition to the indiscriminate disposal of State water power sites to the Aluminum Company of America foreshadowed his later demands for stricter regulation of utilities and for State ownership and development of water power sites. He gave clear evidence of his progressive leanings within the Democratic party by his early avowed support of Woodrow Wilson for the presidential nomination in 1912, and by his unsuccessful primary contest against a Tammany designee for the United States Senate in 1914.

His administrative experiences as Assistant Secretary of the Navy insured a stable foundation for his governorship and for the presidency. His contact with spokesmen of organized labor, and with laboring men and women, enlarged his scope of understanding of our social and economic system. It was also during this period that he came under the direct influence of proponents of social welfare legislation.[2]

Roosevelt's very strenuous campaign for the vice-presidency in 1920, in which he strongly defended Wilson's League of Nations, indicated his basic understanding of the international responsibilities the United States had to assume after World War I.

Through dint of courage and perseverance Franklin D. Roosevelt found himself, within seven years of his tragic bout with infantile paralysis, in the forefront of Democratic politics. By 1928, he was in a position to decline the chairmanship of the National Democratic Committee. The normal, healthy outlook which by determined efforts Eleanor Roosevelt and Louis Howe tried to reinstill in him was evident within one year of the tragedy when Roosevelt vigorously and successfully opposed the attempt of William Randolph Hearst to capture the Democratic gubernatorial nomination.[3]

Roosevelt's understanding of social and economic forces in America was broadened during his period of convalescence by discussions with responsible men and women from all walks of life. Though his choice for the party's presidential candidate in 1924 was rejected by a convention overshadowed by the Ku Klux Klan issue, his Happy Warrior address thrust him once more into the national political cauldron.

Following his party's defeat, and the eclipse of LaFollette's Progressive party in 1924, Roosevelt acknowledged the constructive role played by progressive minority parties on the American scene. Although at first hesitant, Roosevelt eventually agreed that admittance of LaFollette progressives would strengthen the liberal forces in the Democratic party.[4] Subsequent to the 1924 defeat, Roosevelt polled party leaders in an attempt to strengthen the national organization. In the process he gained intimate knowledge of respective local conditions in the Democracy and furthered his contacts with those who would do much to sway the necessary two thirds of national convention delegates in 1932.

Between national conventions Roosevelt persisted in defending the "progressivism" of Southern Democracy.[5] This illustrated his practical approach to politics, for he fully realized that a national Democratic victory was impossible without the combined vote of the rural South, the urban North, and the Far West.[6]

This period also witnessed Roosevelt's persistent, unequivocating, and courageous opposition to bigotry and religious and racial discrimination which he would display throughout his life, with one major exception. The miscarriage of justice which he permitted was the treatment accorded the Japanese residents on the West Coast immediately after December 7, 1941.

Since 1918, Al Smith's personality had dominated New York State politics, in particular the Democratic party. The Happy Warrior had neglected to develop any potentially strong successors. Faced with the loss of their most effective vote-getter, who was the party's presidential nominee, the State organization desperately sought a candidate acceptable to both urban and rural voters. According to these Democratic leaders, essential prerequisites of a winning candidate in 1928 included a record of public service, strong upstate following, a pleasing personality, ability to stump the state and sway listeners, and a straddling position on prohibition. To insure the "proper" religious balance, many party leaders felt it essential that their gubernatorial nominee be a Protestant. Contemplating possible Southern defections, Smith and party chieftains realized that without New York's forty-seven electoral votes they stood little chance of winning the presidency.

In early September, Governor Smith and party leaders were seriously considering Owen D. Young, Franklin D. Roosevelt, Senator Robert F. Wagner, and Herbert H. Lehman for the nomination. The first three had expressed no desire to succeed Smith, with Roosevelt emphasizing that he did "not wish to impede the recovery of his health."[7]

The New York *World*, which had been sympathetic to the Smith administrations, endorsed Roosevelt on the eve of the Democratic State Convention. On September 28, it suggested to convention delegates that the office seek the candidate. In an obvious reference to Lehman's candidacy, it urged that the nomination be given to a man of State-wide reputation who was identified not by his religion but by his capacities to carry on the policies of Governor Smith.

Because Franklin Roosevelt is both an outstanding man of character and ability and comes from upstate he would probably be the strongest candidate to run this year, when Governor Smith, a New York City man, is running for the presidency. It is stated because he is not in robust health Mr. Roosevelt does not wish the nomination. Leading Democrats hope he will reverse his decision, and so far as the vote of the Jewish citizen of Greater New York is concerned, they believe that every man and woman voting for Governor Smith will vote for Franklin Roosevelt, who has so ably championed the Governor for a number of years.[8]

Several upstate leaders, including youthful James A. Farley of Rockland County, urged Roosevelt to reconsider and accept the nomination. But Roosevelt remained adamant. Before leaving for Warm Springs earlier that month he had informed party chieftains that he planned to devote all his energies to restoring his health. He neglected to voice publicly the possibilities of Democratic defeat in 1928.

Meeting in Syracuse on the 29th of September, the Republican State Convention had adopted a platform with no direct mention of prohibition, the overriding issue of the day. It was filled, instead, with bitter invectives against "Democratic misrule" at Albany under Governor Smith. State Attorney General Albert Ottinger of New York City commanded the top of the State ticket, along with Alanson B. Houghton for the United States Senate. Harmony prevailed at the convention, for the enthusiastic orators devoted their lively speeches to condemning the "waste and inefficiency" of the Smith administration.[9] In contrast to the Democratic camp, the Republicans found that their choices had been designated long before the convention met in Syracuse. As the Republican *Herald Tribune* described it:

H. Edmund Machold, State Chairman, Charles D. Hilles, national committeeman, and a half dozen outstanding regional Republican leaders had come . . . to Syracuse to complete their plans in the routine manner for the nomination of the candidates for United States Senator and Governor, whom they selected three months ago on the way home from the Republican National Convention in Kansas City.[10]

The convention ratified the slate with the slogan, "Over the Road to Washington Tammany Shall Not Pass."

Arriving on the Democratic convention scene in Rochester a few days later from a western campaign tour, Al Smith was handed a telegram from Roosevelt in Warm Springs, Georgia. The wire reaffirmed Roosevelt's refusal to run for reasons of health and because of his belief that Smith would win New York State irrespective of the gubernatorial nominee.[11]

The final decision could no longer be put off. But whom would the Democratic leaders select as their candidate? After two lengthy meetings in the inevitable smoke-filled room, Al Smith and party chieftains concluded that the strongest man to help win New York was Franklin D. Roosevelt.[12]

Following this decision Smith sought, unsuccessfully, to contact Roosevelt by phone, for the latter was aware of the Governor's objective and avoided all calls that day. Not until Eleanor Roosevelt put through a personal call, at Smith's request, did her husband answer the phone. Mrs. Roosevelt then handed the telephone to the Governor and left immediately to catch a train for New York City. Smith informed Roosevelt that the convention had reached a stalemate and that no candidate, other than he, would be acceptable to party leaders. Smith made it clear that without his acceptance defeat was imminent, not only for the State ticket, but in all probability for the national ticket as well.[13] In the hushed hotel room with Smith hovered National Democratic Chairman John J Raskob, Dr. Henry Moskowitz, and Herbert Lehman.[14] Smith went on to assure Roosevelt that Lehman, the choice for Lieutenant Governor, would shoulder the bulk of the gubernatorial burden, enabling Roosevelt to continue his extended visits to Warm Springs.

Raskob, a man of great wealth, took the phone when Roosevelt referred to his financial obligations to help expand facilities for the infantile paralysis patients seeking treatment at Warm Springs. Informed that "it would take a couple of hundred thousand dollars" to finance the venture, Raskob assured Roosevelt that he "would assist in getting the money and promised $50,000 himself."[15]

Smith returned to the phone and finally asked Roosevelt what he would do if the convention decided to draft him? After great hesitation Roosevelt felt there was nothing he could do but tell Governor Smith, ". . . not that I would allow the use of my name before the convention, but . . . if, in the final analysis the convention insisted on nominating me, I should feel under definite obligation to accept the nomination."[16]

Why did Roosevelt, in the light of continued "Republican" prosperity, risk his political future in a campaign which he knew would be extremely hazardous, if not fatal, for Democrats? In addition, a Roosevelt victory might well write finis to his struggles to regain the use of his legs, for State Executive responsibilities would keep him away from healing Warm Springs much of the year. Though crippled, Roosevelt was not one to permit others to assume his official responsibilities.

Roosevelt could have been lukewarm during the 1928 campaign, like a great many other Democrats, or he could have announced his support of Smith and then left the work to others. As James A. Farley described it nine years later: "The mere fact that he had placed his stamp of approval on a member of Tammany Hall had a tremendous effect on producing good will for the Happy Warrior around the country."[17]

Since 1918, when he buried the hatchet with Tammany Hall, Roosevelt's respect and admiration for Governor Smith had steadily increased. Yet they never became warm friends, because of their varied personal tastes and social acquaintances. Despite Smith's Tammany background, Roosevelt came to view him as New York's greatest Governor. Roosevelt had seconded Smith's nomination for the presidency in 1920. Four years later, and again in 1928, he brought the national Democratic conventions to great heights with his nominating orations for the Happy Warrior. Roosevelt's loyalty constrained him to do his utmost for Smith, even though he and Louis Howe did not believe that the Happy Warrior, nor any Democrat, could win the presidency in 1928. A decisive national victory for Herbert Hoover could easily mean defeat for the Democratic State ticket in New York. If Roosevelt was rejected at the polls his presidential aspirations might be permanently sidetracked.

On the other hand, Smith had won New York in 1924 despite a smashing national Republican victory. Roosevelt knew he would have the support of the Democracy in New York City and in other urban centers. He had a strong upstate following, because of his known independence of Tammany Hall—whose methods repelled most of the state's farmers—and because of his rural background. If elected Governor, Roosevelt's national stature would increase tremendously; and should "Republican" prosperity collapse in the interim, the presidential nomination, and election, would be within grasp.

In Warm Springs, Georgia, Roosevelt made the most crucial decision of his mature political life when he permitted himself to be drafted for the Governor's race in 1928, over the vigorous opposition of his political mentor, Louis Howe.

Shortly after the Democratic State convention reconvened on October 2, one and one-half hours behind schedule, Mayor James J. Walker of New York City strode to the podium and with oratorical fervor presented the name of Franklin D. Roosevelt as the nominee for Governor. The exhausted delegates quickly endorsed him and the accompanying slate: Royal S. Copeland, of Rockland County, for re-election to the United States Senate; Herbert H. Lehman, of New York City, for Lieutenant Governor; Morris S. Tremaine, of Erie County, for Controller; and Albert Conway, of Kings County, for Attorney General.

The Democratic platform condemned the Republicans while lauding the achievements of the Smith administrations. The power plank charged that the "water power buccaneers" had made their "agent," H. Edmund Machold, Republican State Chairman,[18] and contended that only the vigilance of Governor Smith had prevented the State Water Power Commission, of which Attorney General Ottinger had been a member, from taking from the people vast power rights on the St. Lawrence River.

The platform went on to list a series of pledges which promised continued support of all agricultural educational facilities; a commission of experts to study distribution problems; a scientific study of farm assessment and the tax situation by an impartial body; and support of cooperative marketing agencies. The party proposed legislation to guarantee perpetual ownership and control by the State of water power resources, and a complete State-wide park and parkway system. On reorganization of the State government, the platform demanded a four-year term for the Governor, with election in even-numbered years when the President was not being elected; biennial sessions of the State legislature; and election of State Senators for four years and State Assemblymen for two years.

On labor, the Democracy urged an eight-hour day and forty-eight-hour week for women and children in industry; consideration of old age pensions; an advisory minimum wage board for women and children; extension of workmen's compensation to include all occupational diseases; prohibition of the granting of a temporary injunction in industrial disputes without notice of a hearing; and provision that alleged violations of an injunction be tried before a jury.

The platform urged restoration of direct primaries for all State elective offices; the limitation of campaign expenditures; and the publication of campaign receipts before and after election.

Finally, on prohibition, the Democrats suggested that the respective states determine what is, and what is not, intoxicating, and characterized their party as the unequivocal friend of law and order and believer in rigorous and impartial enforcement of "every provision of the Federal and State Constitutions."[19]

General reaction to the Roosevelt nomination was unusually favorable. Edsel Ford wired Roosevelt that he was "greatly pleased to hear of your selection for Governor. I know what a great personal sacrifice that means to you."[20] From mid-Atlantic, Samuel Seabury wired, "Happy Congratulations and best wishes for success." [21] In New York, Frances Perkins wrote the nominee:

Your nomination and acceptance are in the great tradition of Plato —the best of our citizens serving the State at personal sacrifice and for no glory but that of the State. It is a long time since American political life has produced such a situation—and your election, which is certain, will bring a wholesome uplifting quality to our political life. We shall be a better people because of your sacrifice.[22]

The independent New York *World*, edited by Walter Lippmann, maintained that the office had sought the man and expressed the hope that this signal tribute by the Democratic convention would compensate Roosevelt for the sacrifice he was about to make, for the Democrats had found the ideal candidate. For years he had been actively identified with the affairs of the State, as a distinguished legislator and executive. He was a man above reproach and above the squalor of the struggle.[23]

Embarrassed by a Democratic nominee free of Tammany taint, Republican reaction added little to the stature of their own candidate. Frustrated by Roosevelt's seemingly invulnerable record, they could only lament the Democratic decision to burden a crippled man with an exhausting political campaign and, perhaps, the arduous duties of the Governor's office. They accused the Democratic party of disregarding the man's health for purely selfish motives. The Republican *Herald Tribune* managed to comment that the nomination was as unfair to Roosevelt as it was to the people of the State who, under other conditions, would have welcomed his candidacy for any office.[24]

Continuing references to Roosevelt's physical handicap so infuriated Governor Smith that on one occasion he blurted out that the Governor did not have to be an acrobat.[25] To an inquiring reporter Smith elaborated, stating:

Frank Roosevelt today is mentally as good as he ever was in his life. Physically he is as good as he ever was in his life. His whole trouble is in his lack of muscular control of his lower limbs. . . . We do not elect him for his ability to do a double back flip or hand spring. The work of the Governorship is brain work. Ninety-five per cent of it is accomplished sitting at a desk. There is no doubt about his ability to do it.[26]

An unusual number of independent newspapers and columnists endorsed the Roosevelt candidacy, including the New York *Telegram* and the New York *Sun,* which were supporting Herbert Hoover for President. According to one newspaper, Roosevelt was "one in a million" among men in political life.[27]

While Roosevelt and Smith planned strategy for the New York campaign during the second week in October, the American people were busy discussing the fabulous stock market and the remarkable New York Yankees who had just captured the 1928 baseball world series in four straight games. At the same time no one seemed to care about an election in which the Chinese people selected Chiang Kai-shek as their president.[28]

That same month General Motors recorded the highest earnings for one quarter ever shown by an industrial company in peace time.[29] Charles M. Schwab, Chairman of the Bethlehem Steel Corporation, told the Iron and Steel Institute that business was approaching unprecedented activity and forecast greater prosperity for all industries in the months ahead.[30]

Democrats, generally, felt they had little to criticize concerning "Republican" prosperity. A minority party, as is more often the case in American politics, and too few independent voices, had the courage to attack the usually meaningless slogans of the major parties. Norman Thomas, Socialist candidate for President in 1928, reprobated "Republican" prosperity for permitting thousands of sharecroppers to live in abject poverty, if not in virtual slavery. Earlier in 1928 a few sober voices had begun warning the country of a depression which was subverting the Southwest, a development completely ignored by most of the nation's press. As one of these lone voices, Norman Thomas had pointed to homeless families drifting aimlessly over the countryside in battered cars, searching for jobs, homes, and food.[31] He warned of an approaching economic crisis and of growing job scarcity in some regions. Paradoxically, unemployment continued to mount as big business profits rose to new peaks.[32]

From the Pacific Coast, Los Angeles trade unions reported 70,000 men unemployed, and San Francisco noted the same number. An army of unemployed numbering 60,000 was reported by the Central Labor Union of Boston. In Baltimore they were estimated at 75,000. Socialist periodicals quoted the Labor Department in Washington to the effect that the nation's unemployed totaled some 3,500,000.[33] A survey of the situation in the Empire State by Industrial Commissioner James A. Hamilton verified that New York was also badly hit. His report indicated "an extensive amount of unemployment, and that serious distress has been caused. . . . One has to go back to 1921 to find an employment situation rivalling the present." [34]

Prohibition, however, remained a more stimulating subject, generating more heat and emotion than logic and reason. Before the conclusion of the campaign, however, Herbert Hoover was to hurl charges of "State Socialism" against the Happy Warrior. Religion, injected as a paramount issue, inverted American sportsmanship and produced one of the most degrading contests in our nation's history.

While the Republican party stressed the need for state implementation of national dry laws, Roosevelt opposed all attempts to revive the Mullen-Gage Act, a New York dry law repealed under Governor Smith. Pointing to Georgia, where Federal and state legislation outlawed alcoholic drinking, Roosevelt contended there were more crimes and misdemeanors in that state due to drunkenness than in New York, which had no local statutes supplementing Federal legislation. On the same day Roosevelt stated this view, a position which confused many before the campaign's conclusion, twenty-one persons died from poisoned liquor served within a twenty-four-hour period in New York City.[35]

Albert Ottinger, the Republican candidate for Governor,

had first appeared in politics as a Republican district leader in New York City. He refused to support John Purroy Mitchell for Mayor in 1913, contending that the latter was too radical for him, "an imitation Socialist" who supported progressive principles. The year before he had denounced the principles of Rooseveltian progressivism as those which "make ultimately for bloodshed, revolution and destruction of government and the Constitution itself."[36] He was elected to the State Senate in 1916 for a brief period, where he did much good according to the Citizens Union, but his reactionary attitude on fundamentals firmly identified him with a group of standpat Republicans. After a few years as Assistant to United States Attorney General Harry M. Daugherty in Washington, Ottinger successfully ran for State Attorney General in 1924 and again in 1926.

The campaign techniques of Ottinger were small-scale models of the national Republican effort. Thousands of billboards and throwaways screamed that Republican Presidents Harding and Coolidge had brought prosperity to the nation. The Republican administrations alone were responsible for a chicken in every pot and a car in every garage. Though Ottinger would persistently denounce the Democratic party in New York as corrupt and graft-ridden, he could not make these charges stick to his Democratic opponent.

The Republicans helped insure their continued loss of the governorship when they selected Ottinger, for he was not a formidable campaigner. In contrast to a progressive, enlightened, and vibrant Roosevelt, Ottinger was an arch-conservative who endorsed a high tariff, private enterprise with a minimum of public interference, a war on crime and graft, the abolition of the personal income tax, and the continuation of "Republican" prosperity. He straddled the prohibition issue, alienating many drys and wets.[37]

The campaign started in earnest on October 15, when Ottinger made his acceptance speech at New York City's Hotel Astor. He supported private development of the State's water power resources, as opposed to public ownership. He promised a reduction of real property tax, which he contended made up from 75 to 85 percent of the State's wealth. Finally, he recommended a policy of saving to be substituted for a policy of spending, and accepted the bond issue method of financing State improvements, as the will of the people.[38]

Officially accepting his gubernatorial nomination at the National Democratic Club in New York City, Roosevelt urged support of public development of power resources, a policy he sustained throughout his political career and which was culminated during his presidency with the Tennessee Valley Authority. He referred to his Republican opponent as

... a consistent advocate of private development, which is in accord with the program of his party. In his speech of acceptance he pledged himself if elected to the appointment of a commission of experts to investigate the entire subject and recommend a water power policy. This, too, is in accord with the stand taken by the Republicans in the legislature in their desire to stave off the carrying out of the Democratic policy of state development advocated by Governor Smith.[39]

Roosevelt urged modernization of the governmental machinery of counties and towns along lines suggested by the reorganization plan applied in the administrative branches of the State departments during Smith's administrations.

On October 17, the Democratic nominee set out on his first campaign tour in eight years. In contrast to 1920 there was hope for victory. Accompanied by Herbert H. Lehman, and youthful Samuel I. Rosenman, he ferried over to the Hoboken, New Jersey, terminus of the Erie Railroad. Their journey took them westward across the southern tier of strongly Republican counties, north to Buffalo, eastward along historic Mohawk Valley to Albany, and finally down the colorful Hudson Valley to New York City.

When Roosevelt stepped down from his train in Binghamton during his 1920 campaign for the vice-presidency, he was greeted by a handful of the party faithful. On reaching that community's Arlington Hotel he found a huge throng in the lobby, though none of them appeared to be facing him. They were all busy gathering about Babe Ruth and Madame Galli-Curci, the operatic star. A mere candidate for the vice-presidency of the United States remained unnoticed on the outskirts of the crowd.[40] In 1928, however, hundreds were at the Binghamton railroad station to greet Roosevelt when he arrived to make the first major address of his upstate campaign.[41] The people's interest in politics had been enormously aroused by the intensity of the presidential contest. Immense crowds flocked to meetings and shocked political experts by their outpouring on election day.

It was in Binghamton, in the heart of Ku Klux Klan country, that Roosevelt put aside his prepared address to lash out at the forces of intolerance which had begun a whispering campaign against Al Smith.[42] Before 2,500 enthusiasts who crowded the high school auditorium, the Democratic nominee assailed these bigots by asserting that "attacks on Smith's religion should be punished by deportation." [43] Roosevelt threw all caution to the winds before the thought of "this un-American, this vile thing that is hanging over our heads." [44]

Roosevelt's heated attack against Smith's "bigoted" enemies did not heighten the former's chances for victory. Immediately following Roosevelt's Binghamton address, Louis Howe sent the Democratic nominee a wire stating that his

Binghamton speech as reported in *Times* being twisted by Republicans as meaning that those who do not vote for Smith because of religious scruples should be deported. We have had several violent comebacks on this today including Congressman Jacobstein who is much disturbed. Belle [Moskowitz] suggests that religion now be dropped from campaign and that you take up one weak point at a time.[45]

At Buffalo, Samuel Rosenman received a wire from Maurice Bloch, Democratic minority leader in the State Assembly, advising him to "tell the candidate he is not running for President but for Governor: and tell him to stick to State issues." [46]

Roosevelt subsequently cushioned his remarks on the religious issue, but did not ignore it. The topics he later stressed were labor, farm problems, power, prohibition, and Smith's social-welfare program. Roosevelt's addresses became more simple, direct, and personal, as he and Rosenman adhered to Louis Howe's advice to emphasize one theme at a time.

It was at this stage of Roosevelt's political career that youthful, scholarly, and stable Samuel I. Rosenman, a former State Assemblyman, began to ply the Democratic nominee with facts and figures for his campaign addresses. That Rosenman accomplished his task with acumen, tact, and success is attested to by the increasingly important roles assigned him by Roosevelt in later years as speechmaker, Counsel to the Governor, and Justice of the State Supreme Court at the age of thirty-six. He subsequently resumed his role as speechmaker, but for a President of the United States.[47]

After two days of campaigning by train, Roosevelt decided to continue the rest of the way by car. He wanted to reach the smaller gatherings at crossroads and villages, as he had done in 1910 during his whirlwind campaign for the State Senate. It wasn't an easy task for a crippled candidate but Roosevelt never complained.

In Rochester, Ottinger stressed the need for the retention of high tariffs, claiming that they had insured the high wages maintained by the national Republican administrations. He told his audience that Herbert Hoover would present for America gigantic constructive programs. He praised President Coolidge's foreign policy and pledged farm surplus aid.[48] Within twenty-four hours Roosevelt informed a large gathering at Elmira that the tariff prosperity praised by his opponent existed only on paper. In Buffalo, Ottinger promised rehabilitation of the State Labor Department and an end to red tape, while listing the accomplishments of his office in enforcing workmen's compensation. He reminded the audience that his ruling as Attorney General had prevented some employers from utilizing an old statute for making women work nine hours a day.[49]

At Jamestown, the following day, Roosevelt pledged his party's efforts to raise the price of goods sold by the farmer, and to lower the cost of goods to the eventual consumer through cooperative marketing agencies. He decried the Coolidge administration as having enjoyed a "beauty sleep" and claimed it was now time to get down to work.[50]

Journeying north to Buffalo, Roosevelt once more underscored the religious issue in the campaign and his profound abhorrence of discrimination against religious minorities when he told his audience that he hoped he would not get a single vote because of the fact that his Republican opponent was of a different faith.[51] As a result of continued pressure from party headquarters, he informed the assembled throng that this was the last time he would mention religion. In Utica, that same day, the Republican candidate outlined his welfare program in which he promised State aid to those handicapped in the "struggle for well-being." [52]

Off to the dimly seen left, Norman Thomas predicted the defeat of Al Smith because of superior party organization and finances in the Republican camp. He warned liberals not to throw away their votes on either of the major parties, accusing them both of bigotry.[53] Progressivism that was humble enough to be content with the Smith and Roosevelt version was a progressivism where the crumbs went to the workers and the banquet to the owners. Thomas warned his listeners

. . . about the dangers of the false propaganda about the "New Tammany." . . . the list of our Tammany scandals in New York City as they have been exposed under the Walker administration is long and terrible not only in its cost in dollars but in human well-being. For this situation I must plainly say that Governor Smith, as Tammany's pet and darling, who gave us Walker, who appointed our blundering Public Service Commission, and vetoed most of the laws to make election frauds more difficult, cannot escape responsibility.[54]

On October 22, a huge throng of 22,000 followers crowded New York's Madison Square Garden to hear Herbert Hoover characterize Smith's policies as "State socialism." [55] At the

University of Syracuse, the following day, Norman Thomas scoffed at Hoover's charges when he stated that only the Socialist party could be accused of advocating government ownership of the means of production and distribution.[56] A day later, Roosevelt repudiated the charge of socialism in Watertown, saying that Hoover was in a panic and was seeing Red. At the same time he complimented the people of Watertown on the social betterment derived from their municipally-owned water power plant.[57]

In Utica, Roosevelt accused the Republicans of obstructing public improvements in the State. He endorsed Smith's stand on the dry law, denying that State prohibition enforcement acts had aided the effectiveness of prohibition and maintaining that it was strictly a Federal issue.[58] Ottinger, meanwhile, continued to stress prosperity as the biggest issue of the campaign, deeming it more important than personalities.[59]

In Schenectady, Roosevelt scored the ancient tax laws of the State and promised a survey of the tax system, looking toward a drastic revision under his administration. He further assailed Ottinger for making pledges without taking into account the amount of expenses involved.[60]

As Ottinger launched his final drive on Long Island, Roosevelt warned an audience in Albany that the election of his rival would be followed by long-term leases to private industry of State power sites. To newsmen, Roosevelt imparted the over-optimistic contention that he would break even upstate on election day. Publisher William Randolph Hearst, who was supporting Hoover in the presidential race, denounced Roosevelt for dragging religion into the campaign.[61]

A few days before the political contest drew to a close, the New York Stock Exchange announced its heaviest trading in any single month when it sold 9,984,445 shares. In Manhattan, Ottinger assailed his opponent for misrepresenting his stand on labor which he maintained had always been friendly and co-operative. Speaking in Queens County, Roosevelt insisted that the Smith program must be continued under a Democratic administration. He elaborated on his distrust of the Republican pledge on parks, and stressed his support of a Fair Wages Bill for women.[62] Before an overflow audience at Flushing High School, Roosevelt hammered away at Herbert Hoover's witch-hunting remarks the week previous. The Democrat recalled to his listeners that "Brother Hoover" had gotten into a panic and had called Smith a Socialist, and by that token Smith would be elected. Roosevelt went on to say, about Smith, that

. . . it is just "nuts" to him to be called a Socialist. He knows just what to do when he is called a Socialist, and he has got a mighty good answer, and it is a true answer. If his program is Socialistic, then we are all Socialists, and if his program for the reduction of hours of women and children is Socialistic, and if his program for public improvements for the hospitals of the State and the prisons of the State is Socialistic, we are all Socialists. And if his program for bettering health in this State, for his great aid to the educational program of the State, if they are Socialistic, we are Socialists and we are proud of the name.[63]

Seeking the support of the labor vote, which was nonexistent in an organized form in 1928, the Democratic nominee addressed a luncheon of the "Labor Committee for Roosevelt and Lehman," at the Hotel Commodore in New York City. Roosevelt bore vocal testimony to the efforts of Rose Schneiderman, Eleanor Roosevelt, and other socially-conscious men and women when his listeners heard him comment on his real friendships with organized labor, with individuals and the movement as a whole. Roosevelt maintained that organized labor, more than any other single factor, had been responsible, during his lifetime, for the advancement of the standard of living.[64]

Franklin D. Roosevelt had good reason to claim friendship with the leaders of a labor movement which lacked the class consciousness of its European counterparts. Throughout much of Roosevelt's early political life runs a theme of support for social-welfare legislation. According to political standards laid down by most of America's labor leaders, these achievements were sufficient to merit Roosevelt their endorsement.

Roosevelt's record, and his support of organized labor's major objectives in New York—which was not difficult for a liberal to espouse—moved the Central Trades and Labor Council of New York City, claiming a membership of 600,000, to endorse the Democratic candidate for Governor.[65]

Endorsement by labor leaders, as events have since shown, does not automatically insure the vote of union members, nor of their families. With the passing years, however, Roosevelt would find the bulk of labor consistently voting for him.

On November 5, Roosevelt wound up his campaign at Poughkeepsie, when an estimated 20,000 people paraded down its narrow Main Street. Afterwards, 200 townsfolk gathered in front of his residence at Hyde Park to pay him homage, as they would do at subsequent major elections until his death.

During this campaign, Roosevelt made some thirty-three major addresses, in addition to scores of informal speeches. This arduous schedule made people forget that Roosevelt was crippled. Even the most hardened political newsman who accompanied Roosevelt conceded that the Democratic nominee was as vigorous a campaigner as he had yet encountered. To many it appeared that the campaign had given Roosevelt added vigor, joy, and confidence.

Two of the legendary figures rising to prominence during this campaign were James Aloysius Farley and Louis McHenry Howe. Through the years Farley had risen from town clerk in a Republican community to the upper tiers of Democratic hierarchy until, in 1928, he was designated Secretary of the Democratic State Committee. Howe, a former newspaperman, had been with Roosevelt since the 1912 campaign for the State Senate, and had devoted himself, as political mentor, to making his Franklin, President of the United States.

Faithful to the party, and in particular to Franklin D. Roosevelt, Farley left few stones unturned as he and Howe sought victory for the State Democratic ticket. The key to previous successes for the Democracy had been the immense Democratic pluralities rolled up in the five counties of New York City.

Farley quickly learned that his major task was to reactivate the rural Democratic machine in an attempt to cut into the overwhelming Republican upstate vote.

Farley worked on the State campaign to the exclusion of the presidential contest. A major problem which confronted him was the lack of accurate information regarding the Democratic organization in upstate counties. In some instances even the list of county chairmen and local workers was either missing or too old to be of much use. Farley and Howe whipped an organization into shape and sought to cut into the upstate vote.[66]

Farley's green-inked messages soon had his headquarters staff mailing pungent directives to Democratic county chairmen, election inspectors, and county committee members upstate. These Democratic chieftains were urged to present a full slate of local candidates in order to develop greater interest and increased votes for the party. Where there was annual registration Democratic leaders were directed to get independents and enrolled Democrats registered. They were exhorted to visit voters, distribute handbills, hold campaign rallies, and get every registered Democrat and independent to the polls on election day.[67] Farley and Howe sought to have the party faithful undertake a serious canvass of voters in regions where Democrats hadn't conducted an effective campaign for years. During the previous Smith administrations no well-organized attempt had been made to revive the Democratic machine in the Republican hinterlands. The Happy Warrior had depended mainly upon urban voters.

It was not unusual for Farley to find upstate Democratic leaders in alliance with the Republican machine, if not on their payroll. These "Democrats" often traded State-wide and national Democratic votes for local patronage. In some communities Democratic leaders had not seriously distributed a campaign leaflet, nor held a rally, for twelve or more years. It was even suggested that sections of the upstate organization had been inactive since Grover Cleveland was elected Governor in 1882.

Results of the work of Farley and Howe were observable that very year when upstate returns started trickling in on election night. Full harvest of their efforts, however, would not be evident until the 1930 gubernatorial election.

Although one of the most successful campaign managers in the history of the Democratic party, and ardent supporter of Roosevelt until 1940, James A. Farley was never a New Dealer. He was not a forceful advocate of advanced social-welfare legislation at home, nor was he consistent in his support of democratic, anti-totalitarian forces abroad. He always remained —and still does—a conservative within the party, while helping elect Roosevelt to the governorship and later to the presidency.

One segment of organized labor in New York had a bitter experience with Farley. On May 1, 1929, more than 1,000 drivers, yardmen, and helpers employed in the mason material building supply line in New York City struck for a wage and hours contract. One of the largest concerns in this industry was General Builders Supply, of which James A. Farley was president. Farley had also been president of the industry's association prior to the strike. Union spokesmen later contended they had made every effort to mediate the dispute with Farley, but that the latter had refused to meet with them. During Roosevelt's campaign for re-election in 1930, labor spokesmen informed the Governor:

We had committees to take up the matter with Mayor Walker, J. M. Curry, and other prominent Democratic leaders—all their answers to us were, they could not do anything with Mr. Farley. He even refused to meet them on this situation.

The strike lasted about eight weeks—practically all the men lost their jobs and the entire association is now running as an open shop, which they are carrying on to the present day.[68]

While urging the Governor to intercede in their behalf, the union reminded Roosevelt that they had always supported the Democratic party and had, in the 1928 election, contributed $3,000 to the Democratic campaign fund. The Governor's secretary acknowledged the letter and promised to bring it to

Roosevelt's attention. Nothing further was heard of this case.

One of the most penetrating portraits that was ever recorded of Farley was made by Louis Howe during the summer of 1931. By that time, Howe and Farley had been lining up organization votes throughout the nation for the presidential nomination of Roosevelt. To Colonel Edward House, wartime adviser to President Woodrow Wilson and now adviser to the staff of presidential contender Roosevelt, Howe wrote that he was anxious to have Farley meet with the Colonel, so that the latter might observe Farley's virtues as well as his faults. Howe doubted that

. . . Farley would be a good man to send anywhere in the South . . . but my judgment has been that Farley is temperamentally and physically the ideal man to use in the Western States. He has a wholesome breeziness of manner and a frank and open character which is characteristic of all Westerners. In addition, I think he gives a distinct impression of being a very practical and business like politician as well and reactions I have received from many letters which came to the Governor after his trip have been exceedingly complimentary and favorable to him.[69]

In dealing with the regular Democratic organizations in the Western states, which were overwhelmingly in support of Roosevelt, Howe felt that Farley was exactly the type of man necessary for the job. He impressed those political leaders he spoke with as being a politician of experience himself, and left them with the feeling that the Governor's affairs were being handled by real political experts. But if the Roosevelt forces came into conflict with the regular organization machinery in any state, then Farley, according to Howe, no longer would be a suitable representative, for it would then be

. . . necessary to appeal to the electorate on high economic and moral grounds and we will need someone decidedly more of the intelligentsia to enlist prominent men in such states, who are not ordinary political workers. For this purpose Farly [sic] is utterly unsuited. . . .

He has also one very great recommendation. He does not attempt to dictate, but follows implicitly any advice or instructions which the Governor gives him, and his loyalty and unselfishness are beyond question.[70]

Farley's State-wide organizational efforts were supplemented in New York City by the inevitable "Independent Citizens Committee" for Roosevelt and Lehman. In 1928, the Committee included Arthur Curtis James as chairman; George R. Van Namee, the conservative Democratic member of the Public Service Commission, as campaign manager; and Howard S. Cullman, member of the Port of New York Authority and devoted community leader, as treasurer. Maurice Bloch, dynamic leader of the Democratic minority in the State Assembly, served as executive secretary. This committee secured independent endorsements for Roosevelt and funds with which to conduct an effective campaign.

By 1928, New York gubernatorial contests, in an era when public relations had assumed great importance, required the expenditure of approximately one-half million dollars by a major party. According to Cullman, the Independent Citizens Committee for Roosevelt and Lehman had, by the end of the campaign: "Total contributions and receipts $303,859.55; total disbursements $303,823.21 which gives us the fabulous sum of $36 to have a party, subject to the written approval of the 995 contributors." [71] The campaign expenses for the State Democratic party, as distinct from the Independent Citizens Committee, totaled more than $134,000.

Shortly after the polls closed on election day, and before returns started pouring into national Democratic headquarters in New York, the large hotel ballroom hired for the evening overflowed with noisy, excited supporters. By midnight, the happy, laughing throng had disappeared, leaving behind a handful of despondent followers. From the first returns it had become evident that Smith was a beaten man. New York, New Jersey, Connecticut, and other key states in the New England and Middle Atlantic region had swung to Herbert Hoover. Many Southern states fell into the Republican fold for the first time since Reconstruction days. Thirty minutes after midnight

Governor Smith conceded Hoover's election.[72]

After early acknowledgment of Smith's defeat in his home State, most Democratic leaders were willing to concede Ottinger's victory, rather than wait out the slow trickle of upstate returns for Governor. Significant was the decrease in the usual party plurality in New York City; the early returns indicated that Roosevelt was running some 32,000 votes behind Smith in the City's five counties. Smith, with a 450,000 vote plurality in New York City, had lost the State because of Hoover's overwhelmingly rural tally which had given the latter a State-wide plurality of over 103,000.

To offset his reduced plurality in New York City, and the usual Republican vote north of the City line, Roosevelt had to secure a significantly larger upstate vote than that accorded his party's presidential candidate.

As the hours ticked by after midnight neither camp would concede the gubernatorial race. Some early newspaper editions, however, had given the nod to Ottinger. The few close friends who remained with Roosevelt at Democratic headquarters were increasingly amazed by upstate returns which trickled in at a frustratingly slow pace, for the figures indicated surprising Roosevelt strength in hundreds of towns and hamlets.

In 55 of the 57 counties outside of New York City, Roosevelt edged ahead of Smith by as little as 37 votes in Essex County, and by as much as 11,000 in Westchester County. His loss of 32,000 odd votes in the Democratic column in New York City —32,000 less than that accorded Smith—and a plurality of only 406,505 over Ottinger in the five City counties were barely offset by his leading Smith upstate by some 70,000 votes. Fortunately for Roosevelt, Ottinger ran almost 90,000 votes behind Hoover in upstate returns. The final vote upstate was 1,375,918 for Ottinger and 994,977 for Roosevelt.

Three days after election, as Roosevelt started South for a vacation at Warm Springs, Ottinger still refused to concede defeat. Shortly before boarding his train Roosevelt attacked the Republican state leader, H. Edmund Machold, claiming that the latter had had a "financial reason" in his attempt to elect Ottinger to the Governor's seat. Contending that water power for the people had been saved, Roosevelt remarked, as a sort of afterthought:

It is interesting that only 25,000 votes stood between private development of the State's water power and the Democratic plan of development. That was a narrow escape. It is about 25 to one that if Mr. Ottinger had been elected Governor the coming session of the Legislature would have ended with the enactment of the full 1926 program of the Republicans, and that program called for 50 year leases of power sites, which we contend in effect would be leases in perpetuity for private development.[73]

On November 16, Farley placed the Roosevelt margin at 23,000, with Herbert Lehman's plurality at 13,800, and Controller Tremaine's at 11,000. The Republican candidate for State Attorney General, Hamilton Ward, had managed to win the only State-wide victory for his party by an extremely close margin.[74] Twelve days after election Ottinger finally wired Roosevelt at Warm Springs:

Undoubtedly the final count of the official canvas will declare you elelted [sic] as Governor of the State of New York. You have my heartiest good wishes for a successful administration as you will always have my cordial cooperation to that end.[75]

Official returns by the Secretary of State later gave Roosevelt a plurality of 25,564 votes over Ottinger, out of a total vote of 4,234,822 cast for both candidates. The Lieutenant Governor-elect, Herbert Lehman, surpassed the Smith and Roosevelt vote in New York City but trailed the ticket upstate.

It was Felix Frankfurter, at Harvard University, who voiced the sentiment of many admirers when he wrote the Governor-elect:

Your victory is a great source of consolation and hope. To have the direction of New York affairs in your hands in immediate succession to Smith insures such momentum to those standards of Government which you and Smith typify as to secure for them almost the force of tradition. For you have, as Smith has, the conception of government which seems to me indispensable to the vitality of a Democratic government, namely, the realization that the processes of government are essentially educational processes. And so I shall continue to be heartened by what will come out of Albany. I know you satisfy my own loyalty as a New Yorker, for spiritually I continue to feel that the Governor of New York is my Governor.[76]

Would Roosevelt's administration differ from that of his predecessor?

Smith had returned to Albany in 1919, his first term as Governor, with a tremendous advantage over previous State Executives. His entire political career, except for one term as Sheriff of New York County, had been spent as a legislator in Albany or New York City. As Speaker and majority leader in the Assembly he had frequently sat in the Governor's office debating, counseling, and cooperating on State business. He knew how to handle the Republican legislators who, with one exception during his eight years as Governor, controlled both houses of the legislature. For those eight years the G.O.P. in New York chose the wrong side of almost every public question. This party, which purportedly contained the intellectual elite of the legislature, adopted the policy that anything desired by Al Smith was evil, extravagant, radical, or unscientific, despite the fact that many of the views of the Tammany Governor had been evolved from studies made by eminent Republicans.[77]

In his first gubernatorial message in 1919, Smith sought equality of taxation for all classes, production and distribution of the necessities of life at low cost, improved welfare legislation, and housing relief. At about the same time Governor Smith appointed a reconstruction commission to suggest solutions for these vital problems. Most of the members Smith appointed to this commission were distinguished citizens, and many were Republicans. The Republican legislators, establishing a precedent for subsequent years, refused to appropriate the $75,000 needed for the commission, because it had been Smith's idea. Nevertheless, the commission functioned because its own members supplied the necessary funds.

The Republican majority consistently rejected such Smith proposals as a popular referendum on the prohibition amendment; a scientific water power policy; additional protection for child workers; the creation of a minimum wage commission to pass upon the earnings of women and minors; health and maternity insurance; eradication of deplorable conditions in the State hospitals for the insane; and the suggestion that candidates for public office be required to file an accounting of their campaign receipts before, instead of after, elections.

In November, 1919, voters in congested sections of New York City elected five Socialists to the lower house of the legislature. The Republican-dominated Assembly, which had the right to pass upon the qualification of its members, and which had been overwhelmed by the postwar campaign of Big Business against radical and liberal thought, refused to seat the Socialists for the 1920 session on the basis of their being "Reds" and "Bolsheviks." Governor Smith fought the expulsion with great vigor, publicly denouncing this violation of civil liberties and freedom of representation. Supplementing this action, the Bolshevik-hunting lawmakers enacted legislation granting the Attorney General power to initiate proceedings against "radical" candidates for office before the Appellate Division of the State Supreme Court. This vicious bill, along with many of the other hysterical, conformist-seeking legislation, was promptly vetoed by the Governor. Smith clearly exhibited, at this stage of his political career, rare courage, and sympathy and tolerance for the beliefs of those with whom he did not agree.[78]

Though Al Smith was an unquestioning follower of Tammany Hall and Boss Murphy, prior to 1919, as Governor of the Empire State he made an increasing number of independent appointments which greatly displeased the hierarchy of the Wigwam. Typical of appointments made on merit alone was that of Colonel Frederick Stuart Greene, a Smith Republican, as the State Commissioner of Highways. Smith also appointed Frances Perkins to the Industrial Commission, despite protests against her "radicalism." He also resisted the efforts of Tammany to throw the State courts into politics.

His greatest challenge to patronage-hungry Tammany was his appointment of six Republican cabinet members at the start of his fourth and last term. Created by the State reorganization plan, this new cabinet in 1927 consisted of eight Democrats, in addition to the six Republicans who included Secretary of State Robert Moses and the heads of the departments of Agriculture and Markets, Conservation, Education, the Executive and director of State Charities.

Despite Republican obstructionism, Governor Smith secured repeal of repressive laws inspired by fear of Bolshevism—enacted during the 1921-22 administration of Republican Governor Nathan L. Miller; passage of statutes controlling motor traffic; limitation of rents in congested areas; and referenda by the voters on bond issues authorizing $300 million for grade crossing removal, $50 million for State hospital improvements, and $15 million for State parks. In 1924 he secured a reduction of taxes by some $17 million despite Republican shenanigans.

Smith's achievement in pushing through vital legislation over the opposition of the Republican majority attests to his skill as an executive leader and as a molder of public opinion. His successes were many, but so were his defeats. The Governor supported housing bills which sought to control combinations in building materials, but most of them were shunted aside by the Republicans. He recommended rent legislation and bills permitting tax exemption to stimulate the building of homes. In 1926 he proposed a law to permit corporations agreeing to limited dividends to issue bonds through a State Housing Bank, at low interest, and to condemn land for building purposes. Smith was forced to accept a watered-down compromise because of Republican opposition to his "Socialistic" proposal.

Shortly after becoming Governor in 1919, Smith approved a bill giving equal pay to women teachers. That same year the State contributed about $9 million for education. Nine years later, the State was appropriating over $80 million annually for its school systems.

In 1919, the government of the State was divided among more than 200 boards and commissions, many with independent authority to sign significant financial contracts. Few were responsible to anyone. Smith's reconstruction commission reported on the gravity of this situation but the Republicans, desiring to make this a partisan issue, stalled any action for years. Finally appealing to public opinion through newspapers, over the "raddio," and on the stump, Smith was able to push through legislative amendments to the statute and constitutional law which consolidated these scattered departments into only 18. The heads of the more important State departments were made directly responsible to the Governor as members of his cabinet. New York State finally had a modernized form of government, thanks to Al Smith.

Appalled by the haphazard and irresponsible manner by which State funds had previously been appropriated, Smith pressed for and secured enactment of legislation providing for an Executive Budget which placed the fiscal initiative and responsibility upon the Governor. Instead of the budget being drafted behind closed doors of committee rooms, the Governor would hereafter submit, at the beginning of each year, a list of necessary appropriations. The legislature might add to, or subtract from, the proposals. The G.O.P. leadership fought this enlightened piece of legislation in the legislature and at the polls, but lost out to the wishes of Al Smith and the people.

Having had his eyes opened to the inequities inflicted upon industrial workers as a legislative member of the Factory Investigating Committee in 1911, Smith used all his influence as Governor to further such reforms as minimum wages and the forty-eight-hour week for women. He secured an imperfect forty-eight-hour week law because of the jockeying of Republicans, who likewise stymied his efforts to secure State ratification of the Federal Child Labor Amendment, and who continuously sought to undermine the Workmen's Compensation Act.

Finally, on the question of water power, we come to an issue which Smith had struggled with unsuccessfully since 1919. As Governor, he continuously sought to prevent the power resources of his State, particularly the Saint Lawrence River, from falling into the hands of the du Ponts, the Morgans, and the Mellons. In this struggle he was contending not only with the Republican state machine but also with power-dominated Democrats. His solution was for the State and nation to retain absolute ownership and control of sites, build and operate generating plants, and contract with private enterprises for transmisision and distribution of current.[79]

As we view the Smith administrations in retrospect we can readily see that the foundations for Roosevelt's four years as Governor were well laid by the Happy Warrior. In housing education, budgeting, welfare legislation, parks, and water power, Franklin D. Roosevelt would basically be carrying on the work of Alfred E. Smith.

Faced with the task of preserving and extending the gains of the Smith administrations, Roosevelt quickly responded to the challenges of a recalcitrant, obstructionist Republican majority in the legislature by also going over their heads and appealing directly to the people through the newspapers and with one of the most effective radio voices of his time. He likewise made independent appointments to his cabinet of outstanding men and women. Typical were Miss Frances Perkins, as head of the Department of Labor; Dr. Walter N. Thayer, a psychiatrist and penologist, as Commissioner of Correction; Dr. Thomas J. Parran, Jr., an assistant surgeon general in the United States public health service, as Commissioner of Health; Joseph A. Broderick, as Superintendent of Banks; and Henry Morgenthau, Jr., as Conservation Commissioner. By the summer of 1931, Secretary of State Edward J. Flynn was the only political leader holding a place in the Roosevelt cabinet.

Roosevelt never permitted a letter to go unanswered, strengthening his contact with men and women from all walks of life by a monumental amount of correspondence.

To insure an alert and competent minority in the State legislature, Roosevelt invited Democratic legislators to weekly meetings in the Executive office. Discussions on key legislation, followed by specific assignments to the legislators, resulted in elevated debate on the floor of both houses. No longer could Republicans speedily reject the Governor's proposed legislation, nor hastily push through partisan legislation of their own. The G.O.P. leadership was now confronted with aggressive, argumentative Democratic spokesmen.

Throughout his governorship, Roosevelt was ever careful of his relations with the public and with his administrators, which might well be illustrated by a typical day in Albany.

After breakfast at the Executive Mansion Roosevelt skimmed through eight newspapers published in different parts of the State. He then dictated replies to 25 or 30 letters, mainly from personal friends addressed to him at the Mansion.

At the Executive Chamber he might find 40 or 50 letters for reply or referral to various department heads. At 11 A.M. there began a stream of people who had appointments to see the Governor. The first visitor might be Dr. Frederick W. Parsons, Commissioner of Mental Hygiene, to report on the progress made on the construction of new hospitals for the insane. Dr. Charles W. Johnson, head of the Department of Social Welfare, was the second visitor, who discussed plans for a new hospital for crippled children. He was followed by other department heads who discussed the progress of work on prisons, normal schools, and highways.

The Governor might then take ten minutes off his schedule to meet and shake hands with 100 school children who had come to Albany for the day for some sightseeing around the Capitol building.

Instead of going out to lunch, which was not too easy for a crippled Governor, Roosevelt had his noonday meal in the Executive Chamber, in the company of some person who wanted to discuss a governmental issue. Thus he might spend a half hour with Sam Lewisohn discussing the problems of prison reform, the functioning of the new Parole Board, and the types of new prison buildings to be erected the following year.

The afternoon might be devoted to conferences with a special committee on the unemployment situation; with village officials protesting the high rates of electricity in their community; and with representatives of the Dairy League and the Grange to discuss the depressing agricultural situation.

All of this kept the Governor at his desk until 5:30 or 6 P.M., signing mail and clearing up details. Then he went home to supper with the family and four or five people who were visiting in Albany.

When the legislature was in session the day was a busier one, with dozens of bills and applications for pardons to contend with.

This was a typical day for a Governor who sat at the head of a "corporation" which spent over $300,000,000 a year. The main point, as Roosevelt saw his job, was that the Governor had to be a good manager and at the same time "be sufficiently human and sufficiently interested in the people of the State that he will be thinking constantly about ways in which their welfare can best be promoted."[80]

Most successful Governors have been those who had a real familiarity with the State as a whole and with the needs and desires of the different counties and different sections. Franklin D. Roosevelt had obtained his knowledge from serving in the State legislature and from intimate personal knowledge through travel. Did this background insure that he, too, would be a successful Governor?

For personal and political reasons Franklin D. Roosevelt had not sought the Democratic gubernatorial nomination in 1928. Being drafted by the Democratic convention enabled him to assume sole responsibility for the direction of the State administration, since he was beholden to no one, not even to the Happy Warrior. In contrast to Al Smith, Senator Robert F. Wagner, and other contemporary Democrats in New York, Roosevelt had risen to his position as a self-made leader, and as an independent, anti-Tammany Democrat, with a rural background. These factors, in addition to his religion and the most popular political name in the nation, enabled him to garner a sufficient number of upstate votes to insure his election in 1928.

During the campaign Roosevelt tended to straddle the issue of prohibition. He rejected prosperity as the exclusive property of the Republican party. He vigorously denounced religious bigotry, risking his own election in the process. Roosevelt campaigned on a platform which he would support as Governor and as President of the United States: a scientific study of farm assessment and taxation; perpetual state ownership and control of water power resources; county and state reorganization and consolidation; and continued advances in labor legislation, health, and education.

Roosevelt's record as State Senator, Assistant Secretary of the Navy, and as active citizen during his period of convalescence, earned him the wholehearted endorsement of most of labor's spokesmen. With few exceptions they would continue to support him throughout his political career.

The Rooseveltian tactic of personal political campaigning in a contested geographical area was renewed in 1928, and again in subsequent major contests. It was during the 1928 campaign that James A. Farley and Samuel I. Rosenman first assumed their major responsibilities as master political organizer and as legal adviser and speechmaker, respectively, for Franklin D. Roosevelt.

In this election, as in subsequent campaigns, Roosevelt exhibited surprising strength in rural areas, particularly for a candidate who received his first State-wide nomination from a Democratic party overshadowed by corrupt, urban-minded Tammany Hall.

II

"UPSTAIRS IN ALBANY"

THE TRADITION of a strong executive in Albany, initiated by Charles Evans Hughes and Alfred E. Smith, was carried on by Franklin D. Roosevelt in his conflict with the legislature over the issue of the Executive Budget. Within four weeks after taking his oath of office, Roosevelt found himself in a controversy with a recalcitrant legislature which refused to acknowledge that an amendment to the State Constitution had deprived the lawmakers of certain powers of budget-making.

Considered by many political scientists as the most significant of the Governor's executive powers in relation to the legislature, the control of the budget was a question which had plagued executive-legislative relationships in New York since Governor George Clinton.

Today, it is the duty of New York's Governor to develop a financial program, with respect both to revenue and expenditure, to prepare and submit a budget, and to supervise the course of expenditures. While the legislature retains ultimate control of the purse strings, the executive has the fiscal initiative.

This was not the situation, however, at the turn of the century. Until 1900 the Governor had little to do with administration. His secondary position was evident by the large number of independent constitutional officers and independent charitable and correctional institutions. Even the President of the United States was in an inferior administrative position until the twentieth century. With the absence of executive budgets, for example, governmental agencies went directly to the appropriating body, denying chief executives any influence or control over the amount asked for or granted except in the final act of a veto. This disorganized situation made for extravagance, waste, favoritism, and logrolling. It was not until 1910 that the Governor began to secure recognition as an administrator, and it was not until 1921, with the passage of the Budget and Accounting Act, that the President of the United States became more than a political leader. The result of the changes which took place in the years following 1910 established, according to Leonard D. White, "the possibility of unity of command, of effective coordination, of internal responsibility, and of administrative leadership."[1]

Some two decades before Franklin D. Roosevelt took his oath of office, Governor Charles Evans Hughes sought to centralize responsibility and improve the financial procedure of the State with the passage of a law which required that all requests for appropriations be filed and tabulated for use by the legislature and the Governor in advance of the legislative session. The tabulated requests were to be transmitted to the Governor by the middle of December and then to the legislature on the first day of the new session.

Three years later Governor William Sulzer and the legislature established a State Board of Estimate and a Department of Efficiency and Economy, with the responsibility of formulating appropriation bills and studying administrative methods for improving the management of the public services. As a result of antagonism between the members of the agencies both laws were repealed in 1915.

At the New York Constitutional Convention of 1915, Al Smith was instrumental in including provision for an executive budget among the amendments submitted to the electorate later that year. Following rejection of these constitutional amendments by the voters, Governor Charles S. Whitman secured adoption of a legislative budget system, with an advisory budget prepared and submitted by the Governor.

During his first term as Governor, Smith was unsuccessful in securing legislative endorsement of a constitutional amendment providing for an executive budget. Governor Nathan L. Miller, who barely defeated Smith in the November, 1920, elections, permitted establishment of a Board of Estimate and Control, consisting of himself, the Controller, and the chairmen of the Assembly Ways and Means Committee and of the Senate Finance Committee, to share in the preparation of revenue estimates and of appropriation bills. This merely straddled the problem.

In 1926, a new Reorganization Commission headed by Charles Evans Hughes proposed a partially modified version of Smith's original executive budget amendment, which was finally adopted at the polls the following year as Article IV-A.[2]

The amendment granted to the Executive, through the Budget Division, power to study, investigate, and survey the operation of the various departments. Departmental estimates were to be submitted by October 15 of each year, and representatives of the legislative finance committees were to attend the revision of the estimates. The budget formulated by the Governor, with the assistance of his budget director, and containing a complete plan of proposed expenditures and estimated revenues, was to be submitted to the legislature on or before the first day in February.[3]

Up to the time the Governor submitted his budget, the legislature could not constitutionally pass any appropriations. But as soon as the Executive Budget was transmitted by the Governor, the Constitution gave the legislature plenary powers. The lawmakers could request the head of any department to appear before it. The legislative finance committees were given ample funds and expert personnel to investigate the proposed expenditures and to inquire into any aspect of the budget and into every single item contained in it. The legislature was given full power to strike out any item of appropriation or reduce it or add new ones. In other words, the legislature was charged by the Constitution with the duty and responsibility of examining the budget submitted by the Governor and likewise granted full powers to change that budget in its judgment. It had final authority in reducing the budget.

If the legislature did not approve of the revenue plan in the Executive Budget, it could modify or revise it in any way it wished. In fact, the legislature could completely discard all the revenue recommendations made by the Governor. But if the legislature disliked, disagreed with, or disapproved of any part of the revenue program, it then became its duty to sponsor a tax which would produce equal revenues.

Under the constitutional amendment, the legislature could reduce, or eliminate altogether, any item in the Governor's budget. Having given its approval to, or having slashed, appropriations, the legislature enacted the recommendations into law without returning them for the Governor's signature. Increases or new appropriations might also be originated by the legislators, but they had to be incorporated as separate items in new bills which required executive approval.

The first Executive Budget presented by Roosevelt in 1929 was said to have been the result of "scientific" preparation. This budget was begun by former Governor Smith during the summer of 1928, when department heads were invited to list their needs. Although Smith turned his preliminary work over to his successor, he continued to give his advice at conferences and his Director of the Budget, Joseph H. Wilson, remained as Governor Roosevelt's financial expert.

Those who originally advocated the Executive Budget, and who finally saw it written into the State Constitution, did not seek to take away from the legislature any of its essential rights, but rather to restore the just balance between the executive and legislative in the appropriating process. They felt that the Governor should initiate the budget and be responsible for the proper coordination of the many demands arising in the different departments. The Governor, they felt, would be in a better position to prevent logrolling than the legislature. Also, leading members of the appropriation committees, who were usually legislative old-timers, had frequently been the real power behind the administrative scene. In New York, as elsewhere, their power over the purse had been used for political as well as official ends. As long as the State did not adopt an Executive Budget, so long would such legislators have great influence in administrative circles.[4] The legislature, too, had grown accustomed to having its committees spend so much time drafting the annual appropriation bills that there was little time left for their open discussion. In the Executive Budget, the ultimate power, as Henry L. Stimson argued in the 1915 Constitutional Convention of New York, was really restored to the legislature. The Hughes Committee had recommended a constitutional budget amendment as "the only way in which the true order of procedure can be fully established and the Governor relegated to his true function of proposing a budget and the legislature fully restored to its true function of disposing of that budget."[5]

On January 28, 1929, the first Executive Budget to be submitted in strict compliance with the constitutional amendment ratified in 1927 was placed before the legislature by Roosevelt. It showed estimated revenues and other resources, against which appropriations might be made for the fiscal year beginning July 1, of more than 260 millions, and recommendations from the Governor that provision be made by the legislature for aggregate expenditures of some 256 millions for the support of the State government during that period. This represented an increase of more than 23 millions over the previous budget.[6] This budget bill contained a number of lump sum appropriations, not itemized, with provision for segregation or itemizing by the Governor alone. As a result of the reorganization of the State government initiated under Smith, extensive changes were being made in the administrative departments and many expenses could not be precisely estimated in advance. The budget, therefore, contained not only itemized amounts but lump sum appropriations to provide for currently undetermined administrative needs.

Within a month the first battle between the Governor and Republican lawmakers occurred over the proposed budget. The

era of good feeling which had generally pervaded the atmosphere
in Albany since Roosevelt's inaugural was succeeded by one of
storm and stress when Republican orators denounced the Chief
Executive for seeking to usurp the powers of the legislature and
to make it merely a rubber stamp. He was charged with attempting to use State moneys, through patronage, to revitalize the
Democratic party upstate. "Avarice, presumption, and usurpation" were some of the terms hurled at the Governor by Republican legislators.

It was not the budget bill itself that had provoked this dia-
tribe. The incentive was a special message sent by the Governor
demanding the restoration of nearly all of close to three and
one-half millions slashed from the proposed budget by the Republican-dominated fiscal committees.

The message gave the Republican lawmakers the first evidence
that the new Chief Executive possessed all the fighting qualities
generally associated with his name. In language characterizing
restraint, but reflecting a sarcasm reminiscent of his predecessor
in office, the Governor sought to refute Republican arguments
against granting him sole power over the segregation of lump
sum appropriations. He denounced as unconstitutional and as
contrary to good business policy the practice, provided in the
bill which the legislature subsequently passed, of giving the
Republican chairmen of the two fiscal committees the right to
participate with the Governor in the segregation of lump sum
items.

"I raise the broad question affecting the division of governmental duties between the executive, the legislative and the
judiciary branches of the government," Roosevelt said at one
point. "To the same degree that the Governor should never be
given legislative functions, so the legislative members should
never be given executive functions."[7]

The reading of the Governor's special message brought Republican Senator George R. Fearon rushing to his feet to denounce Robert Moses for leading Roosevelt into proposing $36
million lump sum appropriations and demanding that he have

sole power in determining how the appropriations should be segregated.[8] Senator Fearon contended that to let the Governor have his way would prove disastrous for good government, and he hinted that ulterior motives might have inspired the Governor. The Republican chairman of the Assembly Ways and Means Committee, Eberly Hutchinson, was more direct in his comments when he bitterly accused the Governor of attempting to use lump sum appropriations "to build up the Democratic party by providing good jobs galore for Democratic workers."[9]

Following these Republican diatribes, the Governor remarked that despite the efforts of Alfred E. Smith to place the administrative and business phases of the State government on a high level of efficiency, "upstairs in Albany"—a reference to the legislature which meets on the floor above the Executive office—"conditions have not changed; it is the same old crowd of Senators and Assemblymen that used to be there back in the years when I was a member of the Legislature."[10]

Parts of the Executive Budget bill became law after it received favorable action by the legislature. The awards made for several administrative departments and the State's institutions, and items set aside for the construction and maintenance of highways and for huge public improvements, would have, under normal conditions, not required subsequent action by the Governor. This section, however, was amended by the legislature in the form of increases and insertion of new items. Under the constitutional proviso governing Executive Budget procedure, these amendments were subject to the Governor's veto.

In the process of passing the budget bill on February 27, the legislature struck out all the lump sum items to which the Governor had attached his provision for segregation control and substituted similar items to which were attached clauses calling for joint segregation by the chairmen of the legislative finance committees and the Governor, in accordance with section 139 of the State Finance Law of 1921.[11]

When the Governor vetoed these amended items on March 13, he reiterated that the legislative proposal requiring joint approval by two members of the legislature and the Governor before moneys previously appropriated could be expended was contrary to the spirit and letter of the Constitution of the State. The Governor insisted that he was forced to resort to the veto because the future of the Executive Budget was at stake. Either the State was to carry out the principles of the Executive Budget, which embodied years of effort to place the affairs of the State on a modern efficient basis, "or we shall drift into a hopeless situation of divided responsibility for administration of executive functions."[12]

The Governor maintained that it was wholly contrary to the American form of representative constitutional government to give two-thirds of a purely executive duty to the legislative branch. Roosevelt concluded with the ringing statement that he would not "assent to a precedent depriving the present Governor or future Governors of a large part of the constitutional duties which are inherent in the office of Chief Executive."[13]

On March 18, Roosevelt sent the legislature two alternative supplemental budget bills, one containing lump sum appropriations to be segregated by the Governor, the other providing for itemized appropriations. Somewhat doubtful as to the constitutionality of their proposal for joint segregation of lump sum items by the Governor and two legislators, the Republican leadership sought to fortify itself with a legal opinion from State Attorney General Hamilton Ward, also a Republican. Ward's conclusions upheld the Republican leaders in every respect. He maintained that the direction as to what officers shall approve a segregation must come by way of a legislative act. The Governor could not draw that power to himself by anything he might include in his proposed appropriation bill. The Governor could not arrogate segregation powers to himself and make them beyond attack simply because the provisions had to do with a particular appropriation item. Not finding anything in the Executive Budget provisions of the Constitution which gave the Governor control over the expenditure of moneys once appropriated, the Attorney General advised

Republican Senate leader John Knight that Section 139 of the State Finance Law was constitutional and that the legislature had the right to designate the Governor and the chairmen of the finance committees of the legislature as officers to approve the segregation of lump sum items appropriated for the reorganization of State departments.[14]

The Governor immediately retorted that he had taken his position upon the advice of lawyers as learned in the law as the Attorney General. Furthermore, he insisted that the Attorney General's opinion was not law, nor was it binding upon any one.[15]

Fortified by the opinion of the Attorney General, the Republicans adopted their own version of the budget bill. During the debate which preceded its enactment, Senator Knight angrily accused Roosevelt of duplicity and bad faith in negotiations over the budget procedure carried on prior to the introduction of the Executive Budget bill, and of seeking to arrogate to himself unconstitutional powers. After heated debate between spokesmen for both parties, an amended version of the budget bill was adopted with all Democrats voting in the negative,[16] the first time in at least a decade that a budget bill in New York had been passed by a divided vote in either house.[17]

The legislature had struck out a considerable number of detailed items of appropriations for the departments of Law and of Labor and had substituted lump sum appropriations to be jointly segregated according to Section 139 of the State Finance Law.[18] To the large sum of construction items, aggregating some twenty millions, the legislature appended as Section 11, a segregation clause similar to Section 139.

In an attempt to resolve the controversy over the budget Roosevelt took a sensible course while approving the disputed supplemental budget bill. He vetoed those provisions which gave the finance chairmen joint control with him over the expenditures of lump sum appropriations for the construction items[19] but accepted the joint segregation proposal for the appropriations for the departments of Law and of Labor.[20] These

actions afforded the Governor an opportunity to take the issue
to court.

While signing the bill Roosevelt asserted that if the practice
of joint control was followed to its logical conclusion, subsequent legislatures could, by drastically changing the proposed
budget, or altering the controlling language, completely change
the intent and purpose of every item in the budget and set up
a control of every administrative agency by a committee dominated by two of its own members as officers. Whereas the
constitutional amendment reorganizing the State government
had intended to do away with the service of legislators on boards
and commissions, and to centralize executive responsibility,
Roosevelt maintained that if two legislators could be set up
to share this responsibility with the Governor, the whole intent
and purpose of reorganization would be frittered away.[21]

In insisting on the right of the finance chairmen to a voice in
the allocation of lump sum items, the Republicans had the support of the Attorney General. The Governor, on the other
hand, had countered with a formal opinion signed by his
counsel, Edward G. Griffin, and by the distinguished constitutional lawyer, William D. Guthrie, in which they supported his
stand and recommended his recourse to the courts.[22]

Guthrie and Griffin maintained that Section 139 would be
held unconstitutional under the Executive Budget amendment.
They contended that it would be an exercise of executive power
not warranted under the Constitution and an encroachment upon
the powers of the Governor to require approval of expenditures
by the administrative departments from two members of the
legislature who, under the circumstances, virtually would have
been created public officers. They held this a violation of a constitutional provision which explicitly prohibited any civil appointment of a legislator during the term for which he had
been elected.[23]

Before the case was submitted to the courts, Acting Governor
Lehman and Attorney General Ward prepared the way for a
statement of fact agreeable to both sides in order that all con-

stitutional and legal questions arising out of the budget provisions might be promptly determined.[24] It was further agreed that without prejudice in any way to the case the Acting Governor and the chairmen of the legislative finance committees would sign the necessary segregations covering the schedule of positions and salaries of the Attorney General's office in order that that department might function without handicap.[25]

During the fourth week in May the controversy between Roosevelt and the Republican legislature, as to the administration of the Executive Budget, came before the full bench of the Appellate Division of the State Supreme Court. Based on an agreed statement of fact, the Governor requested an injunction to restrain the Controller from issuing Law and Labor Department salary checks drafted on a lump sum item in the appropriation bill which the Governor had not approved as to segregation.

Guthrie and Griffin appeared for the Executive Department and for State Controller Tremaine, who was the defendant in the action. Solicitor General Claude B. Dawes and former Governor Nathan L. Miller, together with Attorney General Ward, appeared for the Republican majority of the legislature.

Guthrie, senior counsel, argued that in the reorganization of the State government there could be no doubt that it was the intention to centralize the power and make the Executive Department the repository of all civil administrative and executive functions. The Governor had never claimed that the legislature could not give segregation power to others, but he did insist that the Governor was the head of the Executive Department and that it was fitting that the segregation of important items be confined to him as head of the State. The legislature could not rest such duty in two of its own members because of the settled doctrine that the legislature must act as a body.[26]

Attorney General Ward quoted former Governor Smith as having told the State Bar Association, several years previously, to "pay no attention to this talk about increasing the power of the Governor. Pay no attention to this talk about decreasing the power of the Legislature. Nothing in the proposed executive budget does either of these two things. It leaves the power just where it is today, but it provides for the exercise of that power in just a little different way than it is now exercised."[27]

The purpose of the legislature as to segregation was summed up by Mr. Dawes when he maintained that ". . . we find in various annual approprations bills, in Section 139 of the State Finance Law, and in several other general statutes of the State, provisions for the approval of segregations by all of the three officers above named in instances where lump sums are appropriations."[28]

Former Governor Miller, in his argument, presented six chief contentions of the legislative leaders when he said that the legislature had the power to appropriate a lump sum and therefore could delegate the power to split up or segregate that lump sum; that the Executive Budget provisions of the Constitution gave the Governor power to make a budget, but not to control the expenditures of moneys appropriated by a budget bill; that under the Constitution the power to approve segregation of lump sum appropriations was a legislative and not an executive power, therefore the legislature could delegate the power to whom it desired, including persons who happened to be members of the legislature; that the Governor had no power to veto the section of the supplemental budget bill that prohibited expenditures for personal service appropriated for construction, except on the triple approval requirement objected to by the Governor; that Section 139 of the State Finance Law setting up the triple approval requirement in the case of lump sum appropriations, to create, reorganize, or consolidate State departments, was constitutional; and finally, that a member of the legislature was not disqualified from performing functions placed upon him by the segregation statutes.[29]

Within a month after hearing the case the Appellate Division ruled against Roosevelt in a split decision. The prevailing opinion upheld the contention of Attorney General Hamilton Ward that the Governor must share with the two financial chairmen of the legislature the work of itemizing lump sum appropriations under the Executive Budget.[30]

The Appellate Division sustained the argument of the Attorney General when it was unable to discover in the constitutional amendments of 1925 and 1927 any intentions to change previous practice materially, or to find any constitutional objections to the exercise of administrative functions by members of the legislature. Speaking of the function of approving segregations, the court said that perhaps this duty fell within the twilight zone where the function was legislative and the act of approval was administrative; and exact classification was unnecessary. It could be designated as a deferred legislative act in aid of the performance of functions which the legislature might fully have performed originally, properly delegated to officers acting in an administrative capacity. "The legislation was complete, but the distribution for particular purposes was to be made by heads of departments with the approval of the governor and legislative officers, furnishing a system of check and balance." The court further held that the duties of the finance committee chairmen, being in furtherance of the legislative plan, were not necessarily illegal because they involved administrative functions. The legislature was not acting in a body, nor were these chairmen acting as legislators in performing their duties.[31]

These nice distinctions were not very meaningful to the man in the street, for they were too technical in character, and uninteresting besides. Lawyers and scholars, however, appreciated their significance. Republican lawmakers were gleeful, while the Governor and his supporters worried about the impact of this decision upon the separation of powers between the legislative and the executive.

Feeling that the consequences of permitting the legislature to delegate such administrative and executive functions, as were contained in the disputed statutes, to members of the legislature was a practical nullification of the intent of the constitutional amendment of Article V in 1925, requiring the legislature to vest "all the civil, administrative and executive functions of the

State government" in the several State Departments, and of the intent of Article IV-A which provided for an Executive Budget and intended to centralize responsibility in the Executive Department, Roosevelt, Guthrie, and Griffin made immediate plans to resort to the Court of Appeals for a review of the lower court's decision.[32]

Meanwhile, all was not harmonious in the Roosevelt camp. Edward Griffin, the Governor's counsel, felt that Guthrie's presentation in the Appellate Division had lacked reality and feared that if the noted constitutional lawyer continued in the same vein he would confuse the Court of Appeals. In addition, Griffin had at first been unable to convince his senior counsel that the question whether or not Section 139 of the State Finance Law applied to the appropriations that year as a matter of statutory construction, and the question whether Section 11 was inserted in the supplemental budget in an orderly manner, were not the important issues in the case. Griffin felt that nothing would be gained by a court decision unless Guthrie made it clear that legislators might not as a matter of constitutional law participate in any administrative function under any of the circumstances cited.[33]

In view of the far-reaching effect the decision of the Court of Appeals would have on New York, and on other states, Roosevelt underscored for his senior counsel some of the most significant issues in the case, and which he hoped would be referred to during the oral presentation. The Governor wanted it clearly understood that his position was not actuated by any personal feelings but that this was wholly a matter of principle. He was on friendly terms with the legislative leaders and recognized that, in a sense, he was a Governor for only a day and would be succeeded by a long line of Governors. Since the legislature had adjourned, and especially since the decision by the Appellate Division, a number of segregations of public moneys had been made with the approval of the two legislative chairmen and himself. No controversy had arisen, and if there had been any Roosevelt was certain that all three would have made every effort to harmonize their decisions pending the final determination by the Court of Appeals.

The existing temporary situation, however, was not to be regarded as a definite criterion for the future. Although harmony had prevailed thus far, the situation could not be assured with future Governors or future legislative chairmen. If a dispute did arise and a compromise was impossible, would the two votes of the legislative chairmen override the vote of the Governor, or would an impasse be created by which no expenditures could be made at all from the particular appropriation involved?

Finally, Roosevelt sought to stress the thought that no one could tell what the future would bring forth. We might again in our history

. . . pass through times of confusion, of bitterness and of attempts at high-handed usurpation. This controversy deals far more with the future than with the present. In days past, the American theory of the separation of the three principal functions of government— the judicial, the legislative, and the executive—has been found to constitute a successful check against excesses by any one of the three. To overthrow even partially the separation of the function of the executive and the legislative, as advocated by the respondents, would, I feel very strongly, not only nullify the definite purpose of the people of this State in setting up the constitutional budget as a part of the reform of the administrative functions, but would also create a definitely dangerous power in the legislative leaders to administer the affairs of every department of the State Government, including the Executive Department itself.[34]

Guthrie acknowledged that the larger questions in the case arose under the asserted power of the legislature to control in great measure the exercise of executive or administrative functions of the State government, and he agreed to argue these questions first.[35]

A little more than a week before the hearing, Griffin received a copy of former Governor Miller's brief to the Court of Appeals. Griffin described it as a clever brief, for it avoided answering the careful legal arguments developed by Guthrie and himself. Ward and Miller had sought to do what they had done in the Appellate Division, namely state that there was no legal or constitutional question involved, because this segregation had been going on for seven or eight years, and that nothing was put in the constitutional amendments forbidding it. In other words, Miller wanted the court to assume that everyone was in agreement concerning this process until Roosevelt precipitated the issue in 1929.[36]

A few days before the hearing, Griffin gave Roosevelt some cogent advice when he informed the Governor that whether Guthrie made a good oral argument or not depended largely upon how the elderly counsel was feeling. Encouragement, sympathy, and praise were needed by the senior counsel and Roosevelt was advised that he could not "lay it on too heavy. Please accept this suggestion and indicate to the old gentleman that the whole power of the State is behind him and that we are absolutely confident that he alone is winning and cannot fail."[37]

Taking this advice to heart, the Governor dispatched a kind, warmhearted letter to the senior counsel in which he assured Guthrie that he was doing a magnificent piece of work and that he would "give anything in the world to be present at the argument, for I know that you are going to make a ten-strike." Roosevelt feared, however, that it would be unethical for the Governor to appear in the Court of Appeals, even as a spectator. Roosevelt went on to remind Guthrie that while there had been little in the public print about the case during the past few months, "the eyes of the whole State are on you, with full sympathy from the vast majority of citizens and with full confidence also that you will win the case and cannot fail."[38]

After reading Governor Miller's preliminary briefs Roosevelt concluded that the former would again try to laugh off the possibility of serious complications under the existing legislative chairmen control. Roosevelt then advised his senior counsel that a certain amount of indignation on the latter's part at the frivolity and cynicism of Miller's attitude would be helpful. Roosevelt raised the very important point that Miller, as Governor, had

had no quarrel with his legislative chairmen, as the group of three had been a friendly committee which Miller was able to dominate. All three were Republicans who had sought to make a good record for future electoral contests. Miller, therefore, was not a competent person to comment on the budget controversy for he had seen things through the eyes of an experience which the voters of New York had made an exception rather than a rule. Except for one term of the Senate, the State's electorate had consistently voted for Republican legislatures and Democratic Governors since 1922.[39]

In mid-October, the Executive Budget controversy reached its final stage when the case was argued before New York's Court of Appeals. In his argument Guthrie contended that the delegation to the two legislative chairmen of powers to approve the segregation of lump sum appropriations was an indefensible encroachment of the legislature upon the administrative departments of the government and was unconstitutional and dangerous. He asserted, further, that if the legislature desired to assume approval of this segregation, it had to do so as a body, but that it was without that power under the Constitution to delegate such authority to the two specific chairmen named in the bills enacted at the 1929 session.[40]

Former Governor Miller contended that the allocation of this approval power to the two chairmen was well within the purview of amendments to the Constitution providing for the Executive Budget and in line with established precedent for some years. The controversy, according to Miller, presented a new aspect of an old conflict between the Chief Executive and the people's representatives over control of finances.[41]

Guthrie contended that the argument that the two chairmen did not assume administrative functions in taking the power to approve segregations, but simply passed upon them, had a faulty foundation in fact. He argued along the line that since three persons, the Governor and two chairmen, were named as the approving officials for segregations, the Governor was in a minority, while the legislators assumed a majority which gave them a practical administrative control unjustified by the Constitution.[42]

Almost a month to the day the Court of Appeals had heard the case it handed down a unanimous opinion reversing the decision of the Appellate Division, when it denied to the fiscal leaders of the legislature the right to participate in the segregation of lump sum appropriations in the Executive Budget.[43]

In the decision written by Judge Cuthbert W. Pound, a Republican, the court held that the attempt of the legislature to have the two fiscal chairmen supervise the expenditure of money appropriated by the legislature was, in effect, an attempt to give these two legislators administrative duties. Judge Pound pointed out that while no one could question the fitness of members of the legislature to hold administrative offices in the absence of constitutional inhibition, such limitation existed in Article III, Section 7, adopted in substance in 1821. The court ruled that designation of the finance chairmen to approve the segregation of lump sum appropriations amounted to the making of civil appointments by the legislature within the prohibition of this article, because the positions were created and filled by the legislature; that the incumbents possessed governmental powers; that the powers and duties of the positions were defined by the legislature; that such powers and duties were performed independently; and that the positions had some degree of permanency and continuity. Their power was not exhausted by a single act but was a general supervisory power over a large group of appropriations to be exercised whenever the occasion arose.[44]

According to the court this was a clear and conspicuous instance of an attempt by the legislature to confer administrative powers on two of its members. The legislature not only made a law, in the form of an appropriation, but it made two of its members ex officio its executive agents to carry out the law, that is, to act on the segregation of the appropriation.

The court added that the legislature could not secure relief from its duties or responsibilities by a general delegation of legislative power to someone else. Also, the legislation was complete when the appropriation was made. The legislature could make the segregation itself but it could not "confer administrative powers upon its members without giving them, unconstitutionally, civil appointments to administrative offices."[45]

The court then held that the State Finance Law, Section 139, and the vetoed Section 11 of Chapter 593 of the Laws of 1929, and all similar segregation provisions in the appropriation bills of 1929, were unconstitutional and void.

In a concurring opinion, Justice Frederick E. Crane offered an interesting and seemingly more realistic conclusion when he maintained that in adopting the amendment to the Constitution known as the Executive Budget, there was an attempt made in Article IV-A of the State Constitution to provide a new method, given in much detail, for the making of appropriations for the various departments of government. Whatever might have been done before, new methods were to be pursued upon the adoption of this amendment, for "laws in force at the time fell by the way—the Constitution was to override all of the laws and start with a clean sheet." Therefore, Section 139 of the State Finance Law had no further application to the budget, and the lump sum appropriations made by the budget bill were to be segregated by the heads of the departments concerned.[46]

The court unanimously ruled that it devolved upon the heads of the departments, to which the lump sum appropriations were drawn, to apportion and allot the funds under such appropriations in accordance with the law, without the approval of the Governor or the legislative chairmen.[47]

While Republican lawmakers reluctantly accepted the unanimous decision of the Court of Appeals and were glad that the "vexed point" was settled, Roosevelt hailed the Court's action as a victory for sound government.[48] Roosevelt insisted it was not a personal triumph but a great victory for constitutional government carrying out the original theory of separation of powers and sustaining the purpose of the reorganization of State government and the Executive Budget. He also believed, and rightly so, that the effect of the decision would be felt in many other states where similar questions had risen in previous years.[49]

Disturbed by some newspaper editors who underscored the court's decision, wherein the Governor was denied the right to participate in the segregation of lump sum appropriations but left it up to the chairman of the affected department, Roosevelt retorted that at no time had he insisted that the Governor should have the sole power of segregation, but that he had spoken constantly of the executive or administrative power as a whole, including, of course, the department heads who were responsible to the Governor.[50]

The court decision, according to Roosevelt, had upheld his one and only contention that members of the legislature could appropriate moneys but could not carry on administrative or executive duties in connection with the expenditures of the appropriations. The Governor was correct when he maintained that this was a far-reaching decision and would be regarded for years to come as one of the pivots on which the government of New York and other states would rest.[51]

In the final analysis it made very little difference whether the Governor or the heads of the departments carried out the actual signing of segregation papers, for almost all the heads of departments were appointees of the Governor, and their acts were in reality those of the Governor.

Thus ended the struggle between a legislature which sought to nullify the budget amendments of 1927 and a newly inaugurated Governor who would not buckle under to a stubborn and jealous opposition. This conflict was typical of the battle which had raged intermittently between Republican-dominated legislatures and Al Smith since 1919, and which would continue during the administrations of Franklin D. Roosevelt and Herbert H. Lehman. Support of the principle of an Executive Budget had been nonpartisan, outside of the legislature, yet the Republican leadership exhibited an obstructionist, out-dated philosophy which colored most of their activities during the four years

Roosevelt served as Governor.

The significance of the change which developed in New York following the decisions of the Court of Appeals in the budget controversy was the grant to the Chief Executive of authority to control both the budget estimates and, to a great extent, the use of the funds subsequently appropriated by the legislature. Coordination, supervision, and control of finance replaced the unregulated and chaotic freedom of the various administrative agencies to deal directly with appropriation committees.

The administrative authority of the Chief Executive was also enhanced—particularly when he is a member of the same political party which controls the legislature—for he who controls finance is in command of policy. Finally, this decision tended to reduce the influence of legislators, except the chairmen of appropriation committees, on administrative problems, for they were no longer the real power behind the administrative scene.

Roosevelt's actions helped insure unquestioned executive authority over the State administration, the dominant position of the Executive in relation to the legislature in the adoption and execution of the budget, and the major role presently played by the Executive's staff budget unit.

Roosevelt's contribution to the development of the Executive Budget in New York was consistent with his activities on the Federal scene before and after his gubernatorial administrations. As Assistant Secretary of the Navy, a decade before he became Governor, he vigorously supported the movement for a Federal budget system. A decade after the Executive Budget was sustained by the New York Court of Appeals, President Franklin D. Roosevelt signed Executive Order No. 8248, which transferred the United States Bureau of the Budget to the Executive Office of the nation's Chief Executive.

III

REBELLION BEHIND BARS

THREE VIOLENT prison outbreaks in New York shocked the nation and afforded Roosevelt a challenging opportunity during his first year as Governor.

It was the last week of July, 1929, when some 1,300 of the State's criminals in Clinton Prison at Dannemora rioted and stormed the walls in an abortive attempt to escape. Three inmates were shot and killed and at least a score of others wounded before a hastily recruited army of prison defenders drove them back to their stone cell blocks with hand grenades, tear gas, rifles, machine guns, and shotguns. Known as the "Siberia of New York," this prison was feared and hated by even the most desperate criminals.[1]

Six days later, many of the 1,700 inmates at Auburn Prison battled guards for five hours. While four of the ringleaders managed to escape over the wall, two others were shot and killed and eleven suffered gunshot wounds.[2]

Prison outbreaks are never accidental or spontaneous. There are always underlying causes to such tragedies and these two outbreaks were the result of a variety of factors. Leading penologists had long deplored the incarceration of a majority of New York prisoners in small, inadequate cells. Auburn, built in 1816, was the oldest State penitentiary in use. It stood on low ground near a river and was damp and depressing. The building was a shell, inside of which were two rows of stone cells, back to back, in five tiers. The old cells were seven and one-half feet long, four feet wide, and seven and one-half feet high. In the newer part of the cell block they were only three and one-half feet wide. Each cell had an electric light but no plumbing. There was little ventilation except that which came through the heavily grated doors. At the time of the outbreak there were 1,700 prisoners in Auburn, which was more than 400 in excess of normal capacity; the extra prisoners slept in crowded corridors and a dormitory.[3]

The overcrowding at Auburn had frequently been alluded to in prison inspection reports. Three years earlier Special Commissioner George W. Alger referred to the cells as "atrocious" and suggested the expenditure of $2.5 million for major requirements at the prison. A few days before this report was made the State Prison Commission had urged the abandonment of Auburn Prison and the construction of a new penal institution on farm property outside of the city limits.[4]

The task at Clinton Prison in Dannemora was also complicated by old structures which had been opened in 1845 with most of the deficiencies of buildings of that time. There were 382 more prisoners than cells. As a result, some inmates slept in corridors and other odd corners.[5]

Just before the outbreak of these riots, New York's prison population and cell facilities, as compared with those of a year before, were:

	July 1, 1928	July 1, 1929	Cells
Auburn (men)	1,563	slightly larger	1,282
Clinton	1,550	1,574	1,192
Great Meadows	1,130	1,094	1,163
Sing Sing	1,713	1,956	1,450[6]

In 1922 the ratio of prison inmates to the population of New York was 48 to 100,000. Five years later it had risen to 52.[7] The continued overcrowding of the State's prisons intensified the suffering of inmates and increased the difficulties of prison officers. It gave the prisoners an opportunity to educate one another in crime and directly promoted the worst vice.

Another cause for prison outbreaks was the lack of sufficient employment. The prison-labor system in New York had been the State-use system, whereby prisoners were employed in the work of the prison or in the production of goods, in making roads, or in other labor for the benefit of the State or counties, cities, or school districts. For a great many years, however, this system had been hampered by restrictive legislation and by inadequate appropriations. In order to keep their men busy prison officials divided up work so that most of the prisoners did less than six hours of productive labor daily, and three or four men were often employed on a task that could have been easily performed by one.[8]

Also to be considered was the failure of the State to make proper provisions for members of prison staffs. In contrast to Great Britain, Massachusetts, and New York City, the Empire State had no systematic plan for the training of prison guards. In addition, these guards were paid less than firemen and policemen from New York communities, resulting in a significant turnover. The average number of prisoners per guard in New York State prisons was 12.8, compared to 10.6 in France, 9.3 in Sweden, 8 in Germany, and 6.5 in Great Britain.[9]

A major cause for the outbreaks, however, was the extraordinary increase in the severity of laws regulating imprisonment of criminals. This change had been expressed in recent penal legislation and in harsh sentences imposed by judges. The recently enacted Baumes Law of New York provided that whenever a prisoner was convicted for the fourth time for a felony the judge was obliged to sentence him to prison for life. There had also been the abolition of the good conduct time allowance, a pattern which had been customary throughout the nation during the previous half century and which was especially helpful to first offenders. By 1929, many prisoners were receiving two, or even three, times as long a sentence as they would have normally received five or ten years previously.[10] These developments inevitably created a tremendous feeling of desperation and bitterness among prison inmates.

Another agitating factor for prisoners was the abridgment of the use of the parole system. For many months prior to the prison outbreaks the State Parole Board had been more than reluctant in its issuance of paroles, besides providing inadequate guidance and encouragement of those to whom paroles had been issued.[11]

Leading penologists, including Hastings H. Hart, Sam A. Lewisohn, and Dr. Walter N. Thayer, Jr., were aware of these underlying causes. Would Governor Roosevelt, however, seek the counsel of such farsighted men, and of conscientious lawmakers, in the search for solutions to these problems?

A week after the riot at Dannemora, Roosevelt made a personal inspection of Clinton Prison. While there he directed Commissioner of Correction Raymond F. C. Kieb to make a sweeping investigation of the Dannemora and Auburn riots.[12] The following day the Governor concluded a 1,000 mile tour of northern New York by visiting the State's Great Meadow Prison at Comstock. There he saw modern sanitary equipment in fireproof buildings and 500 of its inmates at work in the open air. Instead of the tense atmosphere he had experienced the previous day at Clinton Prison, the Governor found Great Meadows more like a large farm than a penal institution.

Meanwhile, State Senator Caleb H. Baumes, who was also chairman of the New York State Crime Commission, denied that his law was responsible for the prison outbreaks. He placed the blame on special privileges, laxity in the guarding of the felons, and overcrowdedness which had existed long before the Baumes Law became effective. He also pointed out that less than 150 criminals had been convicted under the Baumes Law during the three years it had been in effect.[13]

During the weeks and months which followed the Governor received suggestions from leading penologists and organizations throughout the nation, most of them agreeing on immediate basic reforms.

Delegates to the annual convention of the State Federation of Labor recommended enlargement of existing facilities, the segregation of prisoners according to the severity of the crime, psychiatric clinics, development of prison farms, time off for good behavior, and an elementary and vocational educational system.[14]

Former Governor Smith proposed that a competent board of doctors, psychiatrists, and students of criminology make proper disposition of the convicted prisoner.[15]

Dr. Walter N. Thayer, Jr., superintendent of the institution for defective delinquents at Napanoch, recommended that a substantial minimum sentence of five or ten years be meted out on the first commitment or on the "earliest manifestation of habitual tendency to crime." A criminal, he insisted, was not deterred by a sentence that had a definite termination. With all respect to the courts, Thayer felt they were not in a position to prophesy the date when a criminal could be returned to society.[16]

Joseph A. McGinnies, Republican Speaker of the State Assembly, afforded a contrast for penologists when he advised Roosevelt that although the prison situation was a little annoying, "these things did happen." He believed there was too much sentiment expressed in the treatment of the convict class, and that this did not tend to insure the best of discipline. McGinnies always felt that a man condemned for a crime against society should be treated humanely and given decent quarters but should be made to feel that he was an offender against society and that he was being punished for that offense. However, lamented the Republican leader, "I seemed to be the only one that entertained that opinion, so perhaps I was in the wrong, as I usually am."[17]

Roosevelt felt that this serious situation warranted a thorough inquiry into prison administration, the Baumes Law, parole, and segregation. He hesitated, however, in initiating a general investigation because there had been periodic inquiries of this nature during the previous twenty-five years. The State had volumes of reports from expert penologists, and he believed that "almost every penologist has an individual theory and it is difficult to get any unanimity of opinion." Roosevelt's inclination was to ask the Baumes Commission to hold hearings on the whole subject of life sentences for fourth offenders.[18]

Dissatisfied with Roosevelt's approach to the problem, Felix

Frankfurter did well to remind the Governor that the United States was then far behind the best penological thought in the world. For many years there had been no thoroughgoing inquiry into the underlying purposes of penal institutions, their differentiations, their adaptations to different classes of prisoners, and the scheme of training for prisoners for their eventual resumption of participation in civil life. Frankfurter also doubted whether serious thought had been given to the fundamental lines along which prison accommodations ought to be provided. Here, he felt, was an excellent opportunity for New York to take the lead through a body of experts carrying the weight of an English Royal Commission "when charged with the investigation of a grave national problem." Frankfurter hoped that Roosevelt would find it wise to have such a commission appointed, consisting of men and women whose report would mark an epoch in penal administration in the United States.[19]

Within a month after receiving Frankfurter's suggestion, Roosevelt convened a prison parley of State prison administrators, legislators, and leading crime experts and penologists.[20] The conference participants concurred in the desirability of limiting the size of prisons to accommodate between 1,100 and 1,500 prisoners and unanimously endorsed the need for improving the quality of food served to prisoners. The Governor explained that the discussion was based on the $30 million prison building program adopted in 1927, which looked to 1935 as the date when there would be adequate prison capacity.[21] Before the start of the 1930 legislative session, the Governor reconvened this group to evolve the program he would present for action by the lawmakers.[22]

During the last few months of 1929 the State Crime Commission met frequently to hear testimony and receive recommendations from prison officials and leading penologists. Shortly before the convening of the new legislative session, the Commission concluded that $30 million would be needed to rehabilitate the prisons within five years, with an immediate appropriation of $12 million for emergency needs.[23]

Exactly one week after the report of the State Crime Commission, the principal keeper at Auburn Prison was murdered, a dozen other keepers were wounded or gassed, and eight convicts were killed. For the second time within five months a desperate group of long-term prisoners attempted to escape from Auburn. The inmates were partly in control of the prison for six hours before authorities obtained the upper hand. In the process, Warden Edgar S. Jennings was captured and held as hostage by the group of rioting convicts. When the convicts threatened to murder the Warden unless they were permitted to escape, a hurried telephone message to Acting Governor Lehman in Albany received the prompt reply that there would be "no compromise" with the rioting convicts.[24]

Notified of the prison riot while his train was speeding eastward from Chicago, Roosevelt's immediate response was to endorse Lehman's actions and to promise emergency recommendations when the legislature convened within three weeks.[25]

The day following the second Auburn riot, Commissioner Kieb sent the Governor a long, rambling, and repetitive report on the background of the uprising. He disclosed nothing new or incisive, nor did he exhibit a much needed assertion of leadership.[26] Immediately thereafter, Roosevelt directed Colonel George F. Chandler to make a thorough investigation of the riot. Within four days Colonel Chandler reported on the overcrowdedness and physical conditions of the prison with its damp, dark, unsanitary cells three and one-half feet wide—"files in which human beings are stored away." Though it would take some time for the construction of new facilities, there were improvements which could be made immediately, such as a variety in food and sufficient warm clothing. According to the Colonel, the most pressing need was for more and better trained guards. He also recommended the segregation of incorrigible prisoners so that they be kept away from the other inmates who were doing their best to conform to the order of prison routine.[27] The Chandler report added little to the stature of the Commissioner of Correction, and even less to Warden Jennings of Auburn.

While showing no disposition to criticize Colonel Chandler's report, Commissioner Kieb retorted, as had former Governor Smith previously, that he had tried in vain to make many of the changes Chandler advocated but that the legislature had consistently refused to appropriate the necessary funds.[28]

After a hurried conference with Kieb, the chief State Engineer, Senator Baumes, and the head of the State Police, the Governor developed plans for the establishment of seven camps or cantonments for prisoners, in line with one of Colonel Chandler's recommendations.[29]

On the eve of the new legislative session, Lieutenant Governor Lehman outlined Roosevelt's prison reform program in a lucid and convincing address. Lehman offered a "middle course—an intelligent medium between brutality and privilege." He stressed the duty of the State to treat the prisoners and care for them in such a manner that they would not return to their freedom broken in health or dedicated to fight society. For immediate relief the State should erect road or construction camps in which "amenable prisoners" could be housed while employed in outside work. Ultimately, every inmate should be equipped with a trade, both for his own development and for his return to the world outside the prison walls. The most important suggestion made by Lehman was of a Parole Board to consist of three persons, with competent assistance, devoting all their time and energy exclusively to considering the cases of prisoners eligible for parole.[30]

The 1930 legislature had barely convened when Senator Baumes's State Crime Commission introduced eight bills calling for a $10 million prison building program and $160,000 in additional appropriations to improve the food and clothing of convicts and to provide additional prison guards. The proposed legislation also sought to reorganize the Parole Commission, substituting for the existing ex-officio members an independent body of three salaried individuals appointed by the Governor with the consent of the Senate.[31] Representing, in general, the official Republican program, these bills proposed to carry out many of Roosevelt's ideas on prison reform.

In a special message to the legislature Roosevelt pronounced the State's prison system "antiquated" and its penal law in "the experimental stage." Heeding the advice given him by Frankfurter months previously, the Governor declared that in addition to emergencies which should and could be met at once, there had to be a competent study of the prison situation prior to the reform going more deeply to the roots of the evil. Appropriations were requested for the immediate establishment of five prison cantonments to relieve congestion at State prisons, and to cover salaries for additional prison guards.[32]

Immediately after the reading of Roosevelt's communication, and less than twenty-four hours after the Governor's annual message had invited the friendly cooperation of Republican lawmakers, G.O.P. spokesmen launched a concerted attack on the Roosevelt administration. They subjected the Governor to personal abuse and assigned to him responsibility for the breakdown of the Department of Correction. Senator John Knight expressed doubt that there was any "parallel to the present situation in the history of the State." Eberly Hutchinson, chairman of the Assembly Ways and Means Committee, laid at the Governor's door responsibility for the lives lost in the rioting at Auburn.[33]

According to observing newsmen, students of New York history had to go back to the Sulzer administration to find a legislative attack on an administration paralleling this one in bitterness. Even when relations between the Democratic Governor and the Republican legislature were strained to the breaking point during the previous administrations of Alfred E. Smith, no onslaught equal in bitterness was ever staged in the legislative halls. The exhibition by the Republican leaders was petty and ardently partisan as they attempted to blame former Governor Smith for delay in prison construction, and now Roosevelt for prison deaths.

Despite these onslaughts in the Senate and Assembly the legislature unanimously approved Roosevelt's emergency prison requests. Besides providing for five new prison cantonments, the legislature approved an increase of five cents per day per prisoner in the cost of meals and an additional five dollars in the annual clothing allowance for prisoners.[34]

Shortly thereafter, the Governor forwarded another message to the legislature recommending enactment of bills which went to the root of past evils and which amounted to a new State prison policy. Roosevelt wanted the size of new prison buildings decreased rather than increased; improved prison industrial and agricultural facilities; reconsideration of parole and probation; and re-enactment of legislation insuring time off for good behavior by prisoners.[35]

None of the measures for prison reform under discussion at Albany received wider support than the Governor's proposal to reorganize the State's parole system. Roosevelt, Senator Baumes, and independent prison authorities agreed that the part-time board of prison officials should be abolished and a full-time commission established in its place. The idea, however, was not new, for the Prison Association of New York had been urging this reform for many years.

On January 22, Roosevelt appointed a special committee headed by a mature student of penology, Sam A. Lewisohn, to consider the State's parole system.[36] Within two weeks the committee made its report. This group had a comparatively easy assignment, for many of its members were thoroughly familiar with the problem and long ago had made up their minds that the existing system was little more than a farce. The committee members knew that the State Board of Parole which met one day each month in each prison, and considered from fifty to a hundred applications at a sitting, had little opportunity to determine scientifically whether the man about to be paroled had reached a period when further incarceration would be of less service to him and the State, as a reformative measure, than a like period passed in liberty under parole supervision. With little time at their disposal, and even less information, the parole board had little opportunity to make exhaustive and painstaking studies of individual cases. Likewise, parole officers with some 140 men on their list had little opportunity to give parolees aid, counsel, and adequate supervision.

The Lewisohn committee, therefore, proposed the creation of a board of pardon and parole with members giving full-time service. To free it from routine custodial problems, to give it the necessary prestige, and to render it of assistance to the Governor in the exercise of his pardoning power, the committee proposed to set up the new machinery in the Executive Department. In contrast to Colonel Chandler's earlier recommendations, the Lewisohn committee proposed that all employees of the board, except its executive director, be chosen through civil service examinations, and that provision be made for the further training of parole officers after they had joined the staff.[37]

The Lewisohn committee proposals were of major significance. Not only did they insure a more humane and scientific approach to the problem of rehabilitation but they were more enlightened from a materialistic point of view. It was far cheaper to keep a man at large, but under supervision, than to build a million dollar wall around him.

Desiring to keep the prison issue entirely out of partisan dispute and to prevent its becoming a victim of political strategy, the Governor diverged from the usual custom of forwarding the committee's report with a special message to the legislature. Instead, he sent the report to Senator Baumes in the latter's dual capacity as chairman of the Codes Committee of the Senate and of the State Crime Commission.

As a result of unceasing efforts by Lieutenant Governor Lehman, who more than any other official of prominence at the Capitol had shown consistent interest in the parole problems, and by Senator Baumes, the lawmakers in both houses adopted the Baumes-Esmond measure. This compromise between the recommendations of the Lewisohn committee and Senator Baumes's original proposal provided for an enlightened parole system supervised by a board of three full-time members, appointed by the Governor with the consent of the Senate.[38]

Roosevelt also approved the Knight proposal, which created a temporary commission to survey the prison situation and to define a fixed prison policy for the State.[39] This measure was sponsored by the G.O.P. following investigation by the Republican-dominated legislative fiscal committees which blamed the Smith and Roosevelt administrations for inefficiency in the conduct of prisons, for the recent prison disorders, and for the delay in carrying out improvements and extensions at the State prisons for which the legislature had made ample provisions.[40]

Following adjournment of the 1930 legislative session, two important events occurred which did much to further prison reform in New York. After weeks of negotiation, Dr. Walter N. Thayer, Jr., submitted his resignation as Superintendent of Prisons in Maryland to return to New York as State Commissioner of Correction, succeeding the much-criticized Dr. Kieb.[41] The State's penal system was now in good hands, for Dr. Thayer had long insisted that the criminal law should punish men for what they were, rather than for what they did. "Crime is not the cause but the result," he said on one occasion, "not the disease but the symptom. An effort should be made during the period of imprisonment to ascertain just why the man has become a criminal." Dr. Thayer also maintained that no two criminals should be given the same treatment for purposes of reform. "The individual should receive society's attention on the basis of what caused him to commit the crime."[42]

He had also urged that criminal legislation be revised so that instead of inflicting a definite penalty for a definite act, it make possible the commitment to institutions of individuals likely to continue to commit antisocial acts. He maintained that they be held in custody as long as they retained that attitude toward society.[43] Some years earlier Dr. Thayer had submitted a plan embodying these ideas which provided for an institution for defective delinquents and their commitment thereto for indefinite terms. The plan was carried out by the State and the result was the institution at Napanoch which Dr. Thayer headed until 1929.

Dr. Thayer's appointment as State Commissioner of Correction was received with great approval by hundreds of colleagues, penologists, and editors throughout the country. One newspaper described the Thayer appointment as one of the most commendable made by Roosevelt and declared that it "was almost worth the price paid in the three costly prison riots of last year."[44]

Toward the end of July, 1930, Governor Roosevelt, Speaker McGinnies, and Senator Knight, in pursuance to the Knight bill adopted earlier,[45] jointly agreed upon the membership of a Temporary State Commission to Investigate Prison Administration and Construction. Appointed to head the commission was Sam A. Lewisohn, chairman of the committee which had dealt promptly and effectively with the parole problem earlier in the year.[46] The commission members were to bring in a report proposing a prison policy for the treatment, segregation, and classification of prisoners, together with a plan for the expansion of prison industries, and a program of prison construction. Although this was a large order, it was in the hands of men and women who were familiar with the problems. The Governor relieved their burden somewhat by assigning the prison industry problem to another group headed by George Gordon Battle.

While the Lewisohn commission pursued its studies, the coming of fall signaled the start of another gubernatorial campaign. The prison issue was not ignored, for Republican candidate Charles H. Tuttle ascribed the riots at Dannemora and Auburn to gross mismanagement on the part of the Roosevelt administration. He also denounced the long delay in making improvements for which the legislature had provided appropriations.[47] Louis Waldman, the Socialist candidate, saddled both Roosevelt and the Republican legislature with responsibility for the prison outbreaks. The Governor, according to Waldman, had permitted vile prison conditions to continue until they had become unbearable, while the Republican party had passed the Baumes

Laws which filled already overcrowded jails to the point of causing revolt.[48]

Roosevelt scoffed at these charges and replied that there were two principal causes for the prison riots. First was the failure of a quarter of a century of Republican legislatures to give the State new prisons to replace the antiquated, unhealthy dungeons which were built one hundred years ago. Second was the refusal of Republican legislatures to face courageously the problems presented by a new type of young prisoner who was being sent to jail for life, under a series of laws that bore the name of the Republican candidate for Lieutenant Governor, Senator Baumes. Roosevelt then went on to cite, in utterances more partisan than objective, the splendid prison progress initiated under his administration, "without any help from the Republican leaders."[49]

The electorate was not moved by Tuttle's charges and re-elected Roosevelt by a record-breaking plurality.

In its first report to the Governor, the Temporary State Commission headed by Lewisohn proposed a new prison policy: "the replacement of mass treatment and routine organization by a system of constant personal study, individual treatment and training of every prisoner." It expressed strong disapproval of construction of any prisons with capacity for more than 1,000 inmates. It recommended, instead, that the first new prison to be built have a maximum capacity of some 500 prisoners, and that it be of the "medium security" type—a model bridging the gap between the fortress type of prison such as Sing Sing or Auburn and the road camps where actual confinement was almost non-existent. It also wanted the experiment of road camps continued and extended.[50]

In forwarding the commission's report to the legislature, the Governor drew particular attention to the recommendations which would permit certain offenders to earn time off their sentences by good conduct in prison. Roosevelt felt that nothing would facilitate the proper handling of prisoners to a greater degree than the holding out of hope to inmates of an earlier release by reason of good conduct. Along the same lines were recommendations relative to uniform minimum sentences for first-offender felons and modification of the existing fourth-offender act.

Imprisonment, reminded the Governor, had as its basis the theory that it deterred the commission of crime. Bearing in mind that 92 percent of those sent to prison were returned to society, a more enlightened system of penology insisted that the period of incarceration be more than a mere confinement and should include such treatment of individual prisoners as to make more probable their ultimate conversion into law-abiding citizens on their release.[51]

Before the conclusion of the 1931 legislative session, the lawmakers restored the system of time allowance to be deducted from sentences for good behavior of prison inmates, retroactive to 1926, enacted legislation which opened the way for the segregation of prisoners and appropriated money for the construction of a medium security type prison.[52]

With the enactment of much of his prison program by 1931, Roosevelt could well conclude that the State had taken significant strides toward achieving the goal of complete reorganization of prison construction and administration. Two years earlier, at the time of the prison riots, Felix Frankfurter had made it clear to Roosevelt that with proper handling the State could outline and undertake a real program of prison reform, a task which required real diplomacy and constructive ability. Yet, in the short intervening time, the State, through the efforts of leading penologists and Sam Lewisohn, had been able to adopt, according to Roosevelt, "a real prison program for the first time in our generation. Practically everything which we have sought in the way of legislation has become law, with the single exception of the bill to change the fourth offender act." But Roosevelt had no doubt that that would be taken care of at the next session of the legislature.[53]

It was not illogical for Roosevelt, whose activities were being watched by the entire nation, to be hailed as a prison reformer when receiving the medal of the National Commitee on Prison and Prison Labor. This honor had previously been awarded to Presidents Wilson and Coolidge, Samuel Gompers, Thomas Mott Osborne, Alfred E. Smith, Gifford Pinchot, and Dwight W. Morrow.[54]

The most significant impetus to reorganization of the State's prisons continued to be given by the reports and recommendations of the Temporary State Commission to Investigate Prison Administration and Construction. The Lewisohn commission requested the 1932 legislature to modify the law relating to the sentencing of first offenders, because many of them were cruelly long and tied the hands of the Parole Board until the prisoner had served his minimum term.[55]

Discussing the injustice of the "fourth-offender" act, which had fallen into general disrepute, the commission suggested that this penal law be amended to provide for an indeterminate sentence, the minimum of which would be less than the maximum term for first offenders convicted of the same crime. That would ordinarily put the criminal away for fifteen years. If he were released at the end of that time he would be on parole for the rest of his life. With reference to minimum terms for first offenders, the Lewisohn commission receded from its previous position when it suggested a comparatively mild amendment authorizing the Parole Board to apply to the committing court for the resentencing of a prisoner it regarded as having been dealt with too severely.[56]

Before he left office as Governor, Roosevelt approved two important pieces of prison legislation which all but wound up his prison reform program. One bill provided that individuals sent to prisons after July 1, 1932, be able to earn compensation of seven and one-half days each month off their minimum sentence for good behavior.[57] The other bill, "an act to amend the penal law, in relation to the punishment of fourth, or subsequent, conviction of felony," imposed a minimum sentence for the fourth offender—in no event less than fifteen years, and a maximum sentence of life.[58] This meant that the fourth offender would become eligible for consideration for parole at the end of the fifteenth year. The advantage of this legislation was that it made for a uniform practice without the mandatory severity of the original Baumes fourth-offender act. The bill allowed for individual consideration and treatment by the Parole Board.

In December, 1932, Franklin D. Roosevelt could look back upon four years of his administration and observe great changes in the State's prison policy. The prison system was being transformed on the principle of making the punishment fit the criminal as well as the crime. Some needed iron bars, some needed medical attention, and some needed another chance. Attempts would now be made to insure individual treatment rather than mass restraint. The State was building a new type of prison to house and benefit men and women requiring less restraint. The parole system had been reorganized and imbued with a new spirit. The severity of the fourth-offender act had been tempered with some human understanding and foresight. Roosevelt had sought and followed the most competent advice available on better methods of handling prisoners, and his periodic utterances in support of commission reports had effectively focused public attention on the prison problem. Through probation, parole, the indeterminate sentence, classification prisons without bars, and road camps, New York was once more attempting to take the initiative among states in bringing about a more humane and rational treatment of prisoners.

And so the curtain dropped on four years of intensive efforts to reform the administrative and organizational policy of the State toward its prisons and correctional institutions.[59] As Roosevelt left Albany for broader political fields he might have recalled comments he had once inscribed:

If I were asked what I considered the greatest contribution Lieutenant Governor Lehman and I have made in Albany—I would say that it has been along the lines of public social welfare—

We have evolved a definite and clear prison policy and we are unique among the States in this respect in that we have an objective. We have sought to emphasize not so much the punishment, but rather the ideal to send the prisoner back to society a better citizen than when he went in.[60]

IV

PARITY FOR THE FARMER

A L SMITH loved the "sidewalks of New York." But for the few wheat-colored blades of grass between the cobblestones under Brooklyn Bridge, he had, at first, known little of the rural life that provided so much interest and stimulus for his successor. Franklin D. Roosevelt was reared on a large country estate in the heart of the Hudson Valley. With an open receptiveness and interest in people, implemented by developing years in a rural environment, Roosevelt was familiar with many phases of farming long before the 1928 contest. Replying to a Republican newspaper in South Dakota, Roosevelt made certain that if he did not have a log cabin to fall back upon, for future political use, he at least had an earthy origin with plenty of grass roots, when he wrote: "By the way I am not, as you say, an 'Urban leader' for I was born and brought up and have always made my home on a farm in Dutchess County." [1]

As he traveled through the hinterlands of New York in 1928, he talked with hundreds of farmers and agrarian spokesmen. As Mrs. Eleanor Roosevelt described it two decades later, Franklin D. Roosevelt had an "extraordinary acute power of observation and could judge conditions in any section from the looks of the countryside as he travelled through." [2] From her husband, Eleanor Roosevelt learned to observe from train windows and from a car, for he would "watch the crops, notice how people dressed, how many cars there were and in what condition, and even look at the wash on the clothes lines." [3]

It was during his 1928 swing around the State that Roosevelt's keen eyes observed many deserted farmhouses, eroded hillsides, depleted woods, and generally depressed conditions. What he could not see, nor investigate on foot, he learned from conversation with those who approached his open car. Long before the conclusion of the campaign, Roosevelt realized that farm aid was of extreme urgency.

Few of New York's urban residents were aware of the agricultural resources and productivity of their State, let alone its problems. Living in crowded apartment buildings hidden from the sun, with cows and cornfields a mystery to most youngsters, city folk did not know that in 1929, according to Henry Morgenthau, Jr., New York State was

... first in the amount of milk sold; first in income from dairy cows; third in number of dairy cattle; second in value of dairy cows, second in value and number of pure-bred livestock; first in income from hay; second in production of apples; second in production of pears; second in production of grapes; first in production of cabbage; second in production of potatoes; fifth in commercial acreage of all vegetables; fourth in income from poultry and eggs; fourth in value of farm implements; sixth in cash income to farmers and fourth in number of farms operated by owners.[4]

Citizens of other farm states also shared the ignorance of urban New Yorkers. Typical was the reaction of Wisconsin's State Treasurer who, following an address by Roosevelt in 1931, wrote the Governor:

... You spoke of the difference in the price of milk paid by the consumer, which is fifteen cents a quart, and the three cents a quart received by the farmer. I am sure you surprised all of your listeners, as we did not know that the people of New York knew anything about farmers. We thought you were acquainted only with Wall Street magnates.[5]

The era of "Republican" prosperity coexisted with the great agricultural depression which was entering its eighth year when Roosevelt became Governor. During the early summer of 1920 the bottom had fallen out of the agricultural price structure. A few months later industry experienced a postwar deflation. During the latter part of 1920 and much of the following year,

business generally shared the effects of an economic depression
with the farmer. It was not long, however, before the industrial
sector of society regained a semblance of stability. The agricultural depression lingered on and by 1928 the average farmer
looked to the future with more hope than confidence, never
feeling certain that the eagerly awaited new day had really
dawned.[6]

Owing primarily to the great dairy, poultry, and truck farming of the East, the price index of farm products was always
higher in this section of the country than the general level for
the United States. The index for New York farm prices in
November, 1928, stood at 152, compared to 146 for the nation.[7]

Immediately after his arrival in Warm Springs, following
his election in November, 1928, Roosevelt appointed a temporary commission of twenty-one agricultural experts to propose solutions for the many problems facing the State's farm
community.[8]

Among the twenty-one originally appointed—a group which
later became known as the Agricultural Advisory Commission
—were men and women representing virtually every rural
viewpoint, farm organization, and agricultural institution in the
State. The commission included several who lived on their own
land and made their living by farming, or who had demonstrated
their ability as farmers. Eighteen of them were reputed to be
Republicans.[9]

For chairman of this commission, Roosevelt selected Henry
Morgenthau, Jr., publisher of *The American Agriculturist*, who
had early turned his interests toward rural life. He received
his first experience in farming on Western ranches. After high
school he attended the New York College of Agriculture but
soon left it to become owner and operator of a large fruit
farm in Dutchess County. His farm also became well known in
dairy circles because of its outstanding Holstein cows. In
1922 he purchased the *American Agriculturist*, second oldest
weekly farm journal in the United States.

He inherited an interest in Democratic party politics from

his father, former Ambassador Henry Morgenthau, Sr. As late as 1930 the latter was co-chairman of the Finance Division of the Independent Citizens Committee for Roosevelt and Lehman. In 1920, and again in 1928, Morgenthau, Jr., was active in political campaigns for Roosevelt in Dutchess County. Under his chairmanship the Agricultural Advisory Commission was to make some of the most significant contributions of the Roosevelt administration.

Of all the members of Roosevelt's state and presidential cabinets, Henry Morgenthau, Jr., and his wife Elinor, were the two closest friends of the Franklin D. Roosevelts.[10]

Prior to its first meeting the Governor advised his newly appointed commission of farm experts that its major objective was to answer the question: "What can the State of New York do to aid agriculture, give farmers a square deal and help make the farm dollar go as far as the dollar of the city man?"[11]

At their first meeting, within three weeks of the election, the farm experts sought to formulate a tax program which would help reduce the ruinous burden of farm taxes. Mark Graves, of the New York State Tax Department, informed the commission that counties were then obliged to pay 35 percent of the cost of constructing State highways. Under existing conditions, that burden on some agricultural communities was, proportionately, twenty, thirty, or even forty times heavier than on the more populous and prosperous communities. As a result, the commission suggested that the State assume the entire burden of building and maintaining State highways and eliminating grade crossings, in order to equalize the cost of road construction. They contended this would lighten taxes on farm lands and put the burden on State revenues drawn principally from a one-half mill property tax,[12] and from inheritance, income, and stock transfer taxes.

As a means of providing additional State revenues for the construction and maintenance of highways, these farm leaders recommended a tax on gasoline which they estimated would net the State $20,000,000 annually. They felt this would safeguard city residents from increased taxation for road purposes through the provision of ample revenue from motorists. The commission also suggested that the State assume the job of removing snow from State highways; make a readjustment for the distribution of moneys for so-called dirt roads; provide for a study of the costs of local government and assume the minimum salary for local school teachers.[13]

In contrast to the viewpoint of some experts in administration and executive-legislative relationships, the consensus of this predominantly Republican commission was that they continue to function in an unofficial capacity. They believed that if they sought official appointment and expense appropriations from the legislature the lawmakers would, in all likelihood, weigh down the commission with their own selections, and perhaps impair its efficiency. Most members felt they could persuade their organizations to pay for their traveling expenses, while Chairman Morgenthau and his father volunteered to take care of office space and secretarial and mailing expenses.[14]

The group's final recommendation was that the Governor-elect direct the commission to prepare a long-range program and act in an advisory capacity on rural affairs to the Chief Executive and other State officials.

As one of his first official acts, Governor Roosevelt slightly reshuffled the commission, without changing its political complexion, and designated it as his Agricultural Advisory Commission. He added the Republican chairman of the Senate Committee on Taxation and Retrenchmen, Seabury C. Mastick, and the latter's counterpart in the Assembly, Walter L. Platt. By the inclusion of these key Republican legislators Roosevelt demonstrated an administrator's appreciation of the need for close cooperation between an executive-appointed commission and a lawmaking body.

In mid-January, 1929, the Agricultural Advisory Commission held its first session in Albany. Aware that the tax burden had increased more rapidly in the rural than urban sections of the State, and that the rural counties were paying a greater proportion of the cost of highway construction than their use warranted, the commission unanimously recommended a tax of two cents on each gallon of gasoline. From the revenue to be derived, at least 40 percent was to be so applied as to effect an equalization of the burden of constructing county highways, and relieve the towns of their respective shares of the cost of maintenance. The remainder of this 40 percent, they felt, should be apportioned to the counties for the purpose of aiding them in developing a secondary or lateral system of improved highways.[15]

Fearing that the Democratic Governor would use this commission to make political capital at their expense, the leaders of the Republican majority hastily set up their own legislative committee to look into agricultural problems. At a public hearing, held coincidentally in mid-January, spokesmen for the Agricultural Advisory Commission, and Roosevelt himself, indicated their determination to cooperate with the legislature in working out any and all practicable plans.[16]

Speaking for the Agricultural Advisory Commission, Mark Graves advised the legislative committee of the inequities in taxes paid by farmers. His analysis of the increase in the cost of government in rural communities disclosed that on the average at least 66 percent of the increase had been due to schools and highways. A farmer owning a ten thousand dollar farm in Erie County, for example, could pay $5.70 once and would have completed his payment of the cost for the State highway system; whereas, if he owned the same farm in Yates county, it would cost him $464.50. The cost of the State highway system could, without any injustice or any unfairness to other groups of taxpayers, be more equitably distributed by the State.[17] Other spokesmen for the Governor's commission stressed the need for a two cent tax on gasoline so that the cost of building and maintaining roads would then be put on their users.[18]

Underscoring the unfair and unequal burden of taxation for the support of one-, two-, three-, and four-teacher schools,

the Governor's commission concluded that the principles laid
down in the proposed Webb-Rice bills before the legislature
would do much to remedy these inequalities and urged their
immediate adoption.[19] The commission's insistence on State
aid to elevate rural educational standards was in full accord
with Roosevelt's philosophy. His support of improved rural
education was early in evidence when he wrote Morgenthau,
in 1929:

What hits me most is the very high percentage of ignorance. I am
not concerned about prejudice, personal stupidity or wrong thinking
as much as by the sheer, utter and complete ignorance displayed by
such a large number of farmers. . . . I am inclined to think that someday we will not stop compulsory education at the age of fourteen
but will compel every citizen throughout life to attend a school of
information once a week.[20]

Shortly after his commission presented its findings on rural
education, Roosevelt relayed its recommendations in a special
message to the legislature urging their speedy adoption. He
contended that the State had failed to provide equality of
educational opportunity for all children and asked the lawmakers to appropriate $2,450,000 to relieve the rural taxpayers
of this burden in poorer districts.[21]

The Agricultural Advisory Commission met on three subsequent occasions during the 1929 legislative session, each time
recommending additional farm relief legislation. Their third
report recommended State aid for the construction of town
highways.[22] The fourth report recommended State aid for local
snow removal; early completion of added laboratory facilities
at the State Agricultural Experiment Station at Geneva; thorough research work of muck land problems; a stronger animal
husbandry department at the State College; investigations on
new potato diseases; research on problems of potato storage;
studies of city markets; and further studies of the problems of
cooperative marketing and rural government.[23]

The fifth, and final, report for the 1929 legislative session suggested an amendment to the State Constitution permitting any

county, if it wished, to eliminate all town and school tax collectors. It requested the legislature to appoint a joint commission, consisting of legislators, members appointed by the Governor, and representatives of farmers to study the marketing problem of the State. The commission also favored the rapid purchase and reforestation by the State or county of abandoned farm lands.[24]

Ever since the Agricultural Advisory Commission began to function, the Republican legislative leadership was in a quandary. As spokesmen for the rock-ribbed Republican farm areas, they could ill-afford to oppose the commission's recommendations on the basis of partisanship, inasmuch as the overwhelming number of its members were Republicans and included, in addition, the presidents of major farm groups in the State. On the other hand, to place on the statute books such excellent, and urgently needed, proposals would illustrate Republican forfeiture of farm leadership to a Democratic Governor elected primarily by urban votes. Due to the deteriorating farm situation and combined pressure from the major farm organizations, the State College of Agriculture and Home Economics and the State Department of Agriculture and Markets, the Republican majority had little choice but to facilitate passage of much of the basic proposals of the commission. These enactments included some of the most constructive farm legislation adopted in recent New York history. Even the ardently Republican *Rural New Yorker*, leading farm journal in the State, reluctantly placed the blame for this awkward situation on the shoulders of the G.O.P. leadership, when it held that

Republican leaders of the past were too confident of their position. In spite of better counsel in their own ranks they neglected just demands of country people, and actually created an opening for attack. . . . Progress was made . . . both in method of financing roads and in equalizing allotments to country schools. The bills for the purposes were approved by both sides, and the leaders who had worked for them so long felt that the Governor was stealing their thunder, capitalizing their work, and claiming all credit as a newcomer in the field.[25]

On April 10, 1929, in the presence of his Agricultural Advisory Commission, Roosevelt signed into law much of that body's basic recommendations for 1929. An amendment to the highway law liberated towns and villages from contributing to the maintenance of State and county highways, and imposed the cost of such maintenance entirely upon the State.[26] Another measure provided for further tax reduction for county residents by reducing the contribution of counties for grade crossing elimination from 10 percent to 1 percent.[27] Another bill provided for additional funds for the training of rural school teachers at several State agricultural schools so as to improve the qualifications of rural school teachers.[28]

Additional farm relief bills included appropriations of $1,000,-000 in State aid for two-, three-, and four-teacher schools[29] and $2,000,000 in State aid for one-room schools.[30] Twenty-five percent of the gasoline tax, estimated at $6,000,000 was to be paid to the localities, and to New York City, on a mileage basis.[31] The direct State tax on real estate was eliminated, which meant an estimated saving of $13,000,000 annually to tax-paying citizens.[32]

One bill enacted by the legislature permitted the Conservation Department to acquire tracts of land containing not less than 500 adjacent acres for reforestation by the State. Another bill allowed county boards of supervisors to acquire land for reforestation purposes. Finally, the tax law was amended to remove franchise taxes from agricultural cooperative associations.[33]

The immediate impact of part of this farm legislation is seen, for example, on impoverished Putnam County, third smallest in population with 13,744 in 1930. The law which relieved counties from contributing 35 percent of the cost of completing the State highway system saved Putnam County towns and villages $376,000 in 1929, and would continue yearly. The legislation which relieved towns and villages from contributing toward the upkeep of unimproved State highways saved Putnam County towns and villages $3,980. The elimination of the direct State tax on property saved Putnam County taxpayers $15,857 in 1929, and would continue as an annual saving. Two other laws gave additional tax relief to Putnam County taxpayers. One equalized the burden of school taxes and gave relief on a State-wide basis of about $3,000,000 per year. The other, which reduced the counties' share of the cost of grade crossing eliminations to 1 per cent, would save, on a State-wide basis, $2,801,133 in 1929.[34] What had become known as the farm relief program was in essence a rural tax relief program.

However, these savings that taxpayers wanted passed on to them had to be pushed through by themselves. As Roosevelt indicated time and again, whether or not rural taxpayers received the full benefit depended upon their respective boards of supervisors and other local officials.[35]

Although the news and editorial columns of the *American Agriculturist* attempted to convey an impartial attitude toward the Republican and Democratic parties, Morgenthau never lost an opportunity to use his weekly journal to counter the argument of the *Rural New Yorker* [36] and other Republican newspapers that a Republican legislature had insured passage of farm relief legislation. Many issues of the *American Agriculturist* devoted full page articles to the farm bills enacted "under Governor Roosevelt" and the savings to counties in actual dollars and cents. Although reiterating that the success was due to the united efforts of all concerned, the paper consistently reminded its readers that the original recommendations had been made by the Agricultural Advisory Commission, "which had been appointed by Governor Roosevelt."[37] In a memorandum which the Governor hastily wrote on one occasion, he stressed the relative effectiveness of Morgenthau's journal when he contended:

Old man Dillon of the *Rural New Yorker* is principally peeved because I have operated through the editor of his rival newspaper, Henry Morgenthau, Jr. The *American Agriculturist* has more than doubled its circulation while the *Rural New Yorker* has dropped nearly 50 per cent. The trouble with Dillon is that he continues to fight every progressive measure for the farmer. He used to be a good man twenty years ago but I think he is too old and out of date.[38]

In April, 1929, Morgenthau relayed to Roosevelt a conversation he had had with Louis Howe, who was then helping supervise the State Democratic Publicity Bureau. Morgenthau had suggested to Howe that the first of a series of news releases to rural newspapers be on the gasoline tax pointing out how the farmers could get their exemptions. Since the one piece of legislation the farmers were thoroughly acquainted with was the gas tax, which they thought well of, Morgenthau informed the Governor that "Louis agreed with me that we can't get out too much publicity at this time explaining the workings of the gas tax." [39]

In the meantime, one upstate Republican journal, the *Oneida Post*, made a virulent attack upon the Governor, condemning him for his "opposition" to increased farm relief. On this occasion the Governor violated a well-publicized rule not to reply in writing to critical editorials, although he did so over another's signature. Feeling very certain that the editor hadn't meant to print either "unfair or untrue" information in its editorial columns, Roosevelt called attention to the paper's editorial, under the heading "Claims Are Misleading." Confident that the State Executive hadn't "the slightest feeling" in regard to any of the opinions expressed by this paper, Roosevelt did desire, however, to call attention to one or two very glaring misstatements of fact. For example:

You say "Governor Roosevelt does not point out that the Republican Legislature insisted on giving to the rural schools more than he was willing to grant." It is, of course, a matter of record that Governor Roosevelt told the Legislature, in sending in his budget that, if in their judgment, an additional amount could be granted to the public schools, he would only be too happy to approve it.

Your next statement, "He does not call attention to the fact that he vetoed the bill passed to relieve counties of the cost of building and maintaining bridges on the state and county roads" is, of course, the kind of half truth that is worse than a deliberate falsehood. It is true that the bill was passed but it carried no appropriation to build the bridges. Naturally it was vetoed because it was merely a gesture and did not accomplish anything without the money to carry it out.[40]

It was not uncommon for Roosevelt to send letters to editors over another's signature. One of his signatories, Miss Frances D. Lyon, former librarian in the New York State Library in Albany, was told by the Governor in 1931 that it was "perfectly fine of you to sign these letters which I get inspired to write when I read some of these perfectly awful editorials. Even though they do not answer it gives them something to think about." [41]

The Agricultural Advisory Commission continued its investigations through 1932 and periodically offered recommendations to Governor Roosevelt. Though its membership underwent minor changes, its objectives remained the same.[42]

Its sixth report was sent to the Governor on January 10, 1930,[43] and its seventh on January 30.[44] Within three months, Roosevelt signed into law additional farm relief legislation for which Democrats and Republicans had eagerly vied to endorse and introduce. In 1929, the Republican legislators had rejected a commission recommendation that the State assume the cost of removing snow from State highways. The 1930 legislature, however, passed a bill with the Governor's approval, authorizing the State to share joint expense with the counties in snow removal from State and county highways.[45] In 1929, the legislature had also defeated a commission proposal for readjustment of the distribution of moneys for so-called dirt roads. A year later the legislature adopted the Pratt Dirt Road Bill which gave rural counties approximately double the amount of State money they had heretofore received.[46]

At the request of the Agricultural Advisory Commission, the Governor convened a conference of Mayors and health officers to consider establishment of regulations governing the production and sale of milk and cream to insure consumers maximum health protection and to enable cities to take advantage of nearby sources. The result of the conference was the passage of an act to "amend the public health law in relation to the sanitary control and inspection of milk and cream." [47]

The Governor also signed into law the commission's recommendations for investigation of moths and insects which were injuring the peach and apple industries;[48] for additional work in research by the State College of Agriculture on the control of insects or diseases affecting the potato industry;[49] for the construction of a building at Cornell University for agricultural economics, marketing, and farm management;[50] and, finally, for a survey of the agricultural resources of the State in order to make plans for the most profitable use of each kind of land.[51]

Within two legislative sessions all but one of the major proposals of the Agricultural Advisory Commission had been adopted. In glowing terms the editor of the *American Agriculturist* informed its readers that for the first time in the history of the State the Governor, the legislature, and the agricultural interests had worked together in active unison with the result that the agricultural program which had been put through in New York was far and above the most progressive program of accomplishment for agriculture passed by any other state in the Union or by the Federal government itself.[52]

Republican journals, however, showed their sensitivity by their attempts to deny Roosevelt undue credit for the enactment of farm legislation. In a somewhat apologetic tone, publisher Dillon of the *Rural New Yorker* told his readers that to his certain knowledge upstate legislators had been studying and developing plans for this legislation for some years. The changes were inevitable and the gasoline law had already become a certainty even before Roosevelt became Governor. Furthermore, the

. . . laws were written and passed by the majority in the Legislature and no Governor could safely defeat them even if he had desired to do so. In the last analysis they came in response to the incessant

demand of farmers themselves. . . . Everyone is willing to give
Governor Roosevelt credit for his friendly attitude to the legislation and his approval of the laws, but it gets a little monotonous to
hear his repeated child-like pleas for personal and political credit for
the whole program including the accumulating effect of other
men's work.[53]

The year 1931 was unimportant as far as farm legislation was
concerned. The friendly Morgenthau journal explained that
this was a good year to slow up, not only to give people a
chance to see how the new laws worked, but also on account
of decreased State finances and the tax situation.[54] When the
State income tax was paid on April 15, 1931, the amount
collected was less than half what it had been the previous
year and far below the expectations of the legislature. Roosevelt was then faced with the task of vetoing certain appropriation bills for which he had already expressed his support, but
for which there was no money. Nevertheless, the legislature
and the Governor continued to place farm legislation on the
law books. One bill gave the Department of Agriculture and
Markets some $3,000,000 for tuberculosis eradication work
among cattle.[55] The proposed Hewitt Reforestation Amendment to the State Constitution was adopted by the second successive legislature and was to be submitted to the people in
November.[56] The forest preserve was greatly extended when
the former boundaries of the Adirondack forest preserve were
widened to take in a million more acres.[57] By 1931, the forest
preserve lands of New York were larger than that of any other
state in the Union.

On the other hand, the legislature defeated a Roosevelt-
sponsored proposal for the study of the needs of several localities for a State regional market. First suggested by the Agricultural Advisory Commission in 1929, this bill sought to
establish a comprehensive State-wide system of regional markets
for the purpose of providing suitable outlets for farm products
and to insure decreasing food costs to the consumer.

Despite a grueling program as Chief Executive, Roosevelt

retained a directing hand in the family estate at Hyde Park. It was not unusual for him to imform Moses Smith, a tenant farmer on his estate, that

I am writing Mr. Henry Morgenthau, Jr., for full directions about the squash seed. You should plow up the four or five acres as soon as possible, and we should allow about eight loads of manure to the acre and the manure should be harrowed in. The land should be harrowed at least every ten days between now and the time the seed is put in.[58]

Few political leaders have been more active in body and in spirit than Roosevelt. As Governor, and later as President, he traveled without hesitancy to the far corners of his State, the nation, and the world. With members of his family, and on occasion with close associates such as Morgenthau, the Governor covered much of New York State during summers on "The Inspector," a State-owned flat-bottomed ship. Used generally for inspection of the State barge canal system, the craft served the Governor and his party on these trips westward along the Erie Canal, northeast through Lake Ontario and along the St. Lawrence River, and then south through the Canadian-American canals and the Upper Hudson, to the State Capitol. During the day "The Inspector" would make scheduled stops along the shore, where the Governor and his party would transfer to a car to visit State developments, hospitals, mental institutions, and farming centers. This was valuable training, not only for the Governor, but also for his wife. Mrs. Roosevelt had previously visited various State prisons, asylums, and hospitals for crippled children but rarely with the same serious intention of familiarizing herself with the actual running of an institution.

Since it was impossible for the Governor to do a considerable amount of walking he could not, according to Mrs. Roosevelt,

. . . go inside an institution and get a real idea of how it was being run from the point of view of being overcrowded, staff food and medical care. I was asked to take over this part of the inspection, and at first my reports were highly unsatisfactory to him. I would tell him what was on the menu for the day and he would ask me: "Did you look to see whether the inmates were really getting that food?" I learned to look into the cooking pots on the stove and to find out if the contents corresponded to the menu; I learned to notice whether the beds were too close together, and whether they were folded up and put in closets or behind doors during the day, which would indicate they filled the corridors at night; I learned to watch the patients' attitude toward the staff; and before the end of our years in Albany, I had become a fairly expert reporter on state institutions.[59]

During these frequent halts along the waterways the Governor never lost an opportunity to speak with farmers and meet with Democratic leaders. On this "non-political" trip, Roosevelt became a vital human being to thousands of upstate citizens. He spoke with many concerning their farm problems and his trips were extensively reported in upstate papers.

Each year the Governor returned refreshed from these trips and enriched with a fuller knowledge of the State's resources. He had visited its most distant regions, had been seen by, and spoken to, thousands. His meetings with local Democrats did much to strengthen their upstate organizations which was evident in the increased percentage of the vote accorded local Democratic candidates to the State Assembly in 1929, but even more so in the Democratic landslide a year later.[60]

The end of the nineteen twenties found that taxes had not come down, interest charges had not come down, and land values were as yet incompletely deflated. Nearly all the fixed operation and consumer charges against modern farming stayed high.[61] Cold figures concerning the farm situation are sometimes meaningless to urban folk. Nevertheless, the tragic consequences of the agricultural depression become somewhat understandable when we realize that between 1920 and 1925, nearly 100,000 farms ceased to be operated by their former tenants or owners. From 1925 to 1930 an additional 200,000 farm homes were abandoned, totaling more farm families than were found in all New England, New Jersey, Delaware, and Maryland.[62]

The industrial depression which settled over the country like a thick smog by 1930 soon destroyed the last vestiges of hope of the nation's agrarians. New York's farmers, suffering from a contracted market since 1920, saw their remaining outlets tragically depleted. Farmers watched helplessly as their crops rotted in the fields and their farms were foreclosed by banks and insurance companies. Their meager savings quickly disappeared as farm prices dropped to the lowest level since the early eighteen nineties. By 1931 butter was less than twenty-five cents a pound on the farm. Eggs were selling from fifteen to twenty cents a dozen. Wheat was forty cents a bushel, and cotten ten cents a pound. With 1923 to 1925 as the basis for an index of 100, prices received for farm products dropped from 100 in 1928 to 41 in 1932, yet prices paid by farmers for all commodities bought in the same period dropped from 101 to only 70.[63]

As the depression sharpened, the nation's farmers sustained disastrous losses in income and living standards. By early 1930 the president of the local bank in Gering, Nebraska, wrote Roosevelt about his neighbors' woes and loss of faith in the Republican party.

Twenty-five years ago, Nebraska farmers sold their wheat for around eighty cents to one dollar per bushel and paid one hundred and fifteen dollars for a complete grain harvester. The Nebraska farmers are now receiving seventy cents per bushel for their wheat, and paying two hundred and sixty-five dollars for the same binder. That is fair illustration, and carries out all along the line. This national discrimination against agriculture cannot continue forever.[64]

In his reply the Governor referred to what later became the theme and objective of the Agricultural Adjustment Act of 1933. "Unofficially, and not for publication," Roosevelt requested the reaction of the bank president to a proposal for voluntary crop restriction. Was there any possible device, Roosevelt asked, "to be worked out along voluntary lines by which the total wheat acreage of the nation could be gradually decreased to the point of bringing it in line wtih the actual national consumption figures?" [65]

As early as his first annual message to the legislature in 1929, Roosevelt had outlined the objectives of the agrarian policy he would foster as President. At that time he informed the legislators that his ultimate goal was that the farmer and his family be put on the same level of earning capacity as his fellow American who lived in the city.[66] By 1932, Roosevelt's efforts resulted in the passage of much-needed farm legislation which sought, within the limits of State action, to ameliorate some of the worst features of the depressed farm situation in New York.

During this period Roosevelt exhibited his characteristic receptiveness to ideas which seemed to offer hope and encouragement to the downtrodden. In the late nineteen twenties, M. L. Wilson, the simple and forthright agrarian economist, was developing the domestic allotment farm plans.[67] By early 1930, Franklin D. Roosevelt was discussing this proposal with correspondents.[68]

Early in 1932, M. L. Wilson met Rexford G. Tugwell in Washington and convinced him of the need for congressional adoption of a voluntary application of the allotment principle, similar to that eventually included in the Agricultural Adjustment Act of 1933. A short time after the Wilson-Tugwell meeting Samuel I. Rosenman, with Roosevelt's approval, called upon Professor Raymond Moley of Columbia University to assist in the preparation of a national program on which the presidential aspirant might campaign. The individual selected by Moley to suggest a farm program was Tugwell, now an adherent of Wilson's allotment principle. Roosevelt was not, therefore, suddenly presented with an unfamiliar proposal by Tugwell, nor by Henry A. Wallace at their first meeting in August, 1932, nor later by M. L. Wilson himself who visited the Democratic presidential candidate at Hyde Park. At this last meeting, after Wilson had finished describing his farm program, Roosevelt is reported to have suddenly asked: "Have you been telling me your plan, or have I been telling you mine?" [69]

In a major address of the 1932 presidential campaign, Roosevelt told suffering farmers at Topeka, Kansas, that it would be his purpose as President to restore "agriculture to economic equality with other industries within the United States. I seek to give that portion of the crop consumed in the United States a benefit equivalent to a tariff sufficient to give you farmers an adequate price." [70]

According to candidate Roosevelt, his agricultural plan would provide for the producer of staple surplus commodities a tariff benefit over world prices which was equivalent to the benefit given by the tariff to industrial products. It must finance itself; it must operate as nearly as possible on a cooperative basis; and it must be, in so far as possible, voluntary. Underscoring the philosophy which had dominated M. L. Wilson's thinking, Roosevelt said he liked the idea that "the plan should not be put into operation unless it has the support of a reasonable majority of the producers of the exportable commodity to which it is to apply." [71]

Roosevelt also exhibited unusual interest in the potentialities of crop restriction through elimination of marginal land. Adoption of this new farm utilization policy, he felt, would benefit not only New York but the West as well because in the eastern states an average of at least 20 percent of the agricultural acreage should have been abandoned for farm purposes.[72] It was the type of soil which even irrigation would not make good for crops. The result was that farmers working inferior soil reaped harvests of poor wheat or fruit, receiving little in return for their hard labors. To carry out his program, Roosevelt directed Morgenthau, whom he had appointed State Conservation Commissioner in December, 1930, to purchase tens of thousands of marginal acres which were no longer suitable for productive crop planting because of soil exhaustion. On this land were to be planted millions of seedlings, insuring beautiful wooded acres in State parks and camping grounds, and also lumber resources for future generations.

To secure the money necessary to carry out this program,

Roosevelt recommended, and two successive State legislatures adopted, in accordance with constitutional provisions, a joint resolution to amend the State Constitution, providing for a bond issue of $19 million. This constitutional proposal, the Hewitt amendment, was to be voted on as Amendment Three in the 1931 State-wide elections.

Support for the Hewitt amendment came from virtually all sportsmen's and woodsmen's organizations. It was deemed non-partisan after receiving joint endorsement by the Governor, Democratic and Republican legislative leaders, and by James A. Farley and W. Kingsland Macy, chairmen respectively of the Democratic and Republican State Committees.[73] As Conservation Commissioner, and through the columns of his *American Agriculturist*, Morgenthau fought vigorously for upstate support of the amendment. Supporting conservation leaders pointed to the annual abandonment of some 250,000 acres of poor farming land in New York. Reforestation would not only provide more profitable crops but, by retaining moisture in the soil, would regulate the flow of water streams, acting as partial insurance against flood and drought. Water that seeped slowly through forest roots was naturally filtered, while water that rushed down denuded hillsides was muddy and contaminated.[74]

The prime objective of the Hewitt amendment was to establish a continuing program, for it made mandatory a fixed schedule of appropriations beginning at one million dollars in 1932, increasing $200,000 a year until the amount reached two million in 1937, and continuing at that rate for six years. The amendment also sought to make reforestation operations State-wide so that lands best suited could be selected from all parts of the State.

Dillon's *Rural New Yorker* persisted in its opposition to the Democratic Governor. In an emotional, flag-waving editorial, Dillon contended that the ultimate aim and effect of the amendment was

... to create two classes in this country—wealthy landed gentry and impoverished peasants. They heed not and care not that the small farm freeholder created our great institutions and established the greatest nation the world has ever known. Those who understand its far reaching and sinister effects will, we believe, go to the polls next Tuesday and vote against proposed Amendment No. 3.[75]

To the surprise of conservationists in general, and liberals in particular, opposition to the Hewitt amendment was led by Alfred E. Smith. The former Governor made slashing, and at times convincing, attacks on the proposed amendment. He felt it would put New York into the lumber business, since it authorized the State to cut and sell trees on the lands to be bought and reforested. He was further opposed to paying for the purchase of the lands contemplated out of bond issues instead of current revenues because he held it to be wrong in principle. The land, he felt, could just as well be acquired by the action of succeeding legislatures instead of by a constitutional amendment. Finally, former Governor Smith voiced a fear, shared by many, that as a general rule it was a mistake to pile things into the fundamental law of the State.[76]

The renowned conservationist Amos Pinchot voiced the sentiments of many supporting the amendment when he maintained that Smith's objections were ill-founded. Every undertaking in reforestation and modern forest administration, he contended, put the government into the lumber business in the sense that it gave the government, State, or nation, the power to cut and sell trees. In other words, what Smith called putting the State into the lumber business was "an essential and inescapable part of forestry." [77]

Though conceding the theoretical validity of Smith's contention that the lands could be purchased by succeeding legislatures, Pinchot maintained that from a practical point of view it was more than doubtful that succeeding legislatures would vote the money needed for carrying out a plan of such vast scope. Buying this land by constitutional amendment had the one clear advantage that it was the only way that would insure purchase.

Pinchot, however, could find no refutation to Smith's fear

of piling things into the fundamental law of the State, except that "in view of the importance of getting hold of this land while we still may, it seems as if we were justified in making this exception." [78]

Using the radio to reply to Smith's charges, Roosevelt did not once attack the Happy Warrior by name. He spoke on the issues, reiterating the basic reasonings presented by Morgenthau and Pinchot.

Typical of the reaction of many long-time Smith adherents was that of a friend who wrote Roosevelt:

Everybody I have talked to has been left in a complete fog as to Al's motives behind the un-Smithsonian speeches which he has recently made. Nobody seems to know what he is driving at and everyone also feels that the clearcut analysis of this amendment which you made two weeks ago clarified the whole thing in no uncertain terms.[79]

To most liberals, the vigor and warmth with which Smith had attacked Amendment Three was somewhat overwhelming. However, those who had closely observed Smith since 1926 were not unduly surprised. Despite his constructive administrations as Governor, Smith had been veering toward the conservative scene for months before his nomination in 1928. He had surrounded himself with conservative Democrats and with men and women whose standing in society was apparently determined by wealth, not by a fundamental adherence to Progressive Democracy.

By 1931 Smith was also giving serious thought to re-entering the political scene from which he had voluntarily retired in November, 1928. With the nation in the deep throes of a terrible depression, Smith realized that any capable Democrat might win the presidency in 1932. He knew that James A Farley had been actively seeking support for Roosevelt's candidacy, whereas Smith believed that he should have had prior right to the nomination in 1932. Smith could not help but realize, at the same time, that defeat of Amendment Three would weaken Roosevelt nationally.

It is difficult to place Smith's reasoning in any other context, for there had originally been Democratic harmony in support of the Amendment.

Shortly before the polls closed on election day, Roosevelt privately expressed his keen disappointment with the role of the Happy Warrior, and its implications on party unity, when he wrote:

What a queer thing that was for Al to fight so bitterly on No. 3! I cannot help remembering the fact that while he was Governor I agreed with almost all the policies he recommended but I was against one or two during those eight years. However for the sake of party solidarity I kept my mouth shut. I could have readily taken a public position in opposition to the Governor, but, frankly, I did not think the issue was of vital enough importance to cause a party dispute.[80]

The final tally, which assured passage of the Hewitt amendment by a vote of 778,192 to 554,550, was a signal victory for the conservation forces. For Franklin D. Roosevelt it was of much greater import as an omen for the 1932 national nominating convention—Roosevelt had beaten Al Smith in the latter's "home ball park."

In far-off Iowa, a rural newspaper emphasized the national significance of this struggle when it maintained:

There is one thing about Governor Roosevelt of New York that we heartily approve. That is the advocacy of reforestation, the planting of trees in the waste places of New York, and it might well be extended to all other states.[81]

Governor George H. Dern of Utah wrote Roosevelt, ". . . this is my first opportunity to say to you, anent the election, Hurrah for Trees!"[82] This victory elevated Roosevelt's stature and played a role in his capture of tens of thousands of farm votes twelve months later.

Within ten months, presidential candidate Roosevelt sought to extend his State plan to restrict crops through the elimination of marginal land to the Federal scene. Addressing the nation's farmers from Topeka, Kansas, in September, 1932, Roosevelt enunciated his philosophy of planned use of land. The United

States, he felt, already had more than enough tilled soil to meet its own needs for many years to come, because of a decreasing rate in population increase and because of increased efficiency in agricultural production. Throughout the nation there were great areas of relatively poor land hardly worth cultivation, which provided either actual or potential competition with better land. This situation lowered the value of farm products, depressed the price of better farm products, and created great added expense because of the faulty distribution of the population, and consumed public and private resources in "attempting the development of means of living and communication that ought not to be needed." The sum total was waste and hardship. To alleviate this situation, Roosevelt recommended a joint economic soil survey by the nation and the states, initiated by the Federal government and directed toward the problem of proper utilization of the land and future distribution of population along sound economic lines. "It should lead to mapping and classification of land of all kinds, to determine which lands are marginal and which lands are suited only to growing tree crops." [83]

In January, 1932, the Agricultural Advisory Commission met in Albany and informed the Governor that few farmers in New York were without troubles. Aware of the complexity of the milk situation, in which many milk producers were receiving less than their cost of output, the commission recommended that the Governor propose appointment of a joint legislative commision to investigate the entire milk problem. It also requested that the Governor support amendments to the banking and corporation law which would permit New York farmers suffering from a restriction of farm credit to avail themselves of the credit offered by the Federal Intermediate Credit Bank for the northeastern states at Springfield, Massachusetts. Roosevelt included the amendments in a special message sent to the legislature on January 20, 1932. Shortly thereafter the amendments were adopted and then approved by the Governor.[84]

As his governorship drew to a close, Roosevelt devoted a

radio fireside chat to reviewing his farm legislation and the benefits which should have accrued to rural taxpayers. He informed his listeners that the entire tax bill for State and local purposes had been more than $1,000,000,000 for each of the last few years. In 1932 the State budget was in the neighborhood of $300,000,000 of which $100,000,000 was to be returned to localities in the form of school and highway aid. The share of the State government for carrying on its State-wide services, therefore, would be some $200,000,000. Not one penny of taxes on real property—the tax on land—went to the State or was used for any State purpose. The general property tax levy in the fifty-seven counties outside of New York City had risen from $74,000,000 in 1913, to $146,000,000 in 1920, and to $288,000,000 in 1928. This meant that real estate taxes had doubled in the first seven years, and then doubled again in the next eight years. On an average they were nearly four times as high as they were less than a generation before Roosevelt became Governor.[85]

The Governor proudly referred to the enactment of recommendations by his Agricultural Advisory Commission, which meant savings to taxpayers because of the assumption of local expenses by the State government. The amounts assumed by the State in 1930, as contrasted with 1928, were estimated at more than $31,000,000. It was the Governor's contention that every penny of this could have been passed on in the form of savings to property owners who paid taxes for the support of local government. Yet taxes in many of the fifty-seven counties had been increased. The net amount of increase for these upstate counties totaled $13,000,000 instead of an expected decrease of some $31,000,000.[86]

One basic objective of Roosevelt's farm program had been to draw taxes from richer counties and channel them into poorer counties. This became evident when glancing at the tax totals mentioned by the Governor in his frequent addresses to farm groups throughout the State. As President of the United States, Roosevelt continued with a program which sought to draw taxes from the wealthier and more populous states and distribute them among the poorer ones in varied forms of relief.

Governor Roosevelt had done much to ease farm problems in New York, yet he knew by 1932 that the major difficulties could only be attacked through congressional legislation. As he prepared to draw the curtain on his four years as Governor, Roosevelt learned from a semiliterate resident of the State that, despite his farm relief program, these remained tragically depressing times for our rural population.

I would like to cite one case which explains the whole situation in Madison County near the little town of De Nuyter a widow woman owns a farm which she and her husband paid in $1100 she owes a mortgage of 4700. The husband died six years ago since then she has leased the farm to halves. That is she gives the man on the farm one half of the proceeds of the farm her interest to pay is 282.00 per year. Her sales total tax is 337, her insurance is $60.00 per year. You see she has to pay $689.00 per year anyhow she can't get away from these 3 items her milk checks from 25 cows has averaged $100 per month for the last 11 months she has to give the man on the farm half of that—that leaves her $50 per month or $600 per year to pay 669 and she has to buy half the feed, half the seed and other needs of the farm and live besides. If she was getting 5 cents a quart for her milk and she and thousands and thousands of farmers would be alright.[87]

During his four years in Albany Roosevelt amassed an outstanding record for remedial farm legislation. By his speedy appointment of the Agricultural Advisory Commission in November, 1928, he exhibited political acumen and administrative ability, for he appreciated the worth of experts and knew how to use them to greatest effect. By his persistent and wholehearted support of this nonpartisan commission, Roosevelt displayed an understanding of the problems confronting the rural community and of the urgent need for aid and reform.

Representing the farm areas of the State, and controlling both legislative bodies during the eight years Smith was Governor, with the exception of one term of the Senate, the

Republican party had had ample opportunity to enact similar legislation. Their failure to do so discredited them in the eyes of many farmers and helped insure Democratic victories in State-wide contests and in the 1932 presidential race.

In contrast to the national Republican administration in Washington, and to too many State Executives throughout the country, Governor Roosevelt actively initiated legislation which sought to ameliorate some of the most pressing difficulties of farmers. From the start, his objective had been to raise the income and standard of living of farmers to that of city workers. He kept abreast of thinking among such farm leaders as M. L. Wilson and Henry A. Wallace. He knew of the proposed domestic allotment principle, on a voluntary basis, before it was broached to him by Tugwell and M. L. Wilson, and before he made it part of his campaign promises in 1932.

Roosevelt's farm record as Governor, his receptiveness to new proposals, and his evident leadership influenced many national farm organizations, farm leaders, and farmers in general to support him for President in 1932.

V

"SECURE OUR SAVINGS"

THE CATASTROPHIC DEPRESSION which brought this nation to its knees after 1929 left its impact upon the financial and banking world of the Empire State, which controlled one fourth of the country's bank deposits.[1] Too many financial and banking executives were unable to cope with this crisis, including, at times, the Governor himself. New York State banking laws were found wanting, and the director of the State Banking Department complicated matters by his dishonesty and corruptness.

Before Roosevelt had taken office the State's Banking Superintendent was directing subordinates to overlook dubious activities of at least one financial institution in New York City. This eventually resulted in despair and hardship for thousands, disquieting days for the Chief Executive, sleepless nights for the Lieutenant Governor, and increasing demands for fundamental reform of New York's banking regulatory system.

Frank H. Warder had been appointed Superintendent of Banks by Governor Smith in 1926. This was the final of a series of political appointments given him with the backing of the New York County Democratic organization. Warder had had no experience in the financial world prior to his initial affiliation with the Department in 1920.

As Banking Superintendent, Warder and his family received numerous gifts which included rent decreases, a car, payment of hotel and travel bills, and ten shares of stock in the Harlem Bank of Commerce. The disburser of these gifts, and the presi-

dent of the Harlem Bank of Commerce—which later became
the City Trust Company—was Francesco M. Ferrari.[2]

On February 1, 1929, one month after Roosevelt assumed
office, Ferrari died following an emergency operation in a New
York hospital. Within eleven days his banking concern closed
its doors. Rumors in financial circles hinted at improper use of
the bank's funds by its directors, and also implicated a judge
of the Court of General Sessions. For almost three months the
bank's officials and Banking Superintendent Warder made
strenuous efforts to sell the institution. During this period
Warder refused to discuss publicly the bank's failure, causing
many newspapers to demand a full-scale investigation of the
Banking Department.[3]

When the State government was reorganized in 1927, the
terms of department heads were usually made coterminous with
that of the Governor. For some unexplained reason the term
of Superintendent of Banks Warder was permitted to run to
July, 1929. On March 23, 1929, before any disclosures concerning graft and corruption involving Warder, Governor Roosevelt
announced that Joseph A. Broderick would become the new
Banking Superintendent on July 1.[4]

Broderick, with considerable experience in the banking field,
as State Bank Examiner, chief examiner of the Federal Reserve
System, and vice-president of the National Bank of Commerce,
assumed office sooner than expected, for Warder suddenly
resigned on the 19th of April. In his letter of resignation,
Warder informed the Governor that due to his efforts, and the
cooperation of many leading bankers, a new institution known
as the Mutual Trust Company had been formed, with a capital
and surplus of five million dollars, for the purpose of taking
over the affairs of the City Trust Company on condition that
the depositors were paid in full.[5]

That same week the District Attorney of New York County
instituted an investigation into possible criminal activities, following receipt of complaints concerning the defunct bank.
Legal counsel for one of the depositors' groups suddenly wired

Herbert Lehman, Acting Governor in the absence of Roosevelt from the State, that Warder was preparing to flee the country.[6] After confirming Warder's secretive plans to leave, Lehman realized that the only effective way to keep Warder in the New York area, in order to secure a satisfactory public explanation of his conduct, was by immediate appointment of a Moreland Act Commissioner.[7] Lehman acted quickly and decisively by designating Robert Moses, former Governor Smith's Secretary of State, for the job.

The Lieutenant Governor directed Moses to undertake a thorough inquiry into the failure of the City Trust Company, and of the activities of the State Banking Department. Under the Moreland Act, Commissioner Moses was armed with the authority to subpoena witnesses, records, and books, powers similar to a legislative committee. The day following Moses's appointment, Warder submissively dispensed with his plans to leave for Europe and agreed to cooperate with the new Moreland Commissioner.

Acting Governor Lehman then wrote Roosevelt, who was vacationing in Warm Springs, that he had chosen Moses for several reasons:

In the first place, I knew that you felt that he was courageous and of great ability; in the second place, I was convinced that he would work very well with the Superintendent of Banks and help in all the steps leading to the reorganization in that department; and finally, I felt that he was so familiar with the various departments of the State government that he would be less likely to disrupt things than would a brand new man. I am sure that you will agree with this judgment on my part.[8]

Although most citizens reacted favorably to the Moses appointment, some Republicans refused to see anything good in the move. Claiming that the City Trust "scandal" had reached proportions of a magnitude which the Governor could not ignore, Republican leader W. Kingsland Macy requested the Chief Executive to convene a special session of the legislature for the purpose of "instituting a broad legislative inquiry into all phases of the State banking situation. Public suspicion had been aroused that mere temporizing will not allay." Although expressing some gratification with the invoking of the Moreland Act by the Acting Governor, Macy felt that this action had been impaired by the selection of Robert Moses, inasmuch as the latter had formerly been affiliated with Warder in the previous State administration.[9]

Roosevelt's reply referred the Republican leader to the diligent investigation undertaken by Moses since his appointment, and to another investigation by the United States District Attorney. The Governor reminded Macy that a legislative inquiry would be regarded by the average citizen as the injection of political issues into a department which, more than any other, should be kept free from politics. Roosevelt explained that the reason a special investigation was not held earlier into the City Trust Company bankruptcy was to protect the innocent depositors of that institution. As a result a new trust company was organized and it was expected that all money on deposit would be guaranteed to the depositors. In the meantime, Roosevelt assured the G.O.P. spokesman that the State administration did not intend to permit the whitewashing or escape of anyone guilty of violating State laws in this instance.[10]

From the very start Lieutenant Governor Lehman had been intimately involved in the meetings of bankers seeking to reorganize the defunct City Trust Company. In subsequent letters of protest to Roosevelt and Lehman, concerning the Banking Department, Republican leader Macy felt it incumbent to acknowledge that the only thought of Lehman "in entering public life [was] to render fine public service unselfishly," and to elevate government "to the highest possible plane." [11]

By mid-June, 1929, Warder was named in three complaints alleging criminal acts. He was arrested on felony charges for accepting gifts while head of the Banking Department, but then released on bail.[12] Shortly thereafter, Governor Roosevelt ordered a special term of the Supreme Court of New York

County to convene on July 22, to investigate the City Trust Company and its relation to the Banking Department.[13]

There were those who, dissatisfied with the actions taken by the Governor, requested a more extensive and thoroughgoing inquiry into the Banking Department. Norman Thomas, for example, felt that the inquiry into the City Trust Company had revealed a "shocking degree of corruption and inefficiency under Warder" and "a shocking complicity of Tammany politicians as dummy directors and go-between lawyers." [14] Thomas was particularly justified in his acrid comments on the recent failure of Clarke Brothers, a private banking concern which, though subject to the State Banking Department, had consistently disregarded the first principles of conservative banking.[15] Thomas insisted that the Governor's refusal to broaden the scope of the banking inquiry was only explicable on the theory that he had to get along with his machine politician friends who had brought him down to help dedicate the new Tammany Hall.[16]

After two months of intensive investigation, Moses compiled some startling information concerning the activities of the Banking Department, of the officers and directors of the defunct bank, and the records maintained by the various business concerns associated with the late Francesco Ferrari.[17]

Throughout the hearings Commissioner Moses was confronted with scattered and falsified records, reluctant witnesses, and the untimely death of the bank president. Despite these obstacles, the Commissioner's report to the Governor conclusively showed that Ferrari had resorted to a long list of illegal acts, graft, and corruption to develop and maintain a weak and tottering financial system, with the connivance of former Banking Superintendent Warder.[18]

Despite numerous difficulties, the City Trust Company was reorganized and the depositors eventually reimbursed one hundred cents on the dollar, due largely to the efforts of Herbert H. Lehman. His knowledge, gained from a lifetime of experience in the financial world, was resorted to at every step of the way by the Governor and the new Banking Superintend-

ent. Earlier, the Lieutenant Governor had reminded Superintendent Broderick of his great desire to see all the depositors
paid in full. To insure this the Lieutenant Governor notified
those working on the reorganization of the defunct bank that
when assured that the depositors would be paid in full, he was
willing, at their option and on their call, to invest one million
dollars in the new institution.[19]

After directing the blame for the bank's failure to Francesco
Ferrari, his immediate assistants, and the former Banking
Superintendent, Commissioner Moses offered a number of suggestions for improving the State Banking Department which had
become demoralized under Warder. He also recommended
specific legislation to avert repetition of the City Trust failure.

Moses believed that every banking institution in New York
should be under Federal or State jurisdiction. He cited the
failure of Clarke Brothers to sustain his claim that no further
private banks be permitted since there was no good reason for
their continued existence. Among his major recommendations,
Moses stressed the need for drastic revision of the Banking Law
to insure responsibility by directors and officers, the most effective way being to impose a statutory duty upon them supported
by criminal as well as civil penalties to diligently and honestly
administer the affairs of the bank.[20]

With foresight and courage Moses recommended that savings
and thrift accounts in commercial banks be made subject to
the same laws which governed the investment of savings bank
accounts. The City Trust Company failure would have been
impossible, he maintained, if the greater part of its deposits had
not been in the form of savings and thrift accounts. There were
no good reasons why a savings bank should be made subject to
exceptionally rigid rules concerning investments, while another
bank around the corner advertised for and maintained similar
accounts without any special restrictions.[21] Moses concluded
his more important legislative recommendations with the suggestion that amendments to the Banking Law should require
the Banking Department to investigate original capital and

increases in capital to see that the cash on hand was actually paid in, and not fictitious; and that in the case of mergers or conversions the assets and liabilities of the existing institutions were correctly stated.[22]

The chairman of the board of directors of the defunct institution, Judge Francis X. Mancuso of the Court of General Sessions, received the brunt of the attacks leveled against the bank's activities, particularly after Commissioner Moses charged that the Judge's testimony before him lacked frankness and accuracy and that his neglect of banking duties showed complete irresponsibility.[23]

These disclosures fostered insistent demands by the press and the public for Mancuso's removal from the bench. Taking note of this rising protest, Roosevelt accepted Moses's suggestion to invite the Bar Association of New York, and the New York County Lawyers Association,[24] to investigate jointly the affairs of Judge Mancuso, to see if there were grounds for recommendation for removal by the Governor.[25]

Two days before Judge Mancuso and other officers of the defunct institution were indicted by a special grand jury on charges of violating the penal law relating to misconduct of directors of moneyed corporations, the Governor received the Judge's resignation.[26] A month later Warder was found guilty of accepting a $10,000 bribe while banking head and was sentenced to a five- to ten-year term in Sing Sing. Within a few days he was out on bail while his new attorney, Max D. Steuer, appealed the decision to a higher court.[27]

Following receipt of the Report on the City Trust affair, Roosevelt approved Moses's recommendation to appoint a special commission to study the latter's proposals for changes in the Banking Law.[28] As wtih the Agricultural Advisory Commission, Roosevelt relied on a committee of experts to investigate the ills of the banking world when he appointed eleven men to his Governor's Commission on the Revision of the Banking Law. Fully aware of the need for legislative cooperation, Roosevelt included the respective chairmen of the Assembly and Senate Banking Committees on the commission.

In contrast to the Agricultural Commission, however, the Banking Commission's viewpoint was too limited, for it was dominated by bankers who were expected to reform their own delinquent methods.[29] In addition, the commission did not include a single modern economist, or representative of the farm or labor elements. To discerning citizens there could be little doubt that the commission members would attempt to guard against a renewal of the fly-by-night methods of Francesco Ferrari. On the other hand, they could be expected to do little to strengthen the belief that banking was an enterprise affected by public interest and therefore necessitating increased governmental regulation. The record of bankers, as witness their early attitude toward the Federal Reserve System, was not one which would readily admit the need for stricter government supervision of savings accounts in commercial banks.

The Governor was equally remiss in neglecting to appoint Moses to the commission, especially in view of his original intentions.[30] Moses could have been of inestimable aid in presenting a point of view which subsequent events showed to be more logical and farsighted.

The Governor's Commission on the Revision of the Banking Law was in the process of preparing its report when Roosevelt's annual message to the 1930 legislature informed the lawmakers that the meshes of the Banking Law had been woven so loosely as to permit the escape of criminals who squandered funds of small depositors in reckless speculation for private gain. The entire Banking Law needed revision and the Banking Department needed far more adequate inspection facilities.[31]

Four weeks later the Banking Commission presented its conclusions and recommendations to the Governor. The commision had not held public hearings nor taken any testimony, but its members had read the testimony given to a joint legislative committee which had been investigating the Banking Law. Conferences had been held with the new Banking Superintendent and with spokesmen of banking associations. Commission members had also conferred with officers of banks, trust companies, savings banks, and private bankers, and had given careful consideration to Moses's courageous and painstaking report.[32]

The commission maintained that by January, 1930, the Banking Department was functioning as efficiently as its funds permitted. The failure of the City Trust Company, they contended, had been due to dishonesty on the part of its officers and of the former head of the Banking Department. An examination of the private banking house of Clarke Brothers would have disclosed that that firm should have been subject to the supervision of the Banking Department.[33]

While agreeing with many of Moses's minor recommendations, the commission dissented from his major suggestions. Rejecting his proposals for greater regulation of banks and their officers, the commission maintained that the only banking institutions with whom the public could safely deal were those whose business was conducted by men of "character, integrity and ability." Governmental supervision would not make a dishonest man honest nor an insolvent institution sound. According to these banking spokesmen, the mere placing of a bank under the supervision of the Banking Department could not serve as a guarantee that its affairs would be conducted in accordance with the best banking practices or that it would continue to be solvent.[34]

The commission also disputed Moses's contention that the existing law be amended to impose additional liability, either criminal or civil, upon directors. The members felt that bank directors who knowingly violated their trust by personal participation in wrongful acts were already liable both under common law and under statutory law. If directors were made responsible for any action they took in good faith in reliance upon the records of the institution or the reports of its executive officers, then banks would not be able to recruit the best type of directors.[35]

Whereas Moses believed that all private banks should be abolished, the commission felt that their right of exemption should be further restricted, and that all private bankers, other than exempt bankers, should be subject at all times to full and complete examinations by the Superintendent of Banks.[36]

The conclusion of the Governor's Commission on the vital issue of thrift accounts in commercial banks underscored the basic philosophy of the banking world. The commission members overrode the dissent of the lone savings bank representative when they opposed the segregation of savings or thrift deposits in State banks and trust companies; or the requirement of those institutions to invest a portion of their assets in trustee securities. They did not feel it necessary to decide whether savings or thrift deposits were safer in commercial banks and trust companies or in savings banks. They were safe in sound and well-run institutions. According to the commission, the safety of these accounts had been well demonstrated by the emerging of all types of banks in New York from the market crisis, which constituted a tribute to the honesty and efficiency of their administration and the thoroughness of their supervision by the Banking Department.[37]

The commission went on, however, to recommend a general salary increase in the Banking Department, the appointment of an Assistant Superintendent, and a significant increase in the existing force of examiners to insure thorough and frequent examinations.

Shortly following this report the Senate and Assembly enacted legislation containing the bulk of the commission's proposals. On April 22, the Governor signed these bills,[38] which he deemed some of the most necessary, important, and constructive banking legislation proposed in recent years.[39] These amendments to the Banking Law gave the Banking Department the right to examine and investigate virtually every financial institution in the State and, with few exceptions, absolute jurisdiction over all private bankers.

Broderick advised Roosevelt that this legislation gave the Department greater responsibility than he had dreamed of. It was much better, however, "for us to have the right to stop practises than to avoid undertaking the work because of the responsibilities. It would have been better for everyone if these statutes had been passed before." [40]

While signing these bills the Governor expressed regret that the legislature had rejected the commission's recommendations relating to permanent organization, salaries of deputies and examiners, and the prohibition of public officials whose duties pertained to the enforcement of the Banking Law from acting as bank directors or officers. [41]

The Governor, however, did not see fit to deplore the lawmakers' neglect to segregate thrift and savings accounts in commercial banks, for he had not recommended the enactment of such legislation. Roosevelt would regret this negligence before the year was out.

There is no doubt that Republican lawmakers would have rejected such a recommendation in 1930, as they did in 1931 and again in 1932. They were much more amenable to the views of the commercial banking world than they were to those of Robert Moses, on this issue. The fact remains, however, that Governor Roosevelt had originally refused to endorse Moses's proposal. The former's insistence on the need for such enactment in 1930 would have exhibited foresight and courage and placed him in a strategic position to saddle the Republican leadership with consistent shortsightedness in the field of banking legislation. Instead, both the Republicans and Roosevelt must be indicted for having failed, in 1930, to comprehend the implications of continued neglect of stricter regulation of thrift accounts in commercial banks.

The effects of this neglect were made clear on December 11, 1930, when some 300,000 residents of New York City suddenly found their life's savings unattainable. On that day the doors of the fifty-seven branches of the Bank of United States were belatedly closed by the State Banking Department. [42] Depositors of this gigantic institution had never conceived the possibility of failure. Too many had naively believed that its name meant exactly what it said; that it was the property of the United States government.[43]

Following disclosures of dishonesty and misappropriation of funds in the City Trust Company affair, the citizenry had assumed that the State Banking Department, and the banking community, had taken every precaution to prevent repetition of such disasters. It is true that banking spokesmen, through the Governor's Banking Commission, had suggested, and the legislature and Governor had approved, amendments to strengthen the State's Banking Laws. Nevertheless, a gigantic financial institution had collapsed. The causes were many.

The Governor's Banking Commission, which had included Henry Pollock, vice-president of the Bank of United States, and which had stressed "character and integrity" as the key to safe banking, was at fault. Its members had rejected Moses's recommendation to strengthen the protection of thrift accounts in commercial banks.[44] The Governor was also at fault, for he had accepted the opinion of banking leaders rather than that of Commissioner Moses. The Republican legislative leadership must also be indicted, for theirs was the viewpoint of banking spokesmen. Their backwardness, their fear to tread new paths, was even more evident after the collapse of the Bank of United States.

Although more than a year before, following Moses's report on the City Trust debacle and the appointment of Broderick, Roosevelt had expressed the belief that "such things can never happen again," [45] the Banking Department had again been remiss in its responsibilities. Broderick's department had neglected to act swiftly when it first learned of the bank's precarious condition, months before it was closed.

Most interested parties offered no reflection on the honesty of Banking Superintendent Broderick, nor on the sincerity of his efforts to save the bank. Yet there were questions of judgment and sound banking practice involved in the way the Banking Department had handled a difficult situation which it had inherited from a previous superintendent already under conviction for what he had done in the City Trust case.

On July 13, 1929, over 100 examiners of the State Banking Department and the Federal Reserve Bank had methodically studied the books of the Bank of United States, as part of the semiannual examinations required by law. The report to Superintendent Broderick made drastic criticisms of the conditions and policy of the bank. The most severe condemnation, however, was reserved for the conduct and policies of its chief officers, Bernard K. Marcus and Saul Singer, who were not deemed qualified to conduct the affairs of such a large bank.[46]

Shortly after completion of the report, Marcus and Singer met with Broderick, who recommended changes in policy and personnel. When informed of plans by Marcus and Singer to remedy the situation and then merge with a stable financial institution, Broderick appeared to make no further attempt to enforce his recommendations nor to take serious action for almost twelve months.[47] Marcus and Singer, meanwhile, never carried out their proposed plans.

Although the banking law required two examinations per year, and despite severe criticisms of the bank's operations in August, 1929, Broderick did not see fit to require a re-examination before July, 1930.

Shortly after the bank's doors were closed it was charged, and later substantiated, that the bank had not protected its great numbers of thrift accounts, and that it had permitted its subsidiaries to resort to all manner of financial jugglery. Marcus had also sent out glowing financial statements to depositors, stockholders, and the general public, despite the fact that the examiners' report of August, 1930, disclosed that the surplus and undivided profits of the institution had been completely dissipated, and that, therefore, the capital of the bank was badly impaired.[48]

As these disclosures slowly leaked out there developed an increasing demand for a thorough investigation of the Banking Department. Since the Department was under suspicion, as far as the wisdom of its policy was concerned, many proposed a Moreland Act investigation of its entire conduct, with a view toward recommending additional changes in the Banking Law and its administration.

During the last week of December, 1930, District Attorney Crain of New York County instituted a grand jury investigation into the bank's failure, to determine if there were grounds for criminal proceedings against officers or directors of the defunct institution.[49] Unfortunately, Crain commanded little public confidence as the result of a dismal record investigating banking, racketeering, and politics.

At the same time, Roosevelt refused to honor pleas for a Moreland Act investigation, explaining to Norman Thomas that he had instructed District Attorney Crain to prosecute vigorously his investigation. Any other action had to await the reports of the Banking Superintendent. "Confidentially for your information," continued the Governor, "I was greatly disappointed that last legislature did nothing about thrift accounts. I expect to recommend such action to this legislature."[50]

That same week the Governor advised Crain that the public was entitled to know all of the facts in the case, and that it was of the utmost importance that any violation of law be promptly and vigorously prosecuted.[51]

Max D. Steuer was a lawyer of unusual ability. He had previously served as defense counsel for former Superintendent Warder, who appeared to have approved many of the practices which later undermined the Bank of United States. Steuer's appointment by Crain as special assistant in charge of the Bank of United States case brought to light one of the complexities of New York City politics. The counsel for the Bank of United States, Isidor Kresel, was at that moment establishing an enviable record as counsel for Judge Samuel Seabury's thorough investigation into Tammy graft and corruption in the Magistrates' Courts. As counsel for the Bank of United States, however, Kresel's acts were subject to investigation. Fear was expressed by some civic leaders that the investigation into the defunct banking institution by Steuer, a close ally of Tammy, might impede the successful investigation of the Magistrates' Courts. This situation would have pleased Tammy no end.

The trial of the indicted bank officers provided many damaging disclosures, including the fact that the defunct institution's president had kept the Banking Department's critical reports from its board of directors. Three months after the trial's commencement, with Steuer in the role of special prosecutor, Marcus and the two Singers were found guilty of violating the State's Banking Laws and given sentences ranging from indeterminate to six years.[52]

While efforts were being made to reopen the institution, intense bitterness developed among afflicted depositors. Through street demonstations they protested the failure of the bank, the deplorable activities of its officers, and the seemingly incompetent role of the Banking Department.

One State official disturbed by the immorality of certain members of his familiar banking world was Lieutenant Governor Lehman. Because of Lehman's financial background and successful efforts to reorganize the City Trust Company, Roosevelt leaned heavily upon him during this banking crisis. With the preponderance of afflicted depositors of the Jewish faith, constant appeals were directed to Lehman, a respected member of New York's Jewry. The publisher of one influential Jewish newspaper wired Lehman:

The Italian community suffered from the catastrophe that closed the City Trust Bank just as the Jewish community is striken in the case of the Bank of United States. . . . Governor Roosevelt has already expressed his deep concern for the depositors in their misfortune. It seems to us that it is within his power now not only to help them with words of sympathy but with practical tangible aid. You are leading banker who shared in reorganization of City Trust. It is not too much to hope that you will come to the rescue of the depositors of the Bank of United States. . . . It is in your power to mobilize these financial leaders. With your cooperation it is possible that every cent will be returned to the depositors.[53]

Toward the end of June, 1931, Republican State Chairman

Macy suddenly demanded Broderick's removal as he charged
the Banking Superintendent with violating the law and pursuing
a course strikingly similar to his predecessor's in the City Trust
affair. The Republican leader maintained that stockholders and
depositors would have been protected, and this tragedy averted,
had the Superintendent discharged his duty and closed the bank
in 1929, when "four of his examiners . . . separately signed reports
severely criticizing the administration of the bank." [54]

Viewing this as a personal request, and not from the Republican State Committee which had refused to go along with
Macy, Roosevelt curtly replied, "I do not accede to your request
for the summary removal of the Superintendent of Banks."[55]

Late in October, 1931, as a result of evidence presented by
Steuer, a grand jury handed down indictments against Broderick and twenty-eight officers and directors of the Bank of
United States. Charged with neglect of duty and conspiracy,
Broderick was immediately defended by the Governor. Roosevelt was so bitter that he feared he could be arrested for what
he thought of the whole procedure by Steuer. [56]

As the year 1931 drew to a close the Governor, from his
Warm Springs retreat, brought a rare smile to the face of his
worried and haggard Banking Superintendent when he wired
him:

. . . warm greetings and congratulations on your birthday. It must
be awful to be so old. I will not equal it for another month.[57]

Broderick was finally brought to trial in February, 1932, with
Steuer as the special prosecuting attorney. The jury had to
decide whether or not Broderick knew that conditions warranted
an earlier closing of the Bank of United States. Throughout his
prosecution Steuer contended that Broderick had neglected his
duty and consequently had violated State laws. A mistrial was
declared when it was learned that one of the jurors had hidden
the fact that he had been a depositor in the defunct bank. When
the trial resumed in April, Steuer contended that Broderick

knew four months before the bank's closing that its surplus had been wiped out.[58]

Delaying his plans to leave directly for Georgia from the Governor's Conference in Richmond, Virginia, Roosevelt returned to New York to take the stand voluntarily in defense of his Banking Superintendent. The Governor assumed partial blame for the failure to close the bank at an earlier date when, during one of the few moments Steuer did not object to his testimony, Roosevelt stated:

If it please the court, I have to go back to the first period of 1929. As I remember it, that autumn there were approximately 200 banking institutions in the State of New York under the jurisdiction of myself and the Superintent of Banks that were in a somewhat weakened condition because of the stock market crash.[59]

In these remarks to the court, the Governor had emphasized the word "myself." Despite objections from Steuer, Roosevelt was permitted to relate his unsuccessful attempts to save the bank by a merger through conferences at his home with Broderick, Lehman, and leading spokesmen of the New York banking world, some two months before the bank was closed.

Prodded on by Defense Attorney Martin Conboy, the Governor testified that of Broderick's reputation "there was none higher in the whole State of New York." Meanwhile, Steuer had objected vigorously to Roosevelt's assuming any responsibility for the bank's delayed closing, contending that Broderick was wholly responsible for his own acts. Steuer refused to cross-examine the Governor.[60]

For nine days Broderick was on the witness stand. He testified that the doubtful status of the Bank of United States was only one of many problems confronting him when he became Banking Superintendent. He complained of the inadequate staff with which he was expected to supervise all of the banking institutions in the State. On September 18, 1930, he had first learned from one of his examiners that the surplus of the Bank of United States had been wiped out. He then sought a merger of the bank with stronger institutions. Unfortunately, Broderick contended, the bank's officers wanted more money for their stock than was offered them by the Bank of Manhattan Trust Company and by other institutions. Leading financiers had met on numerous occasions with Broderick in an attempt to save the bank, but the greed of its officers defeated the merger plans.

On the 27th of May, after twelve hours of deliberation, the jury found the Banking Superintendent innocent of the charge of neglect of duty for failing to close the bank at an earlier date.[61]

Two weeks after the failure of the Bank of United States the doors of the Chelsea Bank were closed, as were those of the State Bank in Binghamton. Legislative action was urgently needed to halt additional bank failures and requests for such were not long forthcoming from the Governor and his Banking Superintendent.

In a special message to the 1931 legislature, the Governor endorsed a special appropriation request from his Banking Superintendent for additional examiners.[62] Immediately thereafter, Roosevelt illustrated his basic receptiveness to new ideas—though somewhat belatedly in this instance—and an ability to profit from mistakes, when in clear and unmistakable terms he broke with the obstructionist banking world. In a ringing message he urged the lawmakers to recognize that one of the Banking Superintendent's latest proposals was a matter of principle which affected some one and one-half million depositors out of the thirteen million people in the State: the better safeguarding of thrift accounts owned by these people. The Governor sharply posed the question when he asked:

What, then, is the issue? It is the simple and inescapable fact that in the mind of the average layman, especially the man and woman of limited wealth, there is no nice distinction between thrift accounts and savings accounts. In their minds both are methods for safeguarding and getting a small return on their hard earned savings. They assume, wrongly, perhaps, but none the less naturally, that their thrift accounts are being protected by our State laws in the same way as the deposits of their neighbors who have put their savings in savings banks.[63]

The Governor reminded the legislators that thrift accounts could be placed in any type of investment, whereas savings bank funds were specifically restricted by the State's Banking Laws. If people continued to confuse thrift accounts with savings accounts, the issue then evolved into a simple question as to whether or not the safeguards applied to savings bank accounts should be extended to thrift accounts. The Governor believed that it was nothing more than ordinary good faith to the public that the 1931 legislature initiate the safeguarding and protection of thrift accounts. The people had a right to demand it and the time to do it was now. Any further delay was inexcusable and a breach of the trust which the depositors had in their legislative bodies. Although the method to be followed was a question for the technical consideration of the banking committees, the Governor firmly insisted that there was no need for additional investigation of the facts; they had been before the legislature in one form or another ever since the failure of the City Trust Company two years earlier.[64]

The Governor not only repudiated his previous stand on the segregation of thrift accounts but denounced the destructive attitude of the banking world. Although it had been obvious for a long time that some action had to be taken, most of the banking world had basically opposed all constructive suggestions. According to Roosevelt, banking spokesmen had consistently "thrown cold water on every plan suggested to protect thrift accounts." [65]

Financial leaders had offered no alternative plan, except a continued prayer for delay. No longer could any reliance be placed upon the wisdom of the banking world, lamented the Governor, for theirs had been a campaign of obstruction from the start. "By merely blocking all reform, as they appear to be doing this year with your honorable bodies, they discredit any claim that their efforts are accompanied by any sincere desire to protect the depositors of the State." [66]

These were strong and vitriolic words for a Governor who only a few months earlier had accepted the bankers' viewpoint on thrift accounts. The Governor quickly gave evidence of his changed attitude when he vetoed a proposed amendment to the Banking Law which would have permitted the investment of savings bank funds in securities of water districts within the State. The Republican lawmakers had sought to circumvent, instead of strengthen, State regulation of savings bank funds, for certain of the water districts of the State had had difficulty obtaining bank loans and this bill would have afforded them an unusual source of credit.[67]

Upon the instigation of George Fearon, who recently succeeded John Knight to the leadership of Senate Republicans, and whose legislative record showed him to be hostile to all forms of progressive and social legislation, the upper house of the legislature retaliated by permitting Broderick's request for the segregation of thrift accounts to die in the Senate. Two days before the 1931 legislature adjourned the Governor reminded the lawmakers of the urgent need to strengthen protection of thrift accounts when he said:

There is still time to pass legislation definitely starting the protection of thrift accounts, and I still hope that wiser counsel will prevail in the ranks of the majority party and that something concrete will be done. I can only repeat that this legislature affects nearly two million actual depositors in this State and through them another two or three million other people.[68]

The Republican leadership rejected the Governor's plea and permitted the 1931 session to pass into history without such legislation. When the 1932 legislature was confronted anew with a proposal to segregate thrift accounts in commercial banks and trust companies, the Republicans persisted in permitting the proposal to die in the upper house.

Having failed to move a Republican-dominated State legislature on this issue, Roosevelt sat on the sidelines during his first year as President while the thrift accounts he had formerly sought to protect were finally insured by Congressional initiative through the Glass-Steagall Act of 1933.[69]

During the last regular legislative session under Governor Roosevelt,[70] the Chief Executive sought a new objective: the strengthening of those laws dealing with the public sale of securities. The Governor expressed the feeling that it was finally time to differentiate between prospects and true values, by which he meant enlightening the public as to the "whole truth about the contents of what in the past has been a package too often sold only because of the bright colors on its wrapper."[71]

Here, too, Roosevelt was stymied by a Republican legislature which refused to look ahead to the future. With the rejection of his recommendation for stricter regulation of the sale of securities, the Governor was reminded that for almost twenty years most states had unsuccessfully sought to regulate so-called blue-sky securities for the protection of the public against fraud. However, Roosevelt now realized that most State laws meant little because of a lack of uniformity and because the absence of Federal legislation permitted evasion of State legislation through the sale of securities on an interstate basis.

After battling four years with a Republican-controlled, laissez-faire legislature, and aware of the inconsistencies and loopholes of State regulation, Roosevelt concluded that the only solution lay with the Federal government. Following his dramatic, precedent-shattering flight to Chicago to accept the 1932 presidential nomination at the Democratic convention, Roosevelt endorsed the proposal for Federal regulation of the sale of securities. He wanted to let in the light of day on issues of securities which were offered for sale to the investing public. Publicity, he contended, was the enemy of crookedness.[72]

Elaborating on this theme in a subsequent campaign address, Roosevelt underscored his philosophy on the role of government in business when he maintained:

Government cannot prevent some individuals from making errors of judgment. But Government can prevent to a very great degree the fooling of sensible people through misstatements and through the withholding of information on the part of private organizations, great and small, which seek to sell investments to the people of the nation.[73]

The Democratic candidate held that government had to prevent the issuance of manufactured and unnecessary securities merely for the purpose of enriching those who handled their sale to the public. The sellers should tell the uses to which the money was to be put, through definite and accurate statements concerning bonuses and commissions the sellers were to receive, the investment of the principal, true earnings, true liabilities, and true assets of the corporation itself. Stressing the ineffectiveness of State regulation of holding companies which sold securities in interstate commerce, Roosevelt maintained, "It is logical, it is necessary and it is right that Federal power be applied to such regulation." Because exchanges in the business of buying and selling securities and commodities could, by the practical expedient of moving elsewhere, avoid regulation by any given State, Roosevelt proposed the use of "Federal authority in the regulation of these exchanges."[74]

By early 1933, the situation concerning the sale of securities had seriously deteriorated. Timely as were Roosevelt's recommendations to the State legislature in January, 1932, they were more urgently needed by March, 1933, when he became President. With the situation demanding, and the people yearning for, constructive leadership, President Roosevelt submitted a short, incisive message to the special session of Congress recommending Federal control of security sales. After six weeks of debate the bill emerged as the Securities Act of 1933, retaining the basic principles set forth in the President's original proposals. Thus was born the Securities and Exchange Commission.[75]

The economic disaster of 1929 was months away when the City Trust Company suddenly collapsed. This bank failure acted as a catalyst in the struggle for fundamental banking reforms. Unfortunately, the basic reforms were not to be achieved until Roosevelt assumed the presidency in 1933. Although Robert

Moses's minor recommendations for banking reforms were generally acceptable to the Governor's Commission on the Revision of the Banking Law, his major request for the segregation of thrift accounts in commercial banks was rejected. The Banking Commission, to which Roosevelt had appointed no economist, farmer, or labor representative, stressed "character, integrity and ability" as the solution to most banking evils. The Governor's acceptance of the commission's viewpoint showed him, in this instance, to be backward and shortsighted, and in concert with virtually all banking spokesmen.

The failure of the Bank of United States, and the obstructionist attitude of banking spokesmen to needed reforms, finally moved Roosevelt to denounce the banking world and endorse Moses's recommendation on thrift accounts. The powerful allies of the banking world—the Republican-dominated legislature—frustrated the efforts of Roosevelt, Moses, and others to insure fundamental banking reforms prior to 1933.

Stymied by Republican opposition to stricter regulation of the sale of blue-sky securities, Roosevelt concluded, by 1932, that State regulation alone was ineffective. After March 4, 1933, he successfully pressed for passage of Federal legislation which rescued the banking world from collapse and possible nationalization, signed a bill to protect the savings of the nation's depositors, and pushed through establishment of the formidable Securities and Exchange Commission to protect purchasers of securities.

VI

"TO PREVENT STARVATION
AND DISTRESS"

Franklin D. Roosevelt became Governor with complete faith in the continued stability of the nation's economy. He agreed with most journals and public officials that the American people were enjoying the highest standard of living in the history of the world. Those who did not wander into the stifling slums of New York's urban centers and rural areas generally concluded that people were employed, well fed, well clothed, and well housed. Overlooked by too many were thousands of depressing hovels and developing unemployment.[1] New York's lower East Side, the birthplace of Al Smith, was scarred by thousands of old-law tenements with windowless bedrooms and either yard toilets or a single bathroom to a floor of apartments, a bathroom which usually lacked a bathtub or other facilities.[2] But the new Governor would not give much thought to the economics of the nation until after the stock market collapse and the default of Republican leadership.

Two days after Roosevelt's inauguration the chief economist of the Industrial Conference Board informed advertisers that the prosperity talk they were hearing was pure propaganda, and warned them of increasing inflation. He foresaw major problems ahead, citing a real depression in basic industries despite gains from investments.[3]

A few weeks later the stock market began a significant decline. At the close of the trading day on February 7, stocks dropped from fractions of a point to more than nineteen points. Nothing was spared, the good going down with the rest.[4]

On April 4, 1929, the Federal Reserve Board warned banks and financial speculators that loans had to be cut or that it would step into the picture. A few days before, stocks had crashed in the biggest market day in the history of the stock exchange. Nervous and apprehensive over lost profits and quickly mounting losses, speculators had dumped their stocks on the market.

With the stock market crashing all about him in October, 1929, the Governor received a wire inquiring for his outlook on fundamental industrial and trade conditions following the heavy stock market slump. Roosevelt replied that he did not know detailed conditions but firmly believed that fundamental industrial conditions were sound.[5]

Within a month, Socialist spokesman Norman Thomas felt that while the crash itself did not directly measure or directly affect the industrial productivity of America, such a crash was usually something of a barometer to indicate rainy days ahead. More significant, however, was the great decrease in building contracts and the laying off of thousands of men in the automobile and steel industries.[6]

Two months later the Governor sent a brief message to Louis Howe concerning some shopping to be done in New York City. It conveyed, in part, the Governor's reaction to business tendencies when he wrote:

It is just possible that the recent little flurry downtown will make the prices comparatively low. I have marked several items. Will you take a look at them first and see if the condition is good.

Here also are some sheets from another sale of Chinese things at the Anderson Galleries. Neither Missy [Miss Marguerite Le Hand] nor I know anything of the value of these.

Incidentally you may be able to do some Christmas shopping of your own at the Chinese sale for the things might go fairly cheap.[7]

Roosevelt was aware of New York's slums, for on April 18, 1929, he signed into law the much disputed Hofstadter-Story Multiple Dwellings Bill, despite its many weaknesses.[8] He realized that the State's rural population had not shared proportionately in the material and social advances of the twentieth century, and thus he had initiated significant remedial farm legislation. Yet he veered away from any studious or profound thoughts concerning the general state of the nation's economy until months after the stock market collapse. Roosevelt had not come to the governership with formalized economic principles. He was not conversant with the doctrines of well-known economists on either side of the Atlantic, nor had he given aid or comfort to political forces to the left of the old Populist or Bull Moose movements.

His annual message to the legislature on January 1, 1930, contained not a single reference to rising unemployment nor to increasing privations of the people. It was some time after factories started closing their doors, after public soup kitchens mushroomed throughout the State, and after hundreds of letters poured into his office pleading for aid and sustenance, but above all else for work, that the Governor felt impelled to act upon the changing state of affairs. And then act he did.

Following a survey of over 200 industrial centers in March, 1930, Roosevelt acknowledged that unemployment had reached serious proportions, varying from 5 to as much as 75 percent in certain localities. The State Labor Department's index of factory employment had fallen off almost 10 percent in the previous five months.[9] Roosevelt attributed the accumulation of unemployment to three factors: seasonal fluctuations, technological unemployment, and the "depression due to the business cycle which is an economic phenomenon recurring with some regularity throughout the nation as well as in this State." [10]

Faced with the reality of increasing unemployment, the Governor resorted to two approaches. For the short-range, immediate problem, he suggested to county and municipal officials a census of the unemployed, joint cooperation of community relief agencies, active stimulation of small job campaigns, establishment of free employment clearing houses, and the initiation of local public works.[11] As a long-range project he appointed four business and labor representatives as the Committee on Stabilization of Industry for the Prevention of Unemployment, to work out practical methods for the future control of unemployment.[12] New York became the first state to appoint a commission to coordinate efforts to stabilize business and reduce unemployment.

Inasmuch as the Governor felt that "the depression would be short-lived" and that the nation would be spared unusual hardships, he urged the committee to concentrate on the study of preventive measures for future depressions, not on solutions to immediate economic problems.[13] Like most public officials, New York's Governor did not, at first, appreciate the extent to which the State would have to assume dynamic leadership in the midst of a swiftly deteriorating economy. At this time Roosevelt made no reference to the possible need for unemployment insurance, nor did he recommend other far-reaching reforms. His alert and open mind, however, eventually enabled him to realize the seriousness of the times and to assume a dynamic initiative among governors.

While announcing the appointment of his new Committee on Stabilization of Industry, the Governor remarked to newsmen that he counted on the State's industrialists to strive to overcome recurring unemployment in their industries "with the same good will as they have overcome so many other adverse conditions, such as industrial accidents, industrial diseases, child labor, long hours, etc."[14] This statement, by itself, appears to indicate that Roosevelt was somewhat of a stranger in the struggle for social legislation in New York. The powerful industrialists of the State, like their Republican spokesmen in the legislature, had rarely shown any good will or initiative in eliminating "industrial accidents, industrial diseases, child labor, [and] long hours." Virtually every bill introduced since 1910 to reduce industrial hazards, eliminate industrial diseases, or to curb child labor had been bitterly opposed by the great mass of industrialists. Every effort to reduce hours of labor, through legislation or trade union activities, had met with stubborn resistance from factory spokesmen. These facts were indelibly written into the industrial and legislative history of New York, yet Roosevelt indicated little awareness of them when he recommended the increasing number of unemployed to the good will of industrialists.

When 5,000 women stood in line in the nation's capital during the summer of 1930, trying to get application blanks for 200 openings as charwomen in the government service, a former associate wrote Roosevelt that if conditions got any worse "... we are certainly heading for what took place in Russia.... We will all have to join the Reds soon and if present conditions and the present attitude of big business men and women in responsible positions continue any man will be justified in doing so." [15]

In March, 1930, President Hoover confidently issued statements reaffirming his faith in the return of prosperity within two months. These expressions so jarred Felix Frankfurter that he suggested to Roosevelt that the latter give the President a "tongue-lashing" in the near future. "You will recall," wrote Frankfurter, that

... Hoover announced that at the end of sixty days the unemployment problems will be over. ... have a sharp watch kept for the expiration of this prophecy and then take a very prompt occasion thereafter to show how the facts compare with his "dope"—and make clear how all these statements from the White House about prosperity and unemployment are in truth efforts to dope the public.[16]

Within a month the Governor deplored Hoover's lack of courage to state the "true facts" about the unemployment situation when he maintained that while it was a good thing for the President to call various conferences to prove that the fundamentals were sound, it was silly to claim that within two months unemployment would be normal again.[17]

Unlike some of his predecessors, however, President Hoover later developed some sort of policy for dealing with the business depression and unemployment. It included support of a program of building operations in which he sought cooperation of big corporations and state and local government bodies with the

Federal government; reduction of income taxes; and a tentative agreement between employers and workers in which the former promised not to seek to reduce wages and the latter not to seek to increase them. In contrast with the economic individualism which characterized candidate Hoover during the 1928 campaign, President Hoover had recognized, by 1931, that the world about him required some form of social control. He was pushing public works in a depression, albeit hesitantly.

On April 28, 1930, Secretary of Commerce Robert P. Lamont requested Roosevelt to survey economic conditions in New York. Although Roosevelt was constantly checking State Labor Department figures, he wired Lamont at the White House that he was unable to answer adequately the questions on the basis of existing information because of the well-known lack of current statistical information as to unemployment both in New York and in the United States. In the absence of genuine basic figures as to the amount and distribution of unemployment, Roosevelt felt that attempting to cite exact figures would not only be useless but positively harmful. He did say, however, that there was more than usual unemployment in New York and that indications pointed to a continued increase in unemployment.[18]

A fairly reliable index to the deteriorating employment picture in New York was reflected in annual surveys of Buffalo conducted by the State Department of Labor between 1929 and 1932. In November, 1929, 6.2 percent of men willing and able to work were wholly unemployed. The proportion increased to 17.2 percent by November, 1930, jumped to 24.3 percent by 1931, and by November, 1932, stood at 32.6 percent. At the last date, also, only 44 percent of the male workers in Buffalo had full-time employment.[19]

After a preliminary report in April, 1930, the Committee for the Stabilization of Industry presented lengthy findings to the Governor in November of that same year. The latter report contained a discussion of efforts made by industry to stabilize operations and analyzed the problems involved in regularizing employment, particularly during periods of depression. Although their recommendations were similar to Roosevelt's earlier proposals to county and municipal officials, they did suggest an impartial study of unemployment insurance systems as they might be applied to New York.[20]

As a result of the combined work of the Governor's Stabilization Committee, and a group appointed earlier by Industrial Commissioner Frances Perkins to devise methods of improving the State employment service and the organization of the labor market, every large industrial city except one, and a number of small communities, had a local emergency committee dealing with relief, emergency employment, and stabilization by the middle of November.[21] Following the success of this joint venture, and since he now realized that the emergency demonstrated the need for a continuing stimulation of local communities to meet their unemployment problem, and also for some central coordinating agency representing the entire State, Roosevelt reappointed an enlarged Stabilization Committee in November, 1930. No longer maintaining that the depression would be short-lived, he asked the committee to organize on a more permanent basis, to help communities meet their own problems of unemployment relief by setting up local committees, and to act as a clearing-house and advisory body for relevant plans submitted to State officials.[22]

When the Republican-dominated legislature refused to adopt the Governor's proposal to make the Stabilization Committee an official agency, Roosevelt retorted that the Republican lawmakers had refused to do so because of "the fear of letting me have any credit for the relief of unemployment." [23]

As the tragic year of 1930 drew to a close, William Allen White was painting a picture of foreboding for the country's future. In a most unusual Christmas message to Roosevelt, the famed mid-western Republican editor granted that

These are great days for you Democrats but don't be too cagey. If the old brig rights herself within the next year, whether by reason of good seamanship or by the chance of wind or wave, the people will forget that she ever listed. But what I fear is that if she does not right herself soon, the crew will come running out of Fo'c's'le, and throw the whole brass colored quarter deck crowd into the sea, Democrats, Republicans, and all. Unless the middle class has brains enough to curb the greed of our plutocracy, unless the middle class statesmen can produce some approximate of economic justice for the underprivileged the futile middle class will pass out of power. And we shall segregate into one party the credulous, suspicious, the bigoted, the malicious, the ignorant, led by the crafty and fools. And a majority may assemble with the support of the cynical, the disillusioned and the silly.

With these cheerful forebodings, my dear Governor, I wish you the merriest possible Christmas and the happiest of New Years.[24]

The forebodings of William Allen White, and their implications for the 1932 presidential elections, were not lost on a Governor who now realized that segments of the old economic order were disintegrating. Something had gone amiss with the well-publicized free enterprise system. The laissez-faire ideology and the ancient school slogans seemed antiquated. It was during this critical period in our nation's history that Roosevelt grasped the opportunity to exhibit one of his most constructive traits—a willingness to experiment.

One could almost hear Roosevelt say to his advisers and assistants, "Let's try this proposal. If it doesn't work, then let's experiment with another idea. But let us not sit back on our haunches lamenting 'what was good for our grandfathers should be good enough for us.'"

Roosevelt illustrated this pragmatic approach in a commencement address he made at the Van Hornesville School in upper New York—an institution inspired by its famous resident, Owen D. Young. Commenting on the unbalance caused by the new industrial era, and the need for a dramatic approach to existing problems, Roosevelt informed his youthful audience that the splendid achievements of recent years which had brought the nation higher standards of living, greater physical comforts, vastly better education, and a more abundant prosperity had to be maintained and increased. Nevertheless, the machine was out of balance and the principal effort of the next few years was to restore that balance. Roosevelt believed, however, that

The rules and remedies of the past probably do not form an answer to the restoration of the machine. Probably new and untried remedies must at least be experimented with. Everyone of the new factors in our lives is the result of experimentation and it is therefore only logical and not radical to insist that through experimentation also we must solve the social and economic difficulties of the present.[25]

In another commencement address, to the graduating class of Oglethorpe University in 1932, Roosevelt underscored the philosophy which had come to dominate his thinking as Governor when he made it abundantly clear that he would continue to be motivated by this pragmatic approach. To students who looked to the future with fear and trepidation, rather than hope, their president-to-be said:

The country needs and, unless I mistake its temper, the country demands bold, persistent experimentation. It is common sense to take a method and try it; if it fails, admit it frankly and try another. But above all try something. The millions who are in want will not stand by silently forever while the things to satisfy their needs are within easy reach.[26]

During the latter part of December, 1930, representatives and field workers of the State Department of Social Welfare, the State Charities Aid Association, and the State Department of Labor visited fifty-nine upstate cities to survey the unemployment and relief situation. The confidential report of the survey, submitted a month later, indicated that more than a year after the stock market crash only six cities had made any systematic effort to locate or learn the number of those unemployed. The general tendency of officials was to minimize the amount of unemployment and consequent need for relief despite the fact that the six cities of over 100,000 population—Albany, Buffalo, Rochester, Syracuse, Utica, and Yonkers—and twenty-two smaller ones, all had serious unemployment problems.[27]

Forty-eight of the cities had organized Emergency Committees on Unemployment, most of them established within two months preceding the survey. Of these forty-eight, fourteen were more or less responsible for employment registries but few had any definite programs for promoting more opportunities for work.[28]

The number of applicants and expenditures for relief increased in almost every city in 1930, while in a number of them unemployment had been a serious problem for several years due to the closing or moving away of factories or part-time operation. The joint committee found that public and private relief were fairly adequate in thirty-one cities, inadequate in twenty, seriously inadequate in seven of them, with no relief problem in one city. Figures available for fifty-four of the cities canvassed showed that expenditures for home relief in 1930 were almost $4,000,-000, an increase of 73 percent over 1929. By the beginning of December, 1930, forty-eight of the cities had already exceeded their budgeted relief appropriations for the year.[29]

Most city welfare commissioners admitted they were without special training for this type of work. Several functioned only two nights a week. Some were too old and infirm to do home visiting, while a number of them had no staff for home visits or clerical work. With the exceptions of Buffalo and Rochester, the city governments had failed to recognize the need for adequate administration of public relief.

Only a few cities made any attempt to base public home relief on the actual needs of the applicant. Few gave relief in the form of money, for grocery orders of about four dollars a week, regardless of family size, was the practice in about half the cities, and in one city it was $1.50-$2.00 per week. In some cities rent was paid only to save eviction. Gas and electricity were rarely paid for and clothing was usually provided through private relief agencies.[30]

Persons formerly in the higher income group usually found it difficult to bring themselves to apply for relief. Painstaking efforts to discover those in need through the schools in one city showed that the people of this type would let even their children suffer rather than apply for public relief. These families permitted themselves and their children to endure prolonged hardships and insufficient food, clothing, and warmth. Physical and mental health, earning power, and morale were beginning to deteriorate. Irreparable damage was being done to the health of children and parents who received insufficient assistance from the community or who were ashamed to seek aid, which they had never done before.

The survey report concluded that what was needed immediately was the stimulation of additional work by cities and private employers, public works projects, additional and expert staff for public welfare departments, central registration, and efficient cooperation of all relief-giving agencies.[31]

From the middle of 1931 until his death fourteen years later, Roosevelt was fully aware of the tragic effects of unemployment upon home life and upon the physical and moral fibre of the nation. Implementing one of the major recommendations of his Committee on Stabilization of Industry, and of the joint committee investigating upstate relief, Roosevelt persistently pressed local governments, the State legislature, and his administrative agencies for enlarged public work programs.

His Department of Public Works, headed by Colonel Frederick Stuart Greene, steadily increased its work and labor force to record figures after October, 1929. Contracts were speedily let out for the construction of new hospitals, sanitariums, prisons, highways, and bridges. Special efforts were made to employ a maximum number of workers near large cities. During the calendar year 1930, as much work was placed under contract as in the three previous calendar years combined. In August, 1929, the State actually employed 4,575 men on building contracts. Twelve months later the number had increased to 7,550.[32] In June, 1931, 19,383 men were employed on the construction and maintenance of State highways, as compared to 14,278 for the same period the year before. The total appropriation for highway construction and maintenance in 1931, including Federal aid, amounted to $58,250,000, as compared with $50,700,000 in 1930.[33]

Instead of a deliberate plan to delay work, as some Republican critics charged, the Public Works Department was under the greatest pressure to produce as much work as possible, and as quickly as possible. In July, 1932, the Governor learned from Colonel Greene that financial and labor conditions along the Champlain Canal were as bad as elsewhere. Many local banks had failed and there was practically no employment along the entire valley. Victory Mills looked like a deserted village, and other villages in the section were equally distressed. Greene, therefore, went out of his way "to give a few more weeks of employment in a section of the country where it is badly needed." [34]

In 1930, some Republicans were already condemning Roosevelt for excessive expenditures on public work projects. In contrast, Socialist leaders Norman Thomas and Louis Waldman berated the Governor for appropriating insufficient funds to aid the unemployed. They cited preliminary figures released by the Federal census in 1930 which gave the number of jobless as 364,617 in New York State. Referring to the "New York Industrial Bulletin," they reminded the Governor that the index of factory payrolls in the State had been 91.4 in April, 86.17 in June, and had fallen still further in July, 1930.[35]

It was inconceivable, according to Louis Waldman, that the richest state in the Union was incapable of meeting the problem and providing work or relief for the unemployed, whose condition was not of their own making. He stressed the need for legislative enactments providing for a six-hour day and a five-day week, extensive public works through slum clearance and rural electrification, prohibition of children under sixteen from entering industry, and for immediate allowance to the unemployed in distress coupled with an adequate system of unemployment insurance.[36]

Paradoxically, the New Deal of Franklin D. Roosevelt, incorporating so many of the moderate Socialist proposals in social

welfare, helps explain the speedy demise of the Socialist movement in New York and elsewhere throughout the nation.

However, not until the summer of 1931 did New York undertake to care for its unemployed on a comprehensive scale, one of
the first states to do so. In his annual message to the legislature in
January of that year, Roosevelt referred to rising unemployment
throughout the nation as he underscored the need for enlarged
public work programs. "Public works," the Governor insisted,
"are being speeded to the utmost; all available funds are being
used to provide employment; wherever the State can find a place
for a man to work it has provided a job." [37]

By the beginning of 1931 events had moved Roosevelt to conclude that unemployment and labor legislation were issues which
could no longer be adequately handled by individual State
action. Instead, he felt that fundamental solutions could be effective only when instituted on at least a regional basis through
uniform labor and social-welfare legislation. Thus, it was logical
for Roosevelt to inform the lawmakers that he had invited the
governors of Massachusetts, Rhode Island, Connecticut, New
Jersey, Pennsylvania, and Ohio to meet with him in Albany on
January 23, to discuss unemployment in its broader aspects. It
was the Governor's thought that the northeastern industrial
states could cooperate in a joint study of facts and existing or
proposed methods of relief both here and abroad, so that State
legislation in the future might be made more nearly uniform.
Recommendations adopted at the conference, which the Governor felt might promote a far-sighted policy of prevention and
relief, would be forwarded to the legislature for action.[38]

By the summer of 1931, Roosevelt not only believed in regional cooperation but also concluded that American private
industry had largely failed the people. On the eve of a special
legislative session he wrote a friend:

. . . many of the so-called business men and financiers, even now,
after two years of depression, have not the foggiest idea of what
happened. . . . As to the suggestion that "the great silent body of
American people" believe that any either [*sic*] minor regulation of

certain business by government has been responsible for our troubles, I am inclined to think that the contrary is true. Most average citizens with whom I talk are impressed with the rather serious failure of business to prevent present conditions when they had a chance to do so.[39]

The "present conditions" which Roosevelt referred to included an estimated one-million unemployed in New York State. The national index of factory employment had dropped from 110.3 in September, 1929, to 78.1 in 1931.[40]

A terribly depressing, though more descriptive, picture of the situation was contained in a report of a canvass of forty-five New York cities by the Joint Committee on Unemployment Relief. The outstanding fact shown by this report was that practically every city had spent nearly as much or more for home relief in the first half of 1931 as for the entire year of 1930, and equally large expenditures were expected in the second half of 1931. Especially depressing for social workers was the inadequacy of the relief and the knowledge that unemployment would continue to increase during the winter of 1931-32.[41]

Private agencies could no longer cope with the situation. Private and public relief expenditures during the first quarter of 1931, in New York cities of over 30,000 inhabitants, had increased fourfold over the amount expended for the same period in 1929.[42] The director of the Welfare Council of New York City estimated that during the winter of 1931-32, the municipal authorities would have to provide not less than $20,-000,000 for emergency work and wages.[43]

As a result of these discouraging reports Roosevelt concluded that the coming winter would find twice as many unemployed as the previous year, and since private charity was unable to meet the added burdens, the State would have to step in to avert a complete breakdown of local relief. From all corners came increasing pleas for State aid to cope with the problem. Realizing that if he delayed action until the regular session of the 1932 legislature half of the winter would be gone before the necessary legislation was passed and the work or organization set up,

Roosevelt convened an extraordinary legislative session in August, 1931.

With the nation yearning for positive leadership to drag it out of the morass of hunger and fear, New York's Governor forecast a theme of the New Deal when he informed the legislature that the time had come for the State to assume responsibility to provide either work or food for its unemployed. Government, he maintained, was not the master but the "creature of the people." He continued:

The duty of the State toward the citizen is the duty of the servant to its master. The people have created it; the people, by common consent, permit its continual existence. . . . In broad terms I assert that modern society, acting through its government, owes the definite obligation to prevent the starvation or the dire want of any of its fellow men and women who try to maintain themselves but cannot. . . . To these unfortunate citizens aid must be extended by government—not as a matter of charity but as a matter of social duty. . . . When . . . a condition arises which calls for measures of relief over and beyond the ability of private and local assistance to meet—even with the usual aid added by the State—it is time for the State itself to do its additional share.[44]

These were challenging statements by a leading presidential aspirant. Within two years this philosophy would be the basis for a new era for social workers, administrators, political scientists, historians, sociologists, economists, and practical politicians.

Mild though the Governor's remarks may have seemed to many European nations in 1931, the contention that the State must assume responsibility to provide work, food, shelter, and clothing for its unemployed was a challenge to American traditions. Of vital importance for the faith and hope of the people, and for Roosevelt's personal future was the favorable response to the Governor's leadership by increasing numbers of the nation's poor, downtrodden, and unemployed.

As Governor and as President, Roosevelt did not seek to alter fundamentally the American economic system. His objective was to preserve, not destroy. In 1930, Roosevelt had remarked that there was no question but that it was "time for the country to become fairly radical for at least one generation. History shows that where this occurs occasionally, nations are saved from revolutions."[45]

Following Roosevelt's address to the special session of the legislature in August, 1931, in which he recommended creation of a Temporary Emergency Relief Administration and a work relief program, Republican and Democratic legislators exhibited their usual bitterness and distrust. As always, they sought public recognition for party-initiated legislation.

John J. Dunnigan, Democratic minority leader in the Senate, introduced a bill which contained the Governor's proposals. The Republican Wicks Bill differed in that it would have placed the central administrative body within the Department of Social Welfare and would have provided for State aid for home and work relief at a flat rate of reimbursement to all localities. Roosevelt, however, desired creation of an independent State agency, with virtually complete discretion in the expenditure of a proposed appropriation of $20,000,000. He also wanted to invest county and city commissioners of public welfare with local responsibility for the administration of home relief, whereas the Wicks Bill would have continued the town system, in operation in forty-nine counties.

The struggle which developed between the Governor and Republican leaders Senator Fearon and Assemblyman McGinnies also centered around Roosevelt's insistence that the funds for the proposed $20,000,000 appropriation be secured by a 50 per cent increase in the State income tax. It was clear to the Governor that it was the duty of those who

. . . have benefited by our industrial and economic system to come to the front in such a grave emergency and assist those who under the same industrial and economic order are the losers and sufferers. I believe their contribution should be in proportion to the benefits they receive and the prosperity they enjoy.[46]

The Republicans countered with a proposal to avoid an increase in income tax through strict budget economies and short-term loans. If taxation finally proved necessary, they felt there should be a delay of one year before adoption.[47] As the Republicans readied themselves for enactment of the Wicks Bill and then immediate adjournment, Roosevelt warned them that he would veto their proposal and convene another special session unless, and until, they adopted a constructive and realistic bill.

Faced with the prospects of a veto, with Roosevelt's implied threat to appeal directly to the people for their support, and with the knowledge that the Governor would burden them with responsibility for expenses entailed in convening a second special session of the legislature, Fearon and McGinnies capitulated. As amended and finally enacted, the Wicks Bill conformed to the main principles originally proposed by the Governor.[48] It was a signal victory for Roosevelt and for the principle of State aid for emergency unemployment relief.

The Wicks Bill created the Temporary Emergency Relief Administration to administer relief by furnishing employment, food, clothing, and shelter for needy persons who had been residents of the State for two years prior to November 1, 1931. An emergency period was established from the previous date to June, 1932, during which time the T.E.R.A., headed by three persons named by the Governor, would govern the administration of work relief and home relief and allocate grants to municipalities for work relief projects conducted by the State.[49] Half of the $20,000,000 appropriation was for home relief. Those public welfare districts complying with the rules of the T.E.R.A. were entitled to a 40 percent reimbursement of their expenditures for this type of aid. If financial conditions worsened in certain areas, endangering adequate relief, the T.E.R.A. could, at its discretion, grant increased appropriations beyond the 40 percent figure.

Roosevelt set up the T.E.R.A. in October with Jesse I. Straus, of R. H. Macy, as chairman, along with labor leader John Sullivan of New York City and Philip J. Wickser of Buffalo. Harry L. Hopkins, administrative director of the New York Tuberculosis and Health Association, was named T.E.R.A.'s executive director. Before the end of 1931 the organizational structure of the T.E.R.A. was virtually complete. The committee received unusual cooperation from public officials, social agencies, and innumerable public spirited citizens in every community.

At the beginning of 1932, with unemployment still on the increase, Roosevelt estimated that there were at least 1.5 million out of work in the Empire State.[50] By that time it was doubtful whether the $20 million appropriated by the extraordinary session of the previous legislature would carry through to June, 1932, for it had been possible to put to work only a small portion of those who had registered at Emergency Work Bureaus.

In January, the Governor offered the legislators a depressing picture as he told the crowded chamber:

Not since the dark days of the sixties have the people of this State and of this Nation faced problems as grave, situations as difficult, suffering as severe. The economics of America, and indeed of the whole world are out of joint; only the most skillful and concerted care will mend them.[51]

The Governor urged the lawmakers to cooperate, not as political partisans, but as a legislative body speaking for the entire State. Forecasting his famous "one third of a nation" address as President, Roosevelt maintained that the people of New York "cannot allow any individuals within her borders to go unfed, unclothed, or unsheltered." [52]

In an emergency message in March, the Governor advised the lawmakers that the original appropriation of $20 million for State aid was exhausted, and that additional funds were required.[53] Only two weeks previously the Work Bureau had reported that 75,000 persons were receiving work relief, 82,000 were receiving home relief, while 112,000 additional applicants were in need of work relief but had little chance of getting it. A number of cities and counties could no longer finance themselves and were about to close down their Work Bureaus because of lack of funds.[54]

After numerous conferences with Republican legislative leaders, it was agreed that the work of the T.E.R.A. should be extended beyond the original expiration date of June 1, 1932, along with adequate appropriations. Since the citizens of the State were being heavily burdened by State and local taxation levied within the last two years, and with the expectation of additional taxes by the Federal government to make up the huge deficit in the Federal treasury, the Governor and the conferees agreed that the five million dollars needed through November 1, 1932, would be appropriated from current revenues without new taxes.[55] This would help carry on the work of the T.E.R.A. to election day, when a State-wide referendum would be submitted to the people for a bond issue of $30 million to meet the balance of the requirements through January 1, 1934.[56] This was a distinct departure from the pay-as-you-go policy previously adhered to, but Roosevelt felt that the gravity of the situation warranted the change.

Immediately before the November elections, Roosevelt, Fearon, and McGinnies issued a joint statement endorsing Proposition I, the $30 million relief bond issue. The people responded by a four-to-one vote in support of the proposal.

The economy-minded bloc in New York, which condemned these "excessive" expenditures for relief, was spearheaded by Merwin K. Hart, former classmate of Roosevelt at Harvard and now president of the New York State Economic Council. By the winter of 1931-32, Hart and his supporters wanted an "across-the-board" cut of State appropriations by some 10 percent, and postponement of all automatic increments of civil service wages. This was a period of economic crisis, Hart maintained, and the State should show the way to private business.

Following the Governor's introduction of the proposed budget in January, 1932, Hart wired Roosevelt some four hundred words condemning the recommendations as excessive. It was clear to Hart "that if the total ordinary general budget appropriations could jump from $264 million in 1929-30 to $315 million in 1930-31—nearly twenty per cent for that year alone—that a reduction of sixteen millions this year is totally inadequate."[57]

After bemoaning Hart's failure to pay any attention to the need for economy "in these trying times" by sending such a lengthy telegram, Roosevelt asked him just where he would cut the proposed budget. Give me chapter and verse, demanded the Governor.[58] Hart, who had been characterized by Robert Moses as bigoted and unscrupulous,[59] challenged Roosevelt to debate the issue publicly. Hart advised the Governor: "You do not, of course, expect me to enumerate categorically all of the items that should be struck out or reduced to make up this sum. That is up to you and the Legislature. But it is reasonable to ask me to indicate the general directions where this saving can be made." Hart maintained that less necessary activities could be eliminated, such as the Transit Commission, while in remaining activities, including education, personnel should be decreased and salaries exceeding $1,000 should be reduced by at least 10 percent.[60]

To Hart, and to others with this shortsighted concept of economy—and there were many—the Governor had more than an adequate answer. In the first place, State officers and employees were not paid high salaries. Exclusive of the judiciary, the average salary of the State's 31,000 employees, including the Governor, was just over $1,500. Almost half of these employees worked for an average salary of $818. In contrast to private industry, State salaries had not been increased during or following World War I. While skilled or unskilled workers had received very substantial increases in private industry, the salaries of many positions in State service remained unchanged, or if increased did not correspond with the increased cost of living. Because of these considerations Roosevelt insisted that State employees should not be the first to suffer when retrenchment was in order.[61]

Despite the efforts of Roosevelt and the lawmakers, economic deterioration continued unabated in New York. Howard S. Cullman, a member of the Port of New York Authority, wrote the Governor that things were unbelievably bad in New York City, and that it probably was the most depressing place to live in. At one time Cullman thought it was a distinction to be a graduate of Phillips Exeter Academy and Yale University, but in view of the swollen ranks of the unemployed and an ever increasing army of ex-classmates, it had gotten to be a real liability. In his limited experience it was about the cruelest age he had ever lived through.[62]

The supplementary appropriation for relief voted by the regular legislative session in 1932 was exhausted two months before its scheduled expiration date of November 15. Unemployment in the Empire State approached the two million mark while factory wages dropped from 101.7 in 1929 to 46.5 by the end of 1932.[63] So many men and women were still vainly seeking to earn a livelihood that some critics contended that the most that could be said for much of the effort of New York was that it had warded off actual starvation. In contrast to other states, however, New York had not side-stepped some of its most pressing obligations.[64]

Harry L. Hopkins, successor to Jesse Straus as director of the T.E.R.A., painted a most depressing picture when he informed the Governor that existing funds were inadequate, that unemployment and distress were on the increase, and that funds raised from private sources would be less in the future than in the past. Localities were finding it increasingly difficult to finance their own relief, and reports to his office indicated that the amount of unpaid and uncollected local taxes was on the increase. In most parts of the State adequate or satisfactory work or home relief was not being given, and better results were impossible without increased funds. Finally, Hopkins advised the Governor that if the interests of the people of the State were to be protected during the coming year, steps had to be taken to provide more adequate relief.[65]

Contemplating passage of the thirty-million dollar bond issue for unemployment relief in November, 1932, the State was to continue the prevailing unemployment relief program, despite the fact that the sum being spent was totally inadequate. What was needed was more than $30 million worth of bonds for unemployment relief, bonds which could have been paid back within a few years out of heavier income and inheritance taxes on the higher brackets.[66] This would have placed the burden of unemployment relief upon the shoulders of those who Roosevelt had previously stated were best able to bear the brunt of the depression. In the meantime, short-term borrowings could have been used to expand the State's unemployment relief program. The money could have been paid back from the proceeds of the November bond sale. This was an emergency situation and to many in the fields of social work, labor, and social legislation, it required even stronger measures than those initiated by Roosevelt.

When Roosevelt had contended, in 1931, that government owed the "definite obligation to prevent the starvation or the dire want of any of its fellow men or women who try to maintain themselves but cannot," the "government" he was referring to was the State of New York. By early 1932, Roosevelt was endorsing the efforts of Senator Robert F. Wagner to enact a Federal unemployment relief bill, because he felt it would equalize the burden throughout the nation. Such acts, he maintained, were justified because they carried out the definite obligation of the government to prevent starvation and distress in the existing crisis.[67] Thus, Roosevelt had gone beyond State and regional boundaries when he reaffirmed the principle of government responsibility. "I not only reaffirm it," Roosevelt told a radio audience during the 1932 presidential race, "I go a step further and say that where the State itself is unable successfully to fulfill this obligation which lies upon it, it then becomes the positive duty of the Federal Government to step in to help."[68]

When Roosevelt was inaugurated President in March, 1933, the need for Federal intervention had become overwhelming, for the nation had reached a new low in industrial activity and employment. Having shattered traditions while Governor of New York, President Roosevelt established new precedents by involving the national government in direct programs of Federal aid.

During the critical "Hundred Days" after his inaugural,

President Roosevelt established the Civilian Conservation Corps with Congressional sanction—which transferred 250,000 jobless young men from cities to work in the nation's woodlands— approved the Federal Emergency Relief Act, which was the first example of direct Federal participation in relief through grants-in-aid to states; and pushed through appropriations of additional millions for an immense public works program under the Public Works Administration. In November, 1933, the President created the Civil Works Administration, which put more than four million unemployed to work.

In April, 1935, Congress approved the President's recommendation for an Emergency Relief Appropriation Act with just under five billion dollars for work relief on useful projects. The following month the President created the Works Progress Administration, under Harry Hopkins, to coordinate the execution of the work relief program as a whole.

The critical depression which began late in 1929 saw Roosevelt respond with an open-minded, pragmatic approach in the field of economics. Although not alone amongst governors in the sponsorship of remedial legislation,[69] Roosevelt's acts were always in the forefront, for he was the Chief Executive of the richest and most populous state, and a leading aspirant for the Democratic presidential nomination. Besides, people were searching for an inspiring and aggressive personality to replace the bumbling, defaulting leadership of the Hoover administration.

Immediately after the stock market collapse Roosevelt believed that fundamental industrial conditions were still sound. The following March he maintained that the depression would be short-lived and that it was due, amongst other things, to the regular business cycle. When he appointed a committee to investigate long-range solutions to the unemployment problem, the Governor naively placed unquestioning faith in the ability, and in the desire, of industrialists to voluntarily ease the depression and aid the unemployed. He was consistent, however, in urging his administrative agencies to expand State construction projects to the maximum.

Toward the end of 1930, Roosevelt first exhibited a growing cognizance of the seriousness and extent of the depression when he suggested experimentation in an attempt to resuscitate the sickened economy. The following January, he acknowledged that the depression had hurdled State boundaries and proclaimed the need for a regional approach to basic economic problems.

With belated support from a special session of the 1931 legislature, Roosevelt established the Temporary Emergency Relief Administration to make State aid available to localities for work and home relief. This brought Harry Hopkins onto the scene to direct the experiment which became a model for subsequent Federal legislation. When these initial relief appropriations were exhausted before their expiration date, Roosevelt and the 1932 legislature provided supplementary, though still inadequate, funds and a State bond for additional relief.

The beginning of 1932 found Roosevelt extending his concept of governmental aid to the forty-eight states when he supported Federal legislation for unemployment relief. He made this proposal part of his successful campaign for the presidency. During the months and years which followed, various Congressional sessions provided Federal aid to states for work relief and direct Federal participation in securing work for the unemployed on Federal projects. These precedent-shattering enactments in the field of social welfare were justified, according to Roosevelt, because they were "carrying out the definite obligation of the government to prevent starvation and distress in this present crisis."

VII

A BATTLE ON TWO FRONTS

Within the first year of Roosevelt's governorship, Republican leaders were secretly lamenting his incisive grasp of leadership and excellent sense of timing. Through daily press conferences and radio talks he had kept the public abreast of developments in Albany. In one of his numerous messages to the Governor, Felix Frankfurter commented on this Rooseveltian characteristic when he held:

Nothing surprises this particular observer of national events more than the way public men pass up opportunities made to order for them—they are so scared of the so-called prudences. But you *are* seizing your opportunities. And so I rejoice deeply over the leadership which you have asserted on these basic public questions and the lucid education to which you are subjecting the public.[1]

New Yorkers were confronted with another gubernatorial contest in 1930, an election which Roosevelt knew had to be won by a decisive margin in order to strengthen his candidacy for the Democratic presidential nomination. Would he, during this campaign, continue to subject the public to a lucid education on controversial issues, including Tammany graft and corruption?

Roosevelt never lost interest in the national Democratic organization. Following the party's defeat in 1928, he sought to revive the Democracy for the 1932 presidential contest. This activity kept him in the party limelight and moved increasing numbers of Democrats to hail him as the "next President of the United States."[2]

As the effects of tariff wars, contracting foreign markets, and the stock market crash of 1929 were spelled out in decreasing production, increasing unemployment, rotting farm crops, and fear for the stability of the nation, bitter complaint and harsh invectives were hurled at the national Republican administration in Washington. For the first time since 1921, "Republican" prosperity was on the defensive, and each passing month meant increased votes for Democrats. If the depression continued through 1932, Louis Howe might yet see the fruition of his long-range plans.

There was no doubt in the minds of political experts that because of "hard times" and the Governor's constructive achievements, Roosevelt would be re-elected in 1930. The question, however, was by what plurality? Nevertheless, before the end of the campaign, Tammany Hall was to bring renewed life and hope to the Republican cause. But even that was insufficient to upset earlier predictions.

There were times, however, when both Roosevelt and his "good right arm," Herbert Lehman, preferred the quiet and ease of retirement to the hectic political scene. On one such occasion, when rumor had it that Lehman would not seek renomination in 1930, Roosevelt wrote the full-time Lieutenant Governor that both of them had many personal reasons why they should not run. Nevertheless, continued Roosevelt:

. . . You and I both have the same kind of sense of obligation about going through with a task once undertaken and, frankly, the only reason either of us would run again is that sense of obligation to a great many million people who may insist that we shall try to carry on the work for another two years.

And in the long run I am inclined to think that you and I would be more useful for the next two years in our present position than if we were to return to our own private interests and private life.[3]

Youthful Al Smith had moved upward by the boosts of Tammany Hall. He had remained completely loyal to the organization until his governorship, at which time he exhibited an independence of Tammany which enabled him to seek a superficial housecleaning within the party. As one of thirteen

Tammany Sachems, Smith was unable to reform Tammany, but he did bring some cleansing elements into the New York Democracy.

Following his defeat in 1928, Smith announced his voluntary retirement from the political arena. Shortly thereafter, the dual leadership of John F. Curry, Tammany Hall's newly designated boss, and Mayor James J. Walker set about removing the so-called Smith Democrats from power in New York. By 1930, Boss Curry and the Mayor had managed to rid the leadership of virtually all these good-government elements. Dominated once more by a Boss Tweed mentality, Tammany sought to abscond with the bulk of the City's treasury. Graft was now an open practice and included the sale of judgeships to the highest bidder. Norman Thomas, Socialist candidate for Mayor in 1929, described the situation adequately when he remarked that it was the Tammany of the lightest-weight Mayor in the recent history of New York, under whom waste, corruption, and inefficiency had grown like sunflowers in Kansas. Tammany, he maintained, would be Tammany no matter who was chosen leader. It was not something to be reformed but to be fought.[4]

Before the end of Walker's first administration in 1929, a sewer scandal was uncovered in Democratic Queens County. It was estimated that of a $16,000,000 sewer construction project, $9,000,000 represented graft for Democratic Borough President Maurice Connolly and friends. Connolly ultimately wound up in jail. Payroll padding was uncovered in the Street Cleaning Department, where some $4,000 weekly was being credited to dummies. Under the influence of Mayor Walker a bus franchise was awarded by the Board of Estimate to an Equitable Coach Company which existed in name only. A day after the award Walker left for a vacation in Europe with a letter of credit for $10,000 bought for him by the New York representative of the Equitable Coach Company.

In Brooklyn, members of the police motorcycle squad were disposing of traffic court cases by means of rubber stamp facsimiles of judges' signatures at $10 to $30 a signature. Sheriff

Thomas M. Farley of New York County accumulated bank deposits of $360,000 in a seven-year period during which his legitimate income totaled only $90,000. James A. McQuade, the Register of Kings County, deposited more than $500,000 in a six-year period despite a total legitimate income of only $50,000. Michael J. Cruise, City Clerk of New York County and Tammany leader of the twelfth district, deposited $143,000 in six years, although his total salary had been only $80,000. Distinguished citizens, organizing to combat immorality, formed a Committee of Fourteen and issued reports fervently praising the work of a Tammany-appointed deputy prosecutor. This same prosecutor subsequently confessed that he had accepted six hundred bribes to help crooked police frame six hundred women.[5]

Unpublicized salary increases were voted numerous city officials by a subservient Board of Estimate, only to be revoked when uncovered by civic-minded spokesmen during the 1930 gubernatorial race. Many a Tammany Hall leader availed himself of wonderful "tin boxes" in bank vaults to shield newly acquired loot from the light of public investigation.

Despite damaging charges of graft, corruption, and inefficiency hurled at the Walker administration by opposition candidates and the Citizens Union, gay, sophisticated, debonair, night-clubbing Jimmy Walker had been re-elected Mayor in 1929 by some half-million plurality. As the Hofstadter investigation subsequently disclosed, Walker's failure to be a good Mayor was not considered half so serious by the public as any personal dishonesty that might be charged against him.

During the conflict between "Smith" and "Walker-Curry" Democrats, Roosevelt maintained a policy of benevolent neutrality. Opposed to the philosophy and practices of the Walker-Curry elements, Roosevelt nevertheless granted patronage for deserving New Yorkers through Tammany Hall. Although he had led the fight against Tammany while State Senator and Assistant Secretary of the Navy, Roosevelt was now more practical minded. In fact, as a result of a contribution to the

1929 building fund of Tammany Hall, Roosevelt automatically became a member of Tammany after writing, "I am very glad to send you a check . . . and I regret that I cannot make it larger." [6]

Roosevelt's belief in progressive Democracy remained intact, but he realized that he needed Tammany support to insure re-election in 1930. Besides, the 1932 presidential nominating convention was not far off.

Toward the end of 1929, Roosevelt appointed Amadeo A. Bertini to the Court of General Sessions to succeed Francis X. Mancuso of City Trust Company fame. Bertini was a comparatively unknown lawyer, a man without particular experience in criminal law whose appointment was criticized by the Bar Association. But he was a close friend of Tammany Chief Curry.[7] Only a short time before his appointment, Bertini had paid a substantial fine to the Federal government for underestimating the value of goods he had purchased abroad. Tammany designees continued to merit Roosevelt's endorsement.

Irritated by the rising clamor of civic groups opposed to such nakedly partisan and incompetent appointments, the Tammany-minded New York *Enquirer* retorted in the frankest manner possible. It reminded its readers, and the Governor, of the meaning of party loyalty when it held:

Governor Roosevelt is not the man to take lightly, or to reward with indifference, the political rank and influence of Mr. Curry. He knows the importance of party loyalty and of party solidarity. He is unlikely to view with tolerant eye the attempts of certain candidates and their backers to go over the heads of the leader of Tammany. These intrigues have brought disaster to the Republican Party. They are alien to the spirit of Democracy and should find no place in the appointments of office which are in the gift of the Democratic organization.[8]

Shortly thereafter, when respected Joseph M. Proskauer retired from the State Supreme Court bench, Roosevelt designated Joseph F. Crater, another Curry choice, to the vacant post.[9] Crater's appointment was an affront to Al Smith, who had originally suggested the highly esteemed Bernard L. Sheintag, deemed by many liberals as the best choice the Governor could have made. Roosevelt had again selected a relatively unknown member of the Bar, unknown except to Tammany.

In August, 1930, Judge Crater suddenly disappeared from sight after carefully selling his stocks and closing out his bank accounts. It was later disclosed that immediately following his appointment to the bench Crater had drawn $7,000 from his bank account. This raised the question of purchase of his judgeship, a question never answered for Crater was never located.[10]

Such appointments to the judiciary disheartened many liberal Democrats and independents who had come to expect greater things of Roosevelt. The editor of one newspaper in New York City was moved to write the Governor that he did not believe the Chief Executive was serving either candor, fair play, or himself.[11]

In May, 1930, Federal District Attorney Charles H. Tuttle charged that Tammany Judge W. Bernard Vause had received $250,000 for negotiating pier leases for the United American Lines from the City of New York. He also divulged the existence of unethical practices before the financially-minded Board of Standards and Appeals which heard requests for modification of the city's rigid zoning regulations.[12] A lengthy period of silence in the face of the pier lease exposures, and the scandals in the Board of Standards and Appeals, left the entire Walker administration under a cloud. Many citizens unsuccessfully urged Roosevelt to appoint a Moreland Act Commissioner to investigate the leasing of the piers by New York's Sinking Fund Commission, of which Mayor Walker was chairman. Other civic spokesmen wanted to know who had influenced Judge Vause, and to what use he had put the reputed sum of $250,000 paid him by the steamship company. Within a month, however, Vause resigned from his judicial post, which seemed to be the usual method of hushing up Tammany scandals.

A few weeks before the 1930 elections, the staid Democratic New York *Times* reluctantly admitted that Tammany had brought renewed hope to the Republican party, where none had existed previously. Two months before, Roosevelt's election would have been conceded even by Republicans. The reappearance of Tammany corruption, however, had changed the political outlook. According to the New York *Times*, the corruption issue could be turned to Roosevelt's benefit if he met it with frankness and courage.[13]

These disclosures of Tammany corruption greatly disturbed enlightened elements within the Democracy. A close friend, and member of the Governor's campaign strategy board, suggested to Roosevelt that the men and advisers around him, and those who were to offer his name to the Democratic convention, be of "unquestionable integrity, not in anyway connected with the City Administration."[14]

By the summer of 1930, astute political leaders realized that the State Republican machine had been seriously weakened by an internal struggle over prohibition, by the party's disastrous defeat in New York City's 1929 mayoralty contest, and by the intensifying effects of the nation-wide depression. Upstate Republican leaders also acknowledged a significant trend toward Roosevelt which they attributed to his farm legislation, his extended tours, his honesty, his seeming interest in the problems of individuals, and his personal dryness concerning prohibition.

Another factor in Roosevelt's favor was the developing effectiveness of the upstate Democratic machine, resulting from the efforts of Louis Howe and James A. Farley to revitalize old organizations, develop new ones where needed, and maintain year-round activity. Months before the convening of the Democratic convention, Howe and Farley had completed the preliminary work and planning for the campaign.[15] More than three months before the convention, Farley phoned Howard S. Cullman in New York City and asked him to begin collecting precampaign contributions. Cullman responded by writing the Governor that "we will need probably between $300,000 and $400,000 to put over the campaign and it would seem to me that we would block ourselves beautifully if we anticipate what should be substantial contributions with nominal contributions at this time."[16]

The Governor replied to Cullman that he was quite right about campaign funds except that "we simply have to have money between now and the first of October, in order to print and distribute a great deal of literature which is now being prepared, and also carry on the publicity radio, etc. I think we must certainly get forty or fifty thousand dollars before the campaign."[17]

With "talkies and movies" as one of his responsibilities, Howe brought Roosevelt within sight and hearing of thousands of citizens in distant up-state communities who normally would never see a gubernatorial candidate. Talking pictures were made of Roosevelt, Smith, Wagner, and Lehman, and shown on the screens of some 200 theatres in small communities, as part of Democratic campaign strategy. This plan had been initiated two months prior to the State convention.[18]

Four days before the Democratic convention met in Syracuse the campaign strategy board gathered at the Executive Mansion in Albany. Roosevelt, Lehman, Farley, Howe, Samuel I. Rosenman, and Howard S. Cullman discussed campaign itineraries, radio broadcasts, and trips. The group approved Louis Howe's proposed schedule of twenty major radio broadcasts. Circularization, upstate letters, and the like were to be channeled through Farley; speakers' and candidates' upstate tours to be directed by Henry Morgenthau, Jr.; a general speakers' bureau to be under the guidance of Senator Robert F. Wagner, while Louis Howe was to be responsible for the movies, telephone, and telegrams. The Finance Division was to be jointly managed by Henry Morgenthau, Sr. and Howard S. Cullman, with Cullman doing all of the work. The Executive and Budget Committee was to consist of Roosevelt, Lehman, a representative of the Democratic Union, Farley, Mrs. Caroline O'Day, and Henry Morgenthau, Sr. As the Democratic delegates convened in Syracuse, their campaign plans had all but been completed.[19]

Months before the G.O.P. had had opportunity to designate officially its gubernatorial nominee, Republican leaders and newspaper columnists were belittling Roosevelt's expected victory. Mark Sullivan contended that the true explanation for Roosevelt's victory would be found in the Republican cleavage over prohibition. Unfortunately, according to Sullivan, the people would conclude that Governor Roosevelt had been re-elected by his own personal strength and by the issue of sterner regulation of water power, electrical, and other public utilities.[20] The public would not think much about prohibition in connection with Roosevelt, but they would think of public utility regulation as his issue, and would give comparatively little thought as to whether he was wet or dry.[21]

Following Secretary of State Henry L. Stimson's keynote address to the Republican convention in which he paid high tribute to President Hoover's national administration, convention delegates ratified a prohibition repeal plank by a vote of 733 to 258.[22] Echoing the remarks of Senate Majority Leader Fearon who, earlier that month, had stated that in all his experience as a legislator he had "never known of a more vaccilating Chief Executive than the incumbent,"[23] the delegates endorsed a platform which assailed Roosevelt's administration and the scandals of Tammany Hall. "Tiger Tamer" Charles H. Tuttle, who had recently uncovered damaging evidence of Tammany graft and corruption, was nominated on the first ballot, with Caleb H. Baumes of Newburgh as his running mate for Lieutenant Governor. From that moment on, Tuttle made "Roosevelt's subservience to Tammany" his campaign theme.[24]

Walter Lippmann, who two years earlier had urged Roosevelt's nomination upon the Democratic convention, was now extremely critical of the Governor's handling of Tammany. He maintained that Tuttle's record as United States Attorney had earned him the respect and gratitude of the people of New York and would make a powerful appeal to that section of the voters known formerly as "Al Smith Republicans" who, since 1922, had held the balance of power in gubernatorial elections. They would almost certainly feel that at this time the election of a wet Republican might further the movement for repeal more effectively than the election of a wet Democrat. Lippmann also believed that they would feel that the presence of a Tuttle in Albany might be the only effective way to set the forces in motion which would break the grip of Tammany on New York City.[25]

Lippmann was referring, amongst other things, to the case in which Tuttle had produced evidence that the wife of Magistrate George F. Ewald, an appointee of Mayor Walker, had "loaned" Tammany district leader Martin J. Healy $10,000 on the day of Ewald's appointment, on an unsecured note which had suddenly "disappeared."[26] Eventually the evidence in the Ewald case was turned over to Tammany District Attorney T. C. T. Crain, who, not unexpectedly, was unable to secure indictments.

Within days after receipt of messages from Rabbi Stephen S. Wise and leaders of the Bar Association, charging laxity in the inquiry by the District Attorney, Roosevelt decided to supersede Crain. He directed the convening of an extraordinary grand jury by Justice Philip J. McCook, a Republican, with the inquiry under the direction of State Attorney General Hamilton Ward, also a Republican. The scope of the inquiry, which Roosevelt limited to the Ewald affair, tempered the enthusiasm with which leaders of the Bar, and others who had sought State intervention, greeted the news.[27]

Within a week of hearings by the extraordinary grand jury, indictments were handed down against Healy and Ewald. The grand jury, in accordance with the charge of Justice McCook, continued its inquiry to determine whether Ewald's alleged bribe was paid to Healy as a system governing appointments by Tammany. Subpoenas were issued for the Democratic leaders of all twenty-three Assembly districts in New York County, and for John F. Curry. Called to testify immediately prior to the 1930 Democratic State convention, Curry stalked off the witness chair indignantly claiming that he had been "insulted" by the special prosecutor, Hiram C. Todd, when the latter asked him to waive immunity. Seventeen Tammany district leaders who followed Curry to the stand also refused to sign waivers, and of the remaining Democratic leaders to be called after the Democratic convention, only one was expected to defy the precedent laid down by Curry.

This was New York City under Tammany and Jimmy Walker. Nearly every one of the twenty-three Tammany district leaders who declined to testify on the grounds that they might incriminate themselves had been appointed by Mayor Walker as department heads in the city government, at an average salary of $7,300.[28]

Immediately prior to the convening of the Democratic convention, Roosevelt advised Walker to suggest to these Democratic leaders "that they return before the special grand jury and voluntarily offer to waive immunity. They should freely answer all questions relating to their official acts." [29]

Although most delegates who had come to the Democratic convention in Syracuse sought to ignore New York City's scandals, Roosevelt and Wagner had agreed that the latter, in his keynote address, would make a general denunciation of dishonesty in office. Despite demands by Tammany leaders to delete the phrase from the prepared text, Senator Wagner told convention delegates: "I know that I speak for the heart and conscience of the great rank and file of the Democratic party in our State when I say that he who attains judicial or other public office by dishonest means should be driven therefrom, as also from the ranks of our party."[30]

To put a halt to the increasing number of judges and New York City officeholders who refused to waive immunity before the extraordinary grand jury, Roosevelt personally insisted that the convention delegates support legislation requiring immunity waivers from public officials under examination for their official acts.

The Tammany delegation was not pleased with this proposal, nor with the supporting stands taken by Wagner and Smith. The Governor's message to Walker, on the eve of the convention, directing recalcitrant Democratic leaders to waive immunity before the extraordinary grand jury, almost had the force of a mandate, for Tammany knew that Roosevelt was in complete control of the party and of the convention. Calmer minds among Tammany delegates realized that Curry had made a grievous error and had lost votes for the party when he refused to waive immunity. They also reasoned that Roosevelt's letter to Walker, urging Democrats to waive immunity, probably lessened the prospective damage to Democratic candidates.

The more practical-minded Tammany delegates concluded that for purposes of self-preservation they had best give Roosevelt their wholehearted support. Only then could they insure the defeat of "Tammany Tamer" Tuttle, and avert a thoroughly hostile investigation of New York City affairs. Governor Roosevelt's proposal was adopted.

The delegates, however, went beyond the Governor's personal wishes when they endorsed outright repeal of the Eighteenth Amendment. Early in September, Roosevelt had written Senator Wagner that he agreed with those who maintained that prohibition had not furthered the cause of greater temperance but had, instead, fostered excessive drinking of strong intoxicants, led to corruption and hypocrisy, brought about disregard for law and order, and flooded the country with untaxed and illicit liquor. The Governor went on to say:

The force and effect of the Eighteenth Amendment can be eliminated—only by a new constitutional amendment.

The fundamental of a new amendment must be the restoration of real control over intoxicants to the several states. The sale of intoxicants through state agencies should be made lawful in any state of the Union, where the people of that state desire it, and conversely the people of any state should have the right to prohibit the sale of intoxicants, if they so wish, within its borders.[31]

The Governor wished to insure against the return of the saloon, Federal assistance for those states which preferred to remain dry, and "local option" for dry communities within wet states.

Although the actions of both conventions appeared to have deflated prohibition as a major campaign issue, the Democrats had the better of the argument. They consistently pointed to

the Republican nominee for Lieutenant Governor, Caleb H.
Baumes, as an avowed dry who had been endorsed by the Prohibition party and who had refused to endorse his own party's
plank for revision of the Eighteenth Amendment.[32]

At the Governor's insistence, and over the opposition of many
upstate leaders, James A. Farley was selected chairman of the
Democratic State Committee to succeed William Bray.[33]

Acting upon an earlier recommendation by Industrial Commissioner Frances Perkins, the Governor successfully urged
convention delegates to pledge creation of a commission to
study unemployment insurance[34] and unemployment stabilization.[35]

The 1930 Democratic platform went on to propose legislation
providing for adequate compensation to school teachers, equalization of salaries in the civil service, an eight-hour day for labor,
and a minimum wage advisory board. It also supported a bond
issue for State hospitals, enlargement of the home rule principle,
legislation to prevent interminable litigation in public utility
rate cases, and rate fixing by contract. While making no direct
references to irregularities in New York City, the sixteen-page
mimeographed platform devoted four pages to indicting the
national Republican administration for the collapse of prosperity.[36]

While placing Roosevelt's name in nomination for re-election,
Al Smith launched a heated attack on Tammany scandals. He
reminded the delegates that despite Republican charges of corruption in New York and Albany, and of improper and corrupt
practices with respect to the judiciary, they could not be aimed
against the Democratic party as a whole, or against Roosevelt
and his associates in the State administration. At the same time
Smith characterized the Republican program as negative and
consistent with their previous platforms.[37]

In contrast to 1928, when he had presented the name of
Roosevelt to the convention, Jimmy Walker wasn't even
present at Syracuse. After dispensing with roll calls, the delegates renominated Roosevelt and Lehman by acclamation.[38]

The Republican party, in the meantime, was planning a campaign which would bring Tuttle to more than 130 upstate towns, hamlets, and cities. Though increasing numbers of rural citizens had come to view Roosevelt as above reproach on the issues of graft and corruption, the Republican candidate insisted on hammering away at Tammany corruption, Tammany waste, and Tammany governors.

Both campaigners sought a direct appeal to the people. The charges hurled by a candidate in one town were rebuked by the other close by. This situation enabled the voters to become intimately familiar with the appearance, speech, and personalities of their political choice. This was quite an achievement for State-wide candidates in New York before the era of television. The thoroughness with which both men wove through the State served as a stimulant to political interest among many apathetic citizens.

At his first campaign rally in a crowded Brooklyn hall, Tuttle set the tone for his entire campaign when he charged Roosevelt with reluctance to interfere with Tammany until obliged by public opinion. Tuttle was correct when he said:

On the one hand the Governor needs the support of Tammany Hall in the current campaign and in preparation for 1932. On the other hand, the state needs a Governor that leads rather than follows public opinion and is bigger than Tammany Hall.[39]

Tuttle further charged that Roosevelt had been indirectly responsible for the refusal of Tammany chieftains to waive immunity and appear before the grand jury through limiting the jury's scope so that it could not make an issue of the refusals of Tammany leaders.[40] Tuttle then catalogued the succession of scandals that had contributed to the Governor's dilemma: the sewer graft, notorious and unsolved murders, the enforced retirement of several judges from the bench, the City Trust Company failure, payroll padding in the Street Cleaning Department, and graft in the County Clerk's office.[41] The Republican spokesman contended that this condition had compelled the legislature to enact a bill authorizing the Governor to appoint his own commission to investigate the administration and certain local authorities in New York City, which Roosevelt had vetoed. Tuttle then asked why, on the other hand, the Governor had authorized investigations into the Republican counties of Westchester and Saratoga.[42]

Tuttle later insisted that Roosevelt give a fuller explanation of his judicial appointments, hinting at the purchase of judicial posts by citing cash withdrawals made by Justices Crater and Bertini soon after the Governor had appointed them.[43] He derided the note the Governor had sent Mayor Walker urging city officials to waive immunity, because it had referred only to investigation into their "official acts," not their personal acts. This had given Tammany Hall the necessary loophole.[44]

At Syracuse, Tuttle blamed Roosevelt for the prison riots of 1929, and in Plattsburg dared Roosevelt to deny that Tammany had dictated the appointments of Crater and Bertini.[45] In Ogdensburg, Republicans heard Tuttle denounce the Governor for neglecting to consult the Bar Association before appointing Bertini to the General Sessions bench.[46]

A Roosevelt campaign presents many issues, but there is usually one major theme which underlies his campaign oratory. During the 1930 contest, Roosevelt persistently underscored the unbroken record of Republican obstructionism while extolling the advanced economic and social-welfare programs initiated by Democrats under Governor Smith. While the Republican party lived in the past, the Democrats were aware of changing times and concluded that government should, of necessity, assume increased responsibilities to its citizenry.

"I can say without fear," Roosevelt informed an overflow audience at Binghamton, "that every constructive measure of importance, with the possible exception of one, and that one was eventually declared unconstitutional, has been originated by Democratic leadership since 1910." At every point the Republicans had fought constructive legislation and had given way only when forced by public opinion. Typical was the belated

creation of the Water Power Commission and the passage of an
old age pension law.[47]

Many interesting characteristics of a Roosevelt campaign
evolved during the 1930 contest. In the first place, Roosevelt
never mentioned his opponent by name. Secondly, he followed
Al Smith's effective method of usually stressing one major subject during each address. These addresses were carefully planned,
fully discussed in advance, and replete with personal, homey
illustrations. Thirdly, Roosevelt made wise and effective use of
his rural background to convince great numbers of farm con-
stituents that he alone on the political rostrum was their experienced and trusting friend. In addition, Roosevelt emphasized again and again the inability of his Republican opponents
to cope with changing times. Towering above all these factors
in significance and influence was Roosevelt's ability to make his
listeners feel that he was addressing them personally, whether
they were part of a large audience in a meeting hall or sitting
in their home listening to the radio.

Roosevelt opened his upstate campaign in Binghamton with
Eleanor Roosevelt, Herbert Lehman, and Morris S. Tremaine.
The Governor blamed the Republicans for the stock speculation orgy, for failure to cope with the depression and unemployment, and for obstructing water power development to insure
cheaper electric rates. The G.O.P., he maintained, could not be
trusted to put through any plan for cheaper electricity for they
were the same legislators who had been completely indifferent,
for years, to the crying need for farm relief.[48]

Speaking in four counties that same day, Tuttle continued to
score Tammany corruption while charging that Roosevelt was
not using all available funds to ease the effects of unemployment.[49] Trailing Roosevelt into Binghamton, the Republican
nominee reminded his audience that the farm relief bills Roosevelt referred to had been adopted by a Republican-controlled
legislature. At the same time he renewed his challenge to the
Governor to "stand up and fight" on the Tammany issue.[50]

In Buffalo, the Governor blamed Herbert Hoover for the depression, asserting that the President had failed to curb speculation. Prosperity, as he had always contended, was not a Republican monopoly. To the charge that available funds were not being used to aid the idle, the Governor replied that arrangements had previously been made to let out contracts for the full amount enacted before the end of December. In the State's capital, meanwhile, his Republican opponent promised to jail G.O.P. as well as Tammany grafters.[51]

Despite Tuttle's vigorous campaign, the Republican press was preparing its readers for defeat at least two weeks before election. On October 20, the *Herald Tribune* informed its readers that in the uncompromising antagonism of the extreme drys to Tuttle, the falling off of registration,[52] and the superior organization of the Democratic forces, local Democratic chieftains professed to see a substantial reduction in the normal Republican pluralities in the southern tier counties. Although the Governor was serenely confident of a handsome victory, the *Herald Tribune* believed that he was paying little attention to the more "fantastic predictions" of two or three upstate leaders that Tuttle would come down to the New York City line neck and neck with Roosevelt.[53]

Following Roosevelt's journey from Buffalo to Rochester, through the "impermeable" Republican counties of Erie, Wyoming, Genesee, and Livingston, Republican newspapers conceded that the recognition given him in this enemy territory surpassed that accorded him elsewhere on this tour. In Rochester, impartial observers conceded the palm to the motor parade staged for Tuttle, but the attendance at the Roosevelt rally was considerably larger than that at the Tuttle meeting.[54]

Since the disclosures of possible sale of judicial posts, virtually every newspaper in New York City had joined the clamor for an exhaustive inquiry to ferret out the guilty and to end such recreant practices. While the Republican press hurled daily broadsides at the Governor for straddling the issue, the independent, muck-raking New York *World* voiced the sentiments of many responsible citizens when it maintained that Tammany had done a complete job in convincing the citizenry that it was an enemy of good government. This fact had been demonstrated in a long series of investigations and court proceedings. The corruption which had been exposed to date was only the starting point. However, Walter Lippmann and the other editors of the *World* were more than justified in pointing out that far more serious in its implications was the fact that the agencies established by law to investigate corruption—the mayor's office and the district attorney's office—had shown neither capacity nor desire to search out the evil.[55]

Disturbed by the public's reaction to these disclosures of Tammany corruption, Howard S. Cullman advised the Governor to have District Attorney Crain appoint a special assistant to investigate the judiciary system. He recommended that the Governor insure selection of

. . . some outstanding, fearless, and intelligent Republican that has a name that will mean something, like Buckner, Charles Evans Hughes, Jr., William Donovan or Jerome or if you want to go a step further—Morris Hillquit. I think if this was done it would eliminate the suspicion of politics in the whole situation and would bring the public's attention back to the fact that the State of New York is not entirely run by an investigation of our own judiciary system. . . . who knows even Walter Lippmann might be satisfied.[56]

The Republican press and the New York *World* continued to hammer away at Roosevelt's passiveness toward Tammany misdeeds. Faced with an almost unanimous demand by the press and civic leaders for an exhaustive inquiry into New York City, the Governor was finally forced onto the defensive during the last week of the campaign. He told a Bronx audience that "wherever and whenever there have been presented to me facts which would warrant me in acting in an orderly manner and according to my oath of office, I have acted promptly and vigorously." Roosevelt went on to characterize allegations of wholesale corruption in New York City as loose attacks made purely for partisan benefit and insisted that he would order no extensive inquiry until he was supplied with special charges and more proof.[57]

Even the New York *Times*, an ardently pro-Roosevelt newspaper, was justified in reacting unfavorably to these remarks, for the Governor had hardly satisfied New Yorkers who had been repeatedly dismayed by the disclosures of Tammany corruption.[58] The Governor had complained of vague rumors and charges laid before him without specific "evidence." The evidence, as Roosevelt knew but refused to admit publicly, was not lying around the streets for anybody to pick up. It had to be searched for and dug out.

Walter Lippmann and his associates on the New York *World* expressed the fear that progress under Roosevelt had been dubious, because it had been accompanied by some of the worst reaction in civic standards known to this generation and by a serious deterioration within a great section of the party which controlled the State administration.[59]

Organized labor, however, appeared to have no qualms about its choice. Although still playing a minor role on the political scene, most of labor's spokesmen backed Roosevelt for re-election. In endorsing the Governor, William Green of the American Federation of Labor declared: "Labor has very seldom secured the enactment of so many measures which so favorably affect their economic, social and industrial welfare during a single session of a legislative body."[60]

As the campaign entered its final days, the Republican leadership in Washington was deeply worried as to its outcome. If Roosevelt was re-elected by a significant plurality he would automatically become a leading contender for the Democratic presidential nomination. If he won overwhelmingly, there would be no stopping him at the national Democratic convention. The latter prospect was especially frightening, for Republican leaders had come to view New York's Governor as their most formidable opponent for 1932.

In a last-ditch effort to deflate Roosevelt's expected plurality, the national Republican leadership dispatched two cabinet members into the election fracas.

Secretary of War Patrick J. Hurley sought to refute one of the most damaging campaign charges hurled against his party when he assailed as "paid liars" and "muckrakers" those who blamed the ills of the world upon Republicans. They ignored the fact, he contended, that the United States was suffering to a lesser degree from the world-wide depression than any other nation.[61]

In a radio address beamed from the nation's capital, Secretary of State Henry L. Stimson held the transcendent issue of the New York campaign to be the purity of the judiciary. He cited judicial bench exposures and scandals as a basis for characterizing Roosevelt as unfit for re-election. Courage, asserted Stimson, was needed to rip the lid off the Tammany system of judgeship barter, but Roosevelt had not exhibited that boldness for he had his eye on the 1932 presidential race.[62] So did the Republicans.

With the approval of his campaign strategy board, Governor Roosevelt had avoided discussion of Republican charges against Tammany corruption. Not until the very last days of the campaign did he attempt to allay publicly the fears of civic leaders and newspaper editors.

Roosevelt and his counsel, Samuel I. Rosenman, were well aware of the possible effects upon election returns in New York City if they instituted a thorough investigation of Tammany's administration before the November elections. If Tammany Hall felt inclined, word could easily go out to thousands of election district captains to "sit on their hands" and forget to get out the vote on election day. What then would happen to the sizeable plurality Roosevelt needed to strengthen his candidacy for the presidential nomination? And besides, would he not then be in a position to lose the mighty Tammany-controlled delegation at the national convention?

There was nation-wide interest in the New York contest and in the quandary which confronted Roosevelt as the campaign drew to a close. Walter Lippmann aptly described it when he said, "There is no other large city which does not live in a glass house," but "the sins of Tammany happen to be nationally advertised."[63]

Demands for an expanded investigation into Tammany corruption reached their highest pitch as the gubernatorial contest drew to a close. Until the last week of the campaign it appeared that Roosevelt was drawing upon the example set by Republicans who, when confronted by the scandals of the Harding administration in 1924, did not reply to the attacks, whereupon the attackers soon exhausted their ammunition, bored the voters, and lost heart themselves.

Fully cognizant of the pressures about him, Roosevelt devoted much of his last major campaign address to the charges concerning sale of judgeships in New York City. It was the Saturday night before election. After being introduced by Mayor Walker, the Governor faced an excited, partisan audience which had jammed Carnegie Hall in New York City. Holding himself erect with the aid of his strong arms against the lectern, and in a voice which quivered with anger, the Governor sought to undo the damage caused by Tammany Hall, most of whose leaders were in the audience. With calculated emotion Roosevelt lashed out at his Republican opponent as cowardly for making an intemperate and unlimited attack on the city judiciary. Roosevelt couldn't believe that all members of the judiciary were corrupt. To his listeners he said pointedly:

I and the members of my administration do not yield place to any Republican candidate or editor in abhorrence of a corrupt judiciary. We do not yield place to anyone in indignation against any holder of public office who is recreant to his trust. We do not yield place to anyone in the sincere and honest desire to punish those judges who have or who may prostitute their positions.[64]

The Governor pledged himself to remove any corrupt judge still sitting in New York, though he emphasized that removal had to be "by constitutional means, not by inquisition, not by trial in the press, but by trial as provided by law." The Governor promised to use every rightful power of his office to drive out corruption in the courts, if such corruption existed, regardless of whether it affected any Democratic or Republican organization in any one of the five counties of New York, or in any of the fifty-seven counties of the State.[65]

And the curtain dropped on the 1930 campaign. Civic-minded leaders in New York City, the New York *Times*, the New York *World*, and advisers to the Governor were cognizant of graft and corruption in the Tammany administration. Al Smith and Senator Wagner knew of it. Upstate citizens were aware of the low level of civic administration in the great metropolis, yet most of them overcame their inhibitions against Tammany's support of Roosevelt, reasoning that the Governor had had nothing to do with Tammany shenanigans and had never been a captive of Tammany. He had directed his State administration in a manner which permitted of no charges of graft or corruption. In addition, too many Republican voters realized that a Republican party of national oil scandals, of a Boss Vare of Pennsylvania, and of corrupt upstate county machines could not be morally superior to Tammany, no matter what the honesty and integrity of the Republican gubernatorial candidate.

The Governor's severest critics had admitted that Roosevelt was stronger upstate than any other Democrat. Even the independent and critical New York *World* had conceded that Roosevelt was not

. . . personally identified with Tammany, his personal record is unimpeachable, he has no racial or religious disabilities from the point of view of rural voters, he has a name which possesses much political magic, he is regarded not only as personally dry but as temperamentally favorable to the dry point of view, however flatly he may now be opposing Federal prohibition. Finally, he has an excellent and highly constructive record of achievement in matters that interest the rural voter.[66]

The Republican candidate, on the other hand, had failed to placate the drys and had not succeeded in capturing the imagi-

nation of the wets. His crusade against Tammany had hardly
stirred more than perfunctory interest upstate. Wherever Roosevelt spoke, even in Republican districts, he had drawn larger
and more enthusiastic crowds than Tuttle.

Louis Howe and James Farley had left no stone unturned as
they sought to insure a maximum vote for Roosevelt. The
greater his plurality the greater his influence upon Democratic
leaders and national convention delegates two years hence. As
far as Howe and Farley were concerned, the 1930 contest had
been waged from start to finish as a build-up for the national
Democratic convention.

On election eve, Roosevelt dissuaded Farley from issuing a
pre-victory statement estimating the Governor's expected plurality at over 600,000, for fear that it might cause Democratic
workers to become overconfident and neglect the final drive.
Farley then whittled down his forecast to a minimum plurality
of 350,000. The New York *World* predicted victory for Roosevelt by at least 250,000 votes.[67]

The overwhelming majority of New York's citizenry who
went to the polls on election day were determined to re-elect
their Governor, in spite of Tammany. Elderly folk cast their
ballots for him because of his endorsement of old age pensions;
wets because of his opposition to the Eighteenth Amendment;
some drys because he was known to be personally dry; an
increasing number of farmers because of the enactment of
remedial farm legislation; labor because of his support of social-
welfare and labor legislation; and slum dwellers because of his
endorsement of the Multiple Dwellings Law. Above all else,
people voted for Roosevelt as against Tuttle because they blamed
the Republican party for the depression.

Shortly after the polls closed the victor was known. Roosevelt's State-wide plurality soared to the staggering figure of
725,001. He swept New York City with a plurality of more
than 557,000 votes, while his running mate, Lehman, surpassed
that figure by some 50,000 votes. For the first time in the twentieth century a Democratic gubernatorial candidate overcame

his Republican opponent in the fifty-seven counties outside of New York City. Roosevelt reached the New York City line with a plurality of 167,784 votes. Many was the upstate city and county which went Democratic for the first time in the memory of living citizens.[68]

As compared with the previous off-year gubernatorial election in 1926 when Al Smith defeated Ogden L. Mills, Franklin D. Roosevelt polled some 87,000 more votes in New York City than had Smith, and approximately 160,000 more than Smith upstate. The Governor's vote in New York City surpassed that accorded Mayor Walker the previous year by approximately 60,000[69]

Reaction abroad was varied. One French newspaper, *L'Intransigeant* of Paris, informed its readers that Franklin D. Roosevelt had been "re-elected Mayor of New York City."[70] The November 6th issue of the *Statesman* of Calcutta, India, reported that "Franklin Roosevelt, son of Mr. Theodore Roosevelt, had bested his Republican opponent for Governor of New York. Mr. Roosevelt, junior, is regarded as certain to be Democratic candidate at the next Presidential election." [71]

Deeply moved by this victory, Felix Frankfurter expressed the reactions of many in a heartwarming letter to Roosevelt in which he said:

What a crashing victory it was! And never did a statesman receive a more unequivocal vindication from his people. New York wants a continuation of the kind of government you have been giving them, because you educate them to want such a government and to understand that they were getting it. And your friends rightly believe that the forthrighteousness and standards which made you a leader, overnight in the fight against things that twenty years ago were symbolized by "Blue-eyed" Billy Sheehan, guide you also today.[72]

Despite his election to the governorship in 1928, Franklin D. Roosevelt continued his activities on the national scene as he sought to heal Democratic wounds. Within two years the G.O.P. found itself on the defensive when "Republican" prosperity failed it. Although in New York Roosevelt's re-election to the governorship was all but assured early in 1930, the Governor soon found himself confronted with two major opponents: Tammany Hall and the Republican party.

Tammany graft and corruption had not been as blatant under Charles F. Murphy as it became under George Olvany, and even more so under John F. Curry. Roosevelt's policy of benevolent neutrality in the Smith-Curry struggle strengthened the hands of shortsighted Tammany Sachems, while the rumblings of protest against the purchase of judicial posts and a general deterioration of municipal government increased with each passing day. Roosevelt did take speedy action in the Ewald affair, but restricted the scope of the investigation. He did demand that Tammany leaders waive immunity and testify before the special grand jury, but with reference to their "official" acts only.

Tuttle's crusade against Tammany availed him little or no votes but did finally force Roosevelt to speak out against corruption and graft in New York City. Those who voted for Roosevelt generally felt that his two years in office represented a constructive and positive approach to most issues. The spreading depression, and a strengthened Democratic organization upstate, also insured the record-breaking plurality cast for the crippled political leader. Republican and Democratic voters alike had responded to such a degree in 1930 that they all but insured his nomination and election to the presidency two years later.

VIII

"IN QUEST OF SECURITY"

During the third decade of the twentieth century much of American industry discriminated against hiring older men and women as workers. This tendency impelled socially conscious men and women to agitate for a system of old age allowances and old age insurance throughout the nation.

Roosevelt was in the company of these farsighted citizens, and in step with most of the civilized countries of the world, when he urged the enactment of a system of old age pensions during his first gubernatorial campaign. Irritated by charges of radicalism hurled at those supporting old age pensions, Roosevelt told a campaign audience in Rochester that old age pensions were no more radical or socialistic in 1928 than had been the Workmen's Compensation and Factory Inspection Laws seventeen years earlier. Roosevelt recalled that when he was in the legislature in 1911 many respectable and substantial citizens regarded those who advocated Workmen's Compensation and Factory Inspection Laws as radicals and socialists. If the word "Bolshevist" had been invented then it would have been applied, according to Roosevelt, to such men as Assemblyman Alfred E. Smith, State Senator Robert F. Wagner, and himself.[1]

Roosevelt made it clear, however, that he was opposed to any form of a dole, for he felt that the State had no right merely to hand out money. He desired the adoption of a system of mutual contributions by employers and employees.

In his first annual message to the legislature in January, 1929, and in a special message the following month, Roosevelt recommended creation of a commission to study the subject of pensions for the needy aged. The Governor was aware of the effects of technological and medical progress upon the American economy, mores, and average life span, for he informed the lawmakers that new social conditions warranted new ideas of social responsibility. Poverty in old age, he maintained, should not be regarded as a disgrace or necessarily as a result of lack of thrift or energy. Usually it was a mere by-product of modern industrial life. While improved medical science had increased man's span of life, the rapid pace of modern industry had proportionately increased the number of years during which he was an unsought employee. As Roosevelt viewed it, no greater tragedy existed in modern civilization than the aged, worn-out worker who, after a life of ceaseless effort and useful productivity, could only look forward to his declining years in a poorhouse. A more modern social consciousness demanded a more humane and efficient arrangement.[2]

Although the adoption of any plan of old age pensions or insurance would be expensive, the Governor reminded the lawmakers that the existing method of caring for the aged in State institutions was also expensive. The Chief Executive hoped to see the day when poorhouses would be used, if at all, only for helpless incurables who were unable to provide for themselves.[3]

The great industrial State of New York was quite backward in this matter, for Montana, Kentucky, Wisconsin, and Nevada had attempted to deal with this problem by adopting straight pension systems whereby the government distributed a certain periodic stipend to aged persons who fulfilled residence, citizenship, and other requirements. A number of foreign countries had adopted a similar system, or one in which the workers had insured themselves with the aid of the state against old age want.

In his original proposal to the lawmakers, Roosevelt had requested a commission of nine members to study the question of security against old age poverty, seven to be appointed by himself and one each by the President pro tem of the Senate and the Speaker of the Assembly. Republican Senator Seabury

C. Mastick proposed, instead, that the Governor, the Senate leader, and the Assembly Speaker should each appoint three members to the commission. This meant, of course, Republican domination of the investigative body.

Familiar with the long history of Republican opposition to social-welfare legislation, and fearing a plot to sabotage the campaign for old age pensions, Roosevelt threatened to veto the Republican substitute unless it contained his original recommendations.[4] Ignoring the Governor's challenge, the Republican leadership enacted the Mastick proposal. Rather than have no investigating body, Roosevelt reluctantly approved the legislation which created a commission to ". . . study and investigate the industrial conditions of aged men and women and . . . report the most practical and efficient method of providing security against old age want."[5]

By the middle of February, 1930, the Mastick Commission on Old Age Security presented its report to the legislature. The commission found that many of the needy aged were not adequately or properly cared for. Based on partial surveys made in New York and other states, and upon deductions from the application of these findings to New York, the commission estimated that some 51,000 persons, approximately 15 percent of those seventy years of age and over, were in need of assistance. The members suggested that many of the needy aged should be provided for outside of institutions so that they might continue to live among friends and enjoy a sense of freedom, self-respect, and security.

The commission found ample evidence to prove that the older worker in industry was finding it increasingly difficult to secure employment if for any reason he was thrown out of work. The commission concluded its findings with the contention that it was unable to state authoritatively that insecurity and need in old age were increasing or decreasing in the State of New York.[6]

Reinforcing the commission's recommendations, Senator Mas-

tick introduced legislation to have the State assume the obligation of contributing one half the cost, including administration,
of the assistance, relief, and care of needy persons seventy years
of age or over, excluding those who were inmates of public and
private institutions. Mastick proposed establishment of a State
and county system of pensions for citizens seventy years and
over who were residents of the State for ten years and for
whose support no financially able person was legally responsible.
No fixed grant was mentioned. The amount of payment, as
long as it did not exceed $50 per month, was at the discretion
of public welfare boards of the respective counties. The total
cost for the relief of the 51,000 was estimated at $12,400,000
annually.

The responsibility for accepting applications, investigating
cases, and granting allowances was placed on the county commissioner of public welfare. The State Department of Social
Welfare, through a new Division of Old Age Security, was to
have the power to pass on all allowances and to formulate rules
and regulations for applicants.[7]

Reaction to the commission's report was one of general disappointment among proponents of old age pensions. Their
sentiments were echoed by the New York *Sun*, which contended
that the Mastick report "does not propose old age pensions
at all. It is a long way from a comprehensive and satisfactory
solution of the problem of old age pensions."[8] The New York
Times informed its readers that the commission's plan was not
an old age pension system. Essentially, the proposals constituted
a modernized poor-relief scheme.[9]

Roosevelt likewise expressed keen disappointment with the
commission's report, which he felt had not gone to the real
root of the needs. In addition, the form of machinery proposed
for old age relief was primarily an extension of the existing
welfare or poor laws administered by local officials. The Governor felt that a grave question was raised by this issue: "Should
the administration of a comprehensive law for the relief of the

aged poor be left to the discretion of local officials or should a State-wide system of administration be provided?"

Roosevelt feared that the caliber of local administration would vary considerably. In addition, the amount of relief was left wholly uncertain and could range from $5 to $50 a month, which indicated that the bill had to be regarded as a wholly incomplete plan.[10]

The Governor deplored the fact that the Mastick Commission and the Mastick Bill had omitted establishing a State-controlled method to encourage savings by individual workers. According to Roosevelt, those who had given deepest study to this subject and who were familiar with old age legislation believed that a mere dole or pension for the aged poor was wrong in principle and bad in practice.

Indicating the type of legislation he would continue to press for as Governor and as President, Roosevelt insisted that the most successful systems were based on what might be called a series of classes by which a person who had done nothing in his earlier life to save against old age want was entitled only to old age care according to a minimum standard, while opportunity was offered to others to contribute toward increased incomes during their later years. Thus a definite premium was placed on savings, giving the workers an incentive to save based on the prospects not only of food and shelter but of comfort and a higher living standard than the bare minimum.[11]

Viewing them as a small beginning toward a comprehensive plan, the Governor reluctantly accepted the Mastick report and later signed the Mastick Bill with the understanding that it had many grave objections both in the relief to be afforded and especially in the manner in which that relief was to be administered. The Chief Executive expressed the hope, however, that this would be the forerunner of a more enlightened system of security against old age want in the years to come.[12]

A comparison of the Mastick Bill with New York's poor laws tends to substantiate Roosevelt's reasoning that the aged would gain little by its passage. The benefits to the aged alleged to be provided for in the Mastick proposals were, in the main, already incorporated in the State's poor law. In fact, some of the provisions of the poor law were more liberal than the old age pension bill. Whereas the pension bill prescribed numerous limitations and qualifications for those who became beneficiaries, such as citizenship, an age of seventy years or over, and ten years' residence in the State, the poor law purported to give an old person qualified to receive relief under the commission bill the same relief without most of these qualifications.

The Public Welfare Law of 1929[13] provided that:

It shall be the duty of public welfare officials in so far as funds are available for that purpose, to provide adequately for those unable to maintain themselves.[14]

Compared to the Public Welfare Law, Senator Mastick's bill set forth its object as follows:

The care and relief of aged persons in need and whose physical or other condition of disabilities seems to render permanent their inability to provide properly for themselves is hereby declared to be a special matter of State concern and a necessity in promoting the public health and welfare.[15]

The major difference between the stated objectives of the two laws appeared to be that the Public Welfare Law was all-embracing, covering all ages and conditions of men and women, whereas the Mastick Bill limited that policy only to the aged, and not to all aged either.

Supporters of the commission's proposals had claimed that the new legislation established an important principle, that of "outdoor relief." This meant that an aged person might be maintained in his home or in a private home with some member of his family.[16] It appeared, however, that the right to "outdoor relief" was already clearly established in the Public Welfare Law, which provided that:

As far as possible families shall be kept together, and they shall not be separated for reasons of poverty alone. Whenever practicable, relief and service shall be given to a poor person in his own home; the commissioner of public welfare may, however, in his discretion, provide relief and care in a boarding home, the home of a relative, a public or private home or institution, or in a hospital.[17]

Despite all its shortcomings, however, passage of the Mastick Bill signified a step forward, for the State was now assuming partial responsibility for financing aid to the destitute. Federal intervention was only a short time off.

During his campaign for re-election in 1930, Roosevelt contended that with passage of the Mastick Bill the State had at last begun to take care of its dependent aged. He hoped to see the time when old age assistance would not in any way resemble a dole system.[18]

In his annual messages to the legislature in 1931 and 1932, the Governor appealed for drastic revision of the Old Age Pension Law. He reminded the lawmakers that the aged of the State, along with those of the nation, did not want

. . . charity, but rather old age comforts to which they are rightfully entitled by their own thrift and foresight in the form of insurance. It is therefore my judgment that the next step to be taken should be based on the theory of insurance by a system of contributions commencing at an early age.[19]

His pleas fell on deaf ears, for the Republican leadership felt that they had done enough for the elderly folk of the State. Anything more might be inconsistent with their version of the American ideal of free enterprise and individual initiative.[20]

During his campaign for the presidency in 1932, Roosevelt pledged to seek enactment of unemployment and old age insurance under State laws, for the old-fashioned theory of carting off old people to the county poorhouse was not the best thing after all.[21]

Frustrated by consistent shortsightedness of Republican-dominated State legislatures, Roosevelt resorted to the only course left him after 1932. Under the guiding hand of Secretary of Labor Frances Perkins, and with the courageous help of such individuals as John G. Winant, the Committee on Economic Security recommended, and Congress adopted in 1935, the

Social Security Act. This embarked the Federal government on a permanent policy of financial and administrative participation in public assistance to provide a system of security against old age want.

For some years prior to 1929, a handful of progressive labor and liberal spokesmen had agitated for amelioration of the worst effects of periodic unemployment through government-sponsored unemployment insurance. Citing enactment of similar legislation by Germany, Great Britain, and the Scandinavian nations, these socially conscious citizens bemoaned the fact that by the end of the third decade of the twentieth century the most advanced industrial nation in the world was depressingly backward in the protection of its industrial workers. Only with the advent of severe unemployment during the winter of 1929-30 was there a significant increase in the support for unemployment insurance. Typical was the Presbytery of Brooklyn and Nassau, which informed Roosevelt:

In view of the failure of private charity to adequately cope with the situation . . . municipal and state governments be urged to actively engage in the relief of the unemployed. This presbytery goes on record as favoring adequate old age and unemployment insurance.[22]

In sharp contrast was the position of organized labor. Led by President William Green, a majority of the delegates to the 1931 national convention of the American Federation of Labor overrode the capmakers and garment workers to reject unemployment insurance as a dole and handout.[23]

As the army of unemployed increased with each passing day, pressure mounted on Roosevelt to endorse some system of unemployment insurance. When the Governor appointed his unemployment commission in March, 1930, to investigate long-range problems of unemployment, he did not suggest unemployment insurance as a subject for study. During the 1930 legislative session, the Governor made no commitments in support of unemployment compensation. However, later that year he shocked many by his new, unequivocal stand on the issue.

Shortly before the convening of the twenty-second annual Governors' Conference at Salt Lake City, there had been an interesting exchange of correspondence between its secretary, former Governor Cary A. Hardee of Florida, and Roosevelt. The former's efforts to place New York's Chief Executive in a strategic position were evident in the program which scheduled Roosevelt to address the conference the first day on unemployment and old age pensions, and to make a short address at the banquet later that evening.[24] Since the first Governor's Conference at the White House in 1908, the annual meetings had accomplished little and, on the whole, had avoided any controversial issues. Roosevelt, however, helped shatter this tradition before he completed his address on unemployment at the first session of the 1930 conference.

The state executives listened attentively as Roosevelt developed the theme that the United States would always be faced with a serious unemployment situation as a by-product of industrial development. Although granting that a five-day week, shorter hours per day, public building programs, and other palliatives in emergencies would temporarily ease the situation, Roosevelt insisted, for the first time in public, that only through scientific and businesslike forms of unemployment insurance and old age security could the nation evolve permanent solutions to unemployment. Heralding a new stage in his lucid education of the American public, Roosevelt assured his fellow governors that unemployment insurance would come to this country "just as certainly as we have come to workmen's compensation for industrial injury; just as certainly as we are today in the midst of a national wave of insuring against old age want." [25]

While the solution rested wholly with the individual states and the Federal government, Roosevelt warned against those insurance systems which became mere doles and encouraged idleness. Contributions to the fund had to be made by employers and workers. At the same time the Governor sought to pacify his more conservative fellow-executives when he concluded:

That the broad principles of insurance can be made to meet the basic problem of unemployment and old-age want seems to me a business proposal which is sound. It would be far more radical or socialistic to suggest that local or state governments should in the days to come grant pensions or doles to those who are in need. Our economic progress and tendencies call for business-like plans to meet the difficulties of an industrial age.[26]

Proponents of unemployment insurance were greatly heartened. Others were given food for thought.

Ironically, William Green, the former poor miner boy from Ohio, remained allied with the bulk of Republicans on this issue. The president of the American Federation of Labor continued to oppose unemployment compensation as but one step from a demoralizing dole, and asserted that private industry had to handle the jobless problem without state interference.[27] Roosevelt exhibited greater foresight than labor's spokesman when he recommended that Senator Robert F. Wagner include, in the latter's keynote address to the Democratic State convention, ". . . suggestions for an immediate study of the broad subject of unemployment relief by a contributory system and not dole methods."[28]

For its own position, the Republican party was opposed to any system of a dole because of the contention that it had demoralized industry and labor in other nations. According to the G.O.P., experience had demonstrated that such systems put a premium on idleness, vastly increased the burden of taxation, and raised the cost of living. The Republicans did pledge, however, to encourage employers and employees to lay aside voluntarily a portion of the income earned in days of prosperity for use in days of unemployment.[29]

By the beginning of 1931 Roosevelt concluded that the problem of unemployment could only be solved on an inter-state basis. He therefore invited the chief executives of six neighboring industrial states to meet with him in Albany in January, to discuss the broader aspects of the problem.

In his communication to the respective governors, or governors-elect, of Massachusetts, Rhode Island, Connecticut, New Jersey, Pennsylvania, and Ohio, Roosevelt expressed the hope that after a joint study of the fundamental causes of depression and some of the proposed remedies, such as unemployment insurance, public works planning, and the standardization of labor legislation and workmen's compensation laws, the cooperating states would enact uniform social-welfare legislation.[30]

Roosevelt had the support of such liberals as Congressman Fiorello H. La Guardia when he reasoned that anything short of uniform labor laws and uniform provisions for protection of workers in all of the states would not solve the problem.[31] Nearly all of the seven participating states, which contained more than one third of the gainfully employed population in the nation,[32] had felt the competition from other states, particularly the South, which refused to keep abreast of the times and which attracted industry because of low overhead costs.

The theme of the conference, which convened in Albany in January, 1931, with six governors and the representative of a seventh,[33] was "Government Responsibility for Relief and the Prevention of Unemployment." The governors heard arguments in support of unemployment reserves by Professor Paul H. Douglas of the University of Chicago. Dr. Leo Wolman, of the Amalgamated Clothing Workers of America, presented the experience of foreign nations with unemployment insurance. Professors William Leiserson of Antioch College, and Joseph P. Chamberlain of Columbia University,[34] commented on the possible American variations, corrections, and improvements if a general system of unemployment reserves were adopted in the United States.[35]

The conference adjourned on January 24, with the understanding that the governors' representatives would reconvene in New York City at a later date to discuss unemployment insurance in its broader aspects, such as taxation and private insurance, voluntary and compulsory forms. With the nation in its second year of hungry, jobless men and women pounding city streets and rural highways in search of jobs, the governors of seven northeastern industrial states prepared to survey studies made here and abroad on unemployment insurance.

During the 1931 legislative session Senator Seabury C. Mastick, somewhat of a maverick among Republicans, joined with Assemblyman Irwin Steingut, Democratic minority leader, to sponsor a measure setting up a compulsory unemployment insurance system. It proposed optional contributions by employees so as to provide for unemployment reserves of ten dollars a week for workers more than eighteen years old. No worker receiving more than forty dollars a week would be included in the system. A joint legislative committee on unemployment, hearing testimony on the Mastick-Steingut proposal, learned from the secretary of the State Federation of Labor that his organization desired a survey of the entire unemployment situation before they would support the drafting of specific legislation. The National Association of Manufacturers was consistent in its opposition to social-welfare legislation when its spokesmen testified against the bill.[36]

Professor Joseph P. Chamberlain supported the proposal and claimed that there was no question of its constitutionality since the Supreme Court had upheld the workmen's compensation law. Citing the successful functioning of the unemployment insurance fund in the Chicago men's clothing industry, Sidney Hillman, president of the Amalgamated Clothing Workers of America, testified that the Mastick-Steingut proposal would add only three-fourths of a cent to production cost and that this would be too small to raise the question of competition with goods manufactured in other states. State Industrial Commissioner Frances Perkins voiced her personal support of the bill, but added that unemployment insurance was not a panacea for unemployment.[37]

Lacking the support of Roosevelt and of the Republican leadership, this proposal was doomed from the start. Although an avowed supporter of unemployment insurance, Roosevelt exhibited a frustrating cautiousness in his approach to the problem. Immediately after the hearings on the Mastick-Steingut proposal, he recommended to New York's lawmakers the creation of a small body of experts, four appointed by the Governor and two or three by the legislature, to investigate unemployment compensation systems and to submit an enlightened, businesslike plan to the 1932 legislature. According to the Governor:

Any nation worthy of the name should aim in normal industrial periods to offer employment to every able-bodied citizen willing to work. An enlightened government should look further ahead. It should help its citizens insure themselves during good times against the evil days of hard times to come. The worker, the industry and the State should all assist in making this insurance possible.[38]

The Republican lawmakers perverted Roosevelt's proposal when they authorized formation of a joint legislative committee, including one public representative appointed by the Governor, to study and report back the following year on the various proposals for unemployment insurance.

During the summer of 1930 the Governor had stated that unemployment insurance was needed to protect the great mass of America's industrial laborers against periodic distress. In a letter to his brother-in-law, early in 1931, he spoke of a gradual approach to the development of unemployment insurance, reacting not unfavorably to the possibility of commercial unemployment insurance policies.[39] When confronted, shortly thereafter, with legislative ratification of a Republican proposal to grant private insurance companies the privilege of writing employment policies, Roosevelt was momentarily in a quandary. Mounting opposition to this Republican proposal from some of the Governor's most ardent supporters helped insure an effective veto by Roosevelt. In contrast to his message to G. Hall Roosevelt two months earlier, the Governor's veto message exhibited clearer understanding of the implications of such legislation as he reminded the lawmakers that they had already set up a committee to study the whole question of unemployment and unemployment insurance. Under these circumstances the Governor felt that it would be inconsistent to provide for one form of unemployment insurance and thus discriminate against other proposals which had had much greater public consideration. In addition, experience in the field of workmen's compensation had shown that if private corporations were permitted to begin writing unemployment insurance, they would thereafter claim a kind of vested interest in their business and would be united in their opposition to bills providing other forms.[40]

Toward the end of May, 1931, the first meeting of the Interstate Commission for the Study of Unemployment Insurance, an outgrowth of the regional conference of seven governors, was held in New York City. After discussing practical aspects of unemployment and unemployment insurance from the American point of view, and in order to make a more detailed study of special aspects of unemployment insurance, the governors' spokesmen on the commission apportioned themselves among subcommittees to hold public hearings on the matter under consideration.[41]

In its final report nine months later, the Interstate Commission recommended enactment of a uniform industrial plan which provided for the payment by each employer of a 2 percent contribution on his payroll, to be reduced to 1 percent when the accumulated reserve per employee exceeded fifty dollars. The maximum rate of benefit was to be ten dollars a week, or 50 percent of an employee's wage—whichever was lower—and the maximum period of benefit was to be ten weeks of any twelve-month period. The Interstate Commission also recommended establishment of State Unemployment Administrations representing labor, industry, and the public, and a revitalized public employment service.[42] The Governor forwarded these suggestions to the legislature, believing that their enactment would go far toward relieving the distress resulting from unemployment.[43]

Shortly thereafter, Senator Mastick and Assemblyman Steingut again introduced a joint unemployment insurance proposal, this time containing the basic recommendations of the

Interstate Commission. Although receiving the support of Frances Perkins and others who had long fought for unemployment insurance, the bills died in the legislature. The Republican leadership and the National Association of Manufacturers would hear nothing of it.

On March 3, 1932, after almost a year spent studying unemployment insurance proposals, the lone Roosevelt appointee on the joint legislative committee on unemployment issued a fiery blast at the Republican majority for refusing to recommend enactment of a compulsory unemployment insurance system. While conceding that some form of compulsory unemployment insurance system should eventually be adopted, the Republican majority on the committee convinced the legislature to permit it to continue its hearings through 1932 before taking action on specific legislation.[44]

As 1932 drew to a close, it was evident that the Republican party had effectively, and purposefully, delayed adoption of any system of compulsory unemployment insurance.

Not until 1935 did the State legislature, under the able leadership of Governor Herbert H. Lehman, establish a State-wide unemployment insurance fund to be administered by the Industrial Commissioner. Wisconsin, which had adopted an unemployment insurance system in 1932, remained the lone pioneer until 1935, when eight states, the District of Columbia, and the Federal government followed suit. Republican shortsightedness moved Roosevelt to conclude that the most plausible solution was interstate or Federal action.

With great unrest still sweeping the nation in 1935, the 74th Congress accepted the unemployment insurance recommendations of President Roosevelt's Committee on Economic Security and adopted the Social Security Act, which provided a form of security for those who would unwillingly become unemployed in the future. While no Federal unemployment insurance fund was set up, a powerful impetus was given to states to establish such funds since they were permitted to retain nine tenths of the payroll tax for their own unemployed instead of having it all go to the Federal treasury.

Increasing unemployment among middle-aged and elderly folk, due to technological progress, as well as to business management policy, insured demands by Roosevelt and others for a system of insurance against want in old age, but not a dole. The Republican lawmakers responded with an old age pension act which provided basically for an extension of the State's poor laws.

The tremendous wave of unemployment which followed the virtual collapse of the nation's economy in the early nineteen thirties resulted in a groundswell of support among farsighted individuals for compulsory unemployment insurance. Roosevelt responded, in 1930, by dramatically announcing his willingness to support a scientific, businesslike system of unemployment insurance. A year later he moved in the direction of interstate cooperation through regional enactment of social-welfare legislation. Faced with hostile, Republican-dominated legislatures, Roosevelt was unable to secure enlightened old age pension and unemployment insurance systems. Only after years of persistent prodding by Roosevelt and Lehman, and with a realization that Congress would soon adopt an extensive Social Security Act, did the Republicans in New York enact an unemployment insurance system of their own in 1935.

Unemployment compensation is today an accepted fact in the daily lives of American citizens, thanks to the educational efforts of Franklin D. Roosevelt when Governor of New York, and to the Social Security Act adopted during his presidency.

IX

"I STAND FAIRLY WELL WITH LABOR"

FRANKLIN D. ROOSEVELT was reared in an economic stratum which knew little of the struggles and heartaches of American labor. As State Senator, and then as Assistant Secretary of the Navy under the guidance of Louis Howe, he developed an acquaintanceship with the work and aspirations of many laboring men and women throughout the country.[1] During his years of convalescence after 1921, he imbibed considerable knowledge of the labor movement from Rose Schneiderman and from others who had devoted their lives to the cause of the nation's workers.

What then was Roosevelt's concept of labor's role on the American scene in 1928? How contrast it with his attitude four years later?

Al Smith's most successful efforts to protect men, women, and children in industry were made during his years as a legislator in Albany. During his four terms as Governor, he sought valiantly to secure enactment of laws insuring minimum wages and a forty-eight-hour work week for women. A Republican legislature relented sufficiently to grant him an imperfect forty-eight-hour week law. However, Smith had to be constantly on his guard to ward off frequent Republican efforts to undermine the Workmen's Compensation Act.

During the 1928 campaign Roosevelt expressed a more liberal attitude on injunctions and old age pensions than had Al Smith. As part of his appeal to the "labor vote" Roosevelt cited his excellent relations with organized labor while Assistant Secretary of the Navy, during which time he "did not have one single major dispute, no strike, no walkout, no serious trouble in all the Navy yards over the United States."[2]

The State Federation of Labor endorsed Roosevelt's candidacy without hesitation, pointing out that the Democratic platform supported legislation requiring hearings in court before an injunction could be issued against wage earners and a jury trial of persons accused of violating such injunctions, the paramount legislative reform sought by organized labor. The Republican platform, on the other hand, was indefinite on improvements in labor laws and ignored all of organized labor's proposals on the injunction issue.[3]

Following Roosevelt's hairbreadth victory in 1928, labor leaders awaited his actions with keen interest, particularly since he was being mentioned as a presidential possibility for 1932. The Governor's selection of Miss Frances Perkins to head the Labor Department was a great step forward for a division which had been mismanaged during the last four years of Smith's administration.[4]

In his first annual message to the legislature in 1929, Roosevelt's comments on injunctions and old age pensions stamped him, by American standards, as a liberal. He continued in the Smith tradition when he requested establishment of an "advisory minimum or fair wage board" for women and children in industry. Massachusetts already had such a board, which was a small step in itself toward the guarantee to each family of an income at least sufficient for decency and comfort. The newly inaugurated Governor also favored the extension of workmen's compensation to all occupational diseases, a proposal which many liberals mistakenly believed would receive sympathetic support from Republicans and Democrats alike.[5]

Some liberals concluded that his remarks on old age pensions, in which he recommended a study of the subject by a commission of experts, had a timid sound. They too were misled when they concluded that the only experts who would oppose old age insurance at this time would be conservative labor leader Matthew Woll and business spokesmen in the National Civic Federation.

It was inevitable that where Roosevelt enunciated a strong pro-labor policy, considerable controversy would develop. And develop it did following his support of a law prohibiting the granting of temporary injunctions in industrial disputes without notice of hearing, and providing for trial before a jury of any alleged violations of injunctions. This was in advance of former Governor Smith's labor policy, yet it was not in advance of certain other states. Utah, which was not looked upon as a particularly progressive state in 1928, required jury trials in contempt cases involving injunctions. Wisconsin, with its progressive background, had a somewhat similar provision for a jury trial of facts in cases of alleged violation of injunctions.

On the western European scene, many, if not most, of Roosevelt's labor and social-welfare recommendations had long been acted upon and accepted as a matter of course. The United States remained one of the few democratic nations which appeared to be actively using labor injunctions. It was also the only industrially advanced democratic nation which had not gone further with social insurance than Governor Roosevelt was urging in 1929.

Those labor leaders who viewed Roosevelt as a true spokesman of Wilson's New Freedom were encouraged by his message to the legislature. The president of the Wyoming Federation of Labor wrote Roosevelt that he had read and reread the Governor's recommendations concerning labor and humane legislation, and could almost see the satisfied expressions of the millions of wage earners in New York as they became aware of Roosevelt's interest. According to this labor leader, in every instance the Governor appeared to have touched upon some subject of vital concern to the men and women who toiled.[6]

In Albany the Republicans were more than a brake on the Governor's proposals. Other than providing for a commission to study old age pensions, the G.O.P. leadership repudiated their own platform when they rejected enactment of any significant labor legislation in 1929.

Despite bipartisan support by leading citizens, and the 1928 Republican platform which pledged to continue the party's "constructive program to meet all of our social needs . . . to provide proper care and training for our dependent children, . . . to protect women and children in industry [and] to care for the dependent wards of the State,"[7] the Republican lawmakers killed all legislation proposing a minimum wage for women and children in industry.

The G.O.P. platform had insisted that the Republican party in New York had done more for labor than any other party, citing the labor law and the Workmen's Compensation Law as being the best in all the States. "The Republican legislature has established a commission which has considered and is now considering necessary and beneficent improvements in the workmen's compensation law and all other labor laws, and we pledge our party to give full consideration to the recommendations of this commission."[8]

When the commission studying workmen's compensation submitted its report in March, 1929, it recommended the inclusion of a score of occupational diseases, including silicosis,[9] in the compensation system. Roosevelt's reaction was that these suggestions did not go far enough but were at least a step forward. Not content with rejecting all except one of these necessary and beneficent recommendations, the Republican leadership not only reduced the amount of compensation awards in certain other cases but refused to extend the life of the commission for additional study. The lobbyist for Associated Industries of New York was very pleased.[10]

The Republican lawmakers also ignored Roosevelt's pleas for a straight forty-eight-hour law for women and children in industry, and for a bill stating that the labor of a human being shall not be deemed a commodity. Other labor legislation also died in committee upon orders of Republican leaders.

For all practical purposes the Republican-controlled legislature consisted of the chairmen of a few committees, who were themselves not independent of others. As far as the majority of members of the Republican party were concerned, they too were, primarily, rubber stamps showing no independence of their own, with the rare exception of a maverick. The domination of the State's legislative body by a handful of shortsighted Republican chieftains so infuriated the Governor that he lashed out at them in special radio broadcast. Roosevelt was not exaggerating when he portrayed Republican tactics as

. . . un-American and contrary to the whole spirit of our Government. A Legislature is supposed to consider all suggestions of importance, to debate them with an open mind and to pass or reject them according to the arguments for or against. . . . Under the despotic rule of chairmen of important committees, bill after bill has been buried in the committee's file, and any attempt to force the committee to report it has been defeated by the lash of the party whip upon the backs of the members of the majority.[11]

While the legislature was busy rejecting Roosevelt's recommendations, a bomb was discovered in the main post office of New York City addressed to the Governor. A porter's accidental kick of a cardboard carton had purportedly uncovered the deadly weapon. It is not important to recall that this same porter later admitted that he had planted the "bomb" to gain fame and notoriety. Of significance was Roosevelt's response to the reactions of others.

After learning of the "bomb," some individuals immediately directed their suspicions to organized labor. New York City's police commissioner, Grover Whalen, asked the Governor if he had recently approved or disapproved any labor legislation. A former member of Naval Intelligence and of the Department of Justice asked whether he could render the Governor "any services in apprehending any radical who may try the same thing again on or before May 1st, which they generally do about that date."[12] Before it was disclosed that the bomb was a hoax, the Governor replied to these sharp critics of American labor that he was very certain that the bomb was not sent by a radical but, "as I stand fairly well with Labor and the more liberal element in the population, it is my thought that it was sent by somebody with a fancied grievance."[13]

Labor was restless during 1929. Many workers realized that the "return to normalcy" was not as beneficial to them as most business leaders and college presidents contended.

According to the National Bureau of Economic Research, approximately 35,000,000 workers earned in 1927, with an allowance made for unemployment, $1,205 a year, or $23.17 a week. The Department of Labor's standard budgets in 1929 revealed that a minimum health and decency budget for a family of five was approximately $2,200 a year.[14] Wages of women employed in American cotton mills were reduced an average of 13 percent in the four-year period from 1924 to 1928.[15]

In New York City, some 25,000 men and women in the garment industry put down their tools in July, 1929, to force a shutdown of sweatshops. The International Ladies' Garment Workers' Union, led by Benjamin Schlesinger, David Dubinsky, and others who had gained their political maturity in the Socialist movement of Eugene V. Debs and Morris Hillquit, achieved only fair results by the conclusion of the strike. The sweatshops which had come to characterize the largest single industry in New York City, and which State and City authorities had neglected to eradicate, finally appeared to be on the way out.[16]

Sometime after this strike, spokesmen for the garment association and the union appealed to Roosevelt through Raymond V. Ingersoll, newly designated impartial chairman of the industry, to assist in further stabilization of the cloak and suit industry. Upon Ingersoll's suggestion, the Governor extended invitations to industry and union leaders, and to spokesmen of leading business houses and chain stores, to attend a general meeting on December 12, 1929, sponsored by the Cloak and Suit Conference.[17]

Although Roosevelt and Lehman cooperated fully and addressed the delegates, nothing significant developed out of this conference. In a final effort to close the remaining sweatshops, the union called a general strike on February 4, 1930. Immediately after 25,000 dressmakers struck, the Governor intervened by inviting industry and labor spokesmen to meet with him in the Executive Chamber in Albany.[18]

After briefly conferring with the Governor, the representatives accepted Roosevelt's suggestion to arbitrate their dispute, with Herbert Lehman acting as mediator. Within a week, Lehman was able to bring a semblance of peace and harmony to the garment industry when the disputants signed an agreement to end the eight-day-old strike and cooperate in the abolition of sweatshops. The most significant result of the settlement was the establishment of an arbitration system with a full-time impartial chairman in the New York dress industry—to this day a model of its kind. Both parties to the dispute had only praise for the moderation and guidance displayed by Lehman throughout the conferences.[19]

The statesmanlike response of Roosevelt and Lehman to a major industry-labor dispute was a contrast to the irresponsible, partisan-minded emotionalism displayed by too many state executives during this period of increasing distress and unrest. Many governors called upon the national guard, the state police, and deputy sheriffs to break strikes, all in the name of "preserving the peace."

In Marion, North Carolina, six strikers were killed by deputy sheriffs, following weeks of terror by state troopers who blocked highways and suppressed the liberties of thousands of workers on strike against abysmally low wages and long working hours.[20] In Philadelphia, 50,000 mourning men and women attended the funeral of a hosiery worker who had been killed by strikebreakers.[21] In Danville, Virginia, scores of strikers were gassed by tear bombs as efforts to break a strike were temporarily frustrated.[22] Early in 1931, a girl striker was killed by strikebreakers in front of a Stroudsburg, Pennsylvania, hosiery mill.[23] In Allentown, Pennsylvania, state troopers dispersed 1,000 mill strikers with machine guns.[24]

Roosevelt and Lehman gave consistent evidence that it was their policy not to make state troopers or state militia available in industry-labor disputes, until such time as local authorities were unable to control the situation and when it appeared inevitable that overt acts would be committed and the peace disturbed. Typical was the reaction of Acting Governor Lehman to the situation which developed during a strike at the Endicott-Johnson works. It was in May, 1932, when Mayor L. E. Youngs of Johnson City suddenly wired Lehman:

Anticipate serious disturbance here early tomorrow morning small local force unable cope with situation. Strike Endicott-Johnson shoe factories here last Thursday. Mass meeting scheduled Monday seven A.M. About ten thousand employees this company involved. Desire of local officials and officials of Endicott-Johnson Corporation that we have about thirty state troopers. . . . Please wire immediately.[25]

Immediately after receipt of this message the Acting Governor conferred with Mayor Youngs by phone. After acquainting himself with the situation, Lehman rejected the Mayor's request in his usual clear and unmistakeable terms when he said:

. . . I have talked to you by telephone and you have informed me that no overt act has been committed, that the peace has not been disturbed and that there is no injury to life and property. You have also informed me additionally that you have not called on the sheriff of Broome County for assistance. Under the circumstances I reiterate my position that I decline to order state police to Johnson City unless and until I have definite evidence that the local peace authorities of the village and county are unable to care for any situation that may possibly arise.[26]

On another occasion, Lehman answered the pleas of the International Ladies' Garment Workers' Union during a difficult hour of its existence in 1928. He loaned the organization $25,000 to enable it to maintain its integrity and to help preserve the living standards of its thousands of members. While Lehman was anxious not to appear to be taking sides in any labor dispute or situation, he nevertheless felt justified in making the loan, for he was thoroughly convinced that the prosperity of the garment industry could be obtained only through a well-managed and responsible organization of employers and a strong, responsible and honest association of workers. Lehman accordingly felt that he was helping not only labor but the entire industry and thus was serving the interests of the community in which he lived. The $25,000 loan was repaid by the union within eighteen months.[27]

Although Herbert H. Lehman remained consistent, and unusually frank, in his support of justice and social democracy on the American scene, Franklin D. Roosevelt backtracked at times, or refused to take positions on controversial issues which extended beyond the confines of New York.

Shortly after Christmas of 1931, inmate #31921 of San Quentin penitentiary in California sent Roosevelt a four-page typewritten letter detailing the history of his imprisonment. The writer, Tom Mooney, a *cause célèbre* for labor, appealed to Roosevelt to intercede on his behalf with California's Governor James Rolph for an unconditional pardon. Lacking the courage which characterized three governors, eight United States senators, mayors of three major cities,[28] plus scores of public servants who had endorsed Mooney's plea, Roosevelt assumed a hands-off policy. His reply rejected Mooney's request,

. . . irrespective of any sympathy I may have for your cause. As the Governor of a sister state, I do not feel it to be within my proper province to interfere in a matter exclusively within the jurisdiction of the Governor of California, especially when it involves the status of a person who was not a citizen of my own state.[29]

New York's Governor was not exhibiting an antilabor policy in this instance. He simply feared the effect his support of Tom Mooney might have upon many delegates to the national Democratic convention which was only a few months away. Practical politicians may have called this an astute decision.

When a truckers' strike in New York City threatened to halt the shipment of products from upstate farmers, the successful efforts of Roosevelt to arbitrate the dispute moved farm spokesmen to thank him heartily for his "prompt cooperation and support in the settlement of the . . . strike . . . in which our farmers were vitally interested."[30]

On another occasion, some spokesmen of the southern economy became exceedingly disturbed when they learned, from what they deemed reliable sources, that New York's Governor had criticized the tendency of northern manufacturers to move South because of cheaper labor. A sharp wire from the editor of the *Southern Textile Bulletin* in North Carolina, condemning Roosevelt for his purported attitude, elicited from the latter the following reply:

I did not, of course, make any statement that New York mills move South in order to employ child labor. As you know, I spend much time in Georgia and know of the labor laws of that state and of North Carolina. It is true, however, that many efforts to give better protection to working men and women and children in New York State has, in the past, been met by some manufacturers with threats of moving their plants south. The length of working hours is now the chief factor.[31]

When the State legislature convened in January, 1930, the Governor renewed his requests for an advisory minimum or fair wage board for women and children in industry; for the extension of workmen's compensation to all occupational diseases; for a genuine eight-hour day and forty-eight-hour week for women in industry; and for legislation prohibiting the issuance of temporary injunctions without notice of hearing in industrial disputes, with provision for trial before a jury of any violation of injunctions when granted. He also recommended raising maximum payments for workmen's compensation; regulation by the State of fee-charging employment agencies; and the declaration, in the form of a statute, that the labor of human beings was not a commodity or an article of commerce.[32]

It was inconceivable to many liberals that by the end of the third decade of the twentieth century opposition to a forty-eight-hour week law, providing a half-day of rest on the sixth day for women workers, should develop in the leading industrial state of the nation. And yet tremendous pressure developed from the Merchants' Associations of the State as they lobbied among legislators against the Mastick bills containing these provisions.

After its hesitant adoption by the Republican-dominated legislature, with amendments which beclouded the original objectives, the Governor was unsuccessfully besought by the Merchants' Associations to veto the bill.[33] Although some of the Governor's friends became anxious concerning his eventual decision, Rose Schneiderman wrote him subsequently:

At no moment did I doubt that you would keep faith with the hundreds of thousands of women wage earners of the State. I am terribly proud of all you have accomplished. I am sure that the citizens of the State of New York will appreciate the intelligence and deep sincerity with which you have handled the affairs of the State and will send you back to the State House next November so that you may continue the good work.[34]

The Governor replied that slowly, but surely, he was securing some accomplishments even from Republican legislative leaders. What he hoped for was that "just so long as the Democratic Party in our State shows definite progressive accomplishments, we shall get the support of the real liberals and progressives. It is a long, hard, uphill fight, but we seem to be getting somewhere."[35]

While refusing to establish an advisory minimum or fair wage board for women and children in industry, the Republican lawmakers added three more diseases to the list meriting workmen's compensation,[36] and finally prohibited the granting of temporary injunctions in industrial disputes without notice of a hearing.[37] On the other hand, Republican leaders refused to place upon the statute books the sentiment that the labor of human beings was not a commodity or an article of commerce.

Contemplating the possible effects of Roosevelt's elevation to the presidency in 1932, labor spokesmen throughout the nation displayed increasing interest in the Governor's efforts in social-welfare and labor legislation. From one responsible labor spokesman the Governor learned that he had been an object of interest ever since his tenure as Assistant Secretary of the Navy, and that the former's union wanted to express its

. . . appreciation of the work you have done in the difficult position of Chief Executive of New York. Your stand on power, the encouragement you have given labor in its fight on the injunction, and the strengthening you have given every social and labor measure has been heartening indeed.[38]

Shortly thereafter, one of Roosevelt's statements set him back, temporarily, in the eyes of labor. Although organized labor had persistently opposed the sale of prison-made goods on the open market, because it competed unfairly with the products of free labor, it was not until 1929 that Congress enacted the Hawes-Cooper Convict Labor Bill which provided for the regulation of interstate traffic of prison-made goods.[39]

At the annual Governors' Conference at Salt Lake City, the following year, many governors made a general onslaught upon this specific piece of Congressional legislation. They contended that unless the bill was repealed or modified it would so restrict the conduct of manufactures by convicts in the various states as to bring about a serious menace in many of the penal institutions. The governor of Idaho was joined in a denunciation of the bill by New York's Chief Executive. Roosevelt not only believed the bill was unconstitutional but also contended that it was an unwarranted invasion of states' rights.

Roosevelt's castigation of the Hawes-Cooper Bill was immediately criticized by the nation's labor leaders. William Green expressed keen surprise at what Roosevelt had called an invasion of "State home rule," and at his doubts concerning the constitutionality of the bill which had received labor's endorsement. Green reminded Roosevelt that the latter had signed a bill which took advantage of the power given the State to protect free labor from the competition of convict labor of other states.

As to the constitutionality of the act, the Supreme Court has said that Congress which has complete control over interstate commerce has the power to divest goods, wares and merchandise manufactured, produced or mined by convicts or prisoners of their interstate character in certain cases. It does not take any power away from the state but gives power to the state.[40]

The labor chieftain recalled that for many years goods, wares, and merchandise manufactured in the prisons of New York had not been sold on the open market, in order to protect free labor. At the same time, convict-made goods from other states were shipped into New York and sold on the open market to such an extent that it had demoralized certain industries. Green chastised Roosevelt for not giving "these facts consideration before you delivered your address at the Governors' conference. I hope, however, that you will make an investigation as to the injury being done free labor in your state by the wholesale dumping of convict-made goods into New York State from other states."[41]

In the face of this unequivocal stand by labor's chief spokesman, New York's Governor sought a diplomatic retreat from his previous contentions. With regard to the Hawes-Cooper Bill, Roosevelt informed Green that there was absolutely no question about his wholehearted support of the purpose behind the act. His recommendations to the Governors' Conference, he maintained, related "wholly to the question of the growing usuperation [*sic*] of federal privilege at the expense of the states. When I see you next I will give you some examples that limited interstate shipment." The Governor added that there continued some doubt as to the constitutionality of the bill, on the purely local side.[42]

Still finding himself on the defensive a few days later at the convention of the State Federation of Labor, the Governor attempted to clear the minds of his listeners of

. . . any doubt as to my attitude towards prison labor, in view of certain grotesque misrepresentations of my position. . . . No one more clearly realizes the evil of competition of prison labor with free labor than I. The best proof of how seriously I regard this matter is that I have added to the State-created Prison Commission a Governor's subcommittee to consider how we may keep our prisoners employed without competing with the labor of our free workmen. I did this because I felt that otherwise this question, which for years has troubled all penologists, might be ignored or scantily considered as it has been in the past. . . . It is almost unnecessary for me to add that I am wholly and irrevocably opposed to letting one state dump its prison-made goods on the free market of another state.[43]

In contrast to his remarks at the Governors' Conference the previous summer, the Governor was readily admitting by October that the Hawes-Cooper Bill would be sustained by the Supreme Court on the grounds that it came under the interstate commerce clause of the Constitution. What he had been referring to "was the danger of many entering wedges, giving the Federal government more and more control, and I merely raised the point that the proposition of the Hawes-Cooper Bill might have been obtained through State agreements."[44]

"States' rights" has, of late, perhaps been employed more as a slogan than an honest philosophy of governmental power. Roosevelt, as a Democratic Governor, played with the slogan aspect in the Hawes-Cooper Bill. As long as the Republicans controlled the White House, he was suspicious of legislation which increased the power of the Federal government.

In his third annual message to the legislature in January, 1931, the Governor informed the lawmakers that although New York had taken the lead in enactment of labor legislation, it had not kept fully in step with the newest developments in industrial life and the newest conceptions of social welfare. He recommended anew the extension of workmen's compensation coverage; raising the ceiling for compensation to twenty-five dollars weekly; a genuine eight-hour day and forty-eight-hour week for women and children in industry; and an advisory minimum or fair wage board for women and children. He stressed the need for strict regulation of fee-charging employment agencies and for a declaration that the labor of human beings was not a commodity or an article of commerce. In one basically new proposal he urged the lawmakers to establish a special Labor Department bureau for enforcement of those aspects of the labor law relating to the eight-hour work day, the prevailing rate of wages, and preference to citizens of New York State on public works.[45]

Although many of these recommendations had previously received the support of Governor Smith, Roosevelt was still urging their enactment upon a Republican legislature years later.

Of the 1,120 bills which came to the Governor's desk for executive action during the 1931 legislative session, only one contained an original labor recommendation by Roosevelt. The proposal which the Republicans permitted to pass established an enforceable forty-eight-hour week and half-holiday every week for working women.[46]

At an extraordinary session of the 1931 legislature in August, the lawmakers approved the Governor's request for an eight-hour day and a prevailing rate of wages on all State highway contracts, and for a five-day week on all State public works, up to December 1, 1932.[47] On the final day of the extraordinary session, the Governor was handed the two labor measures for his signature along with a telegram from economy-minded Merwin K. Hart. Commenting on these labor measures, Hart maintained that if they became law the Governor would do an injustice to the taxpayers, who could not afford to have a dollar of relief, or other, money spent on construction prices at 30 percent higher than private persons could or would pay, and which would discourage the resumption of private construction work.[48]

Shortly before leaving for a vacation in Warm Springs, the Governor approved the bills and dispatched a revealing reply to Hart. In it, Roosevelt underscored the philosophy which motivated him as Governor, and later as President during a period of domestic crisis, when he maintained:

If you were not an old friend and classmate I would tell you that you were all wet! Honestly, my dear fellow, I cannot at all see the point of your telegram about the five-day week. It will undoubtedly raise to a very small amount the cost of certain types of contract, but on the other hand it will result in the actual employment of a great many more individual human beings, and that after all is what we are seeking during this coming winter. I don't agree with you that the philosophy back of these bills is false. There are lots of very able businessmen who think that all industry ought to go on a five-day week for this coming winter—all you have to do is talk to many members of the U. S. Chamber of Commerce to verify this.[49]

Shortly after Roosevelt left the State, Acting Governor Lehman was involved in settling disputes in New York's millinery industry. Although employers and union spokesmen had been anxious to arbitrate certain issues to insure peaceful industry relations, racketeering elements had ensconced themselves in what Judge Samuel Seabury had called the "millinery racket." Unable gracefully to take the initiative, labor and industry spokesmen appealed to Lehman to convene a conference between the disputants.

After discussing with President Max Zaritsky of the Millinery Workers' Union the need for eradication of illegitimate practices and the inauguaration of collective relations, the Acting Governor asked Raymond V. Ingersoll to initiate meetings between employers and the union looking toward arbitration and conciliation.[50]

Following six months of negotiations, a collective agreement was reached which both parties regarded as promising and constructive. The workers gained a five-day week and some minor points. A brief, but successful, stoppage to organize nonunion shops increased union membership by several thousand and more than doubled the size of the employer's association. President Zaritsky later expressed to Lehman the deep appreciation and gratitude of thousands of union members for his role in helping to eradicate a vicious racketeering system and in rendering conspicuous service to both industry and labor.[51]

During his last year as Governor, Roosevelt was again frustrated in his desire for enactment of major labor legislation. In his last annual message to the legislature in January, 1932, he once more appealed for extension of the Workmen's Compensation Law; State regulation of private, fee-charging employment agencies; the declaration by law that the labor of human beings was not a commodity; and, finally, the establishment of an advisory minimum fair wage board for women and children.[52]

All this was to no avail, for the Republican leadership would grant the Democratic presidential aspirant none of his requests.

Unfortunately for the Republican party, their usual obstructionist, shortsighted tactics boomeranged even more impressively in 1932 than they had in 1930.

As a result of the efforts of Senator Robert F. Wagner, and the effects of Supreme Court invalidation of moderate recovery acts, Roosevelt, as President of the United States, was influenced to support development of a national collective bargaining policy which, by 1935, insured to workers: the right to freely associate and select representatives for collective bargaining; the guarantee that their employers could not interfere in the exercise of those rights; and, finally, the stipulation that employers should recognize and deal with these spokesmen. This development facilitated the large-scale organization of labor which now characterizes the United States.[53]

With too few exceptions the Republican-dominated legislature frustrated Roosevelt's efforts to enact his labor program, but he helped to educate the public lucidly in the process. His consistent support of labor's demands in the legislative field, and the statesmanlike efforts of Roosevelt and Lehman to stabilize industry-labor relations in New York State, in contrast to the roles played by other state executives, earned New York's Governor increasing recognition and support by the nation's organized labor movements. There were times, however, when Roosevelt, in search of the presidential nomination, took the easy way out by refusing to commit himself on controversial issues for fear of alienating key individuals or groups.

In November, 1932, organized labor overwhelmingly supported Roosevelt at the polls. With a sympathetic, and at times dominated, Congress behind him, President Roosevelt helped initiate the National Recovery Act, the National Labor Relations Board, the Wagner Labor Relations Act, and, finally, the Fair Labor Standards Act which established a floor under wages and a ceiling over hours. These, and other enactments, brought to the nation's workers some of the primary goals Roosevelt had sought since his elevation to the governorship in 1928.

X

"POWER BELONGS TO THE PEOPLE"

Almost a half century ago the New York legislature granted to the Aluminum Company of America title to the bed and waters of the St. Lawrence River for water power development. A few years later the charter was revoked by a Democratic-controlled legislature, presumably because the State had surrendered valuable rights without just compensation, and because the Aluminum Company had done nothing with its special franchise.[1]

For years thereafter, no efforts were made by utility corporations to develop the latent water power along the St. Lawrence. Eventually, those interested in the development of these power resources split into two groups. One maintained that development of electrical energy should be directed by private interests and private capital, while the other group contended that this great natural resource should never pass from State control.

Following Smith's election to the governorship in 1918, the Frontier Power Company applied for a legislative charter. However, not until after Smith's defeat in 1920 by Republican Nathan L. Miller could the utility company secure enactment of a water power bill which granted to a handful of legislators and State officials, and which was geared to insure Republican domination, the right to lease State power properties.[2] The final efforts of the Frontier Power Company to secure a lease of the St. Lawrence rights for fifty years were blocked at the last moment by Smith, now victorious in the 1922 gubernatorial race, not only on the technical ground that the lease actually proposed was illegal, but on the broader ground that it was contrary to a sound public policy.[3]

The years following were studded with renewed conflicts of these two philosophies. Although Republican leadership was more than willing to grant long-term leases for all the State's rights and properties, it now admitted that nominal ownership should remain with the State. Governor Smith vainly urged succeeding legislatures to develop a dam and power house on the St. Lawrence through a quasi-public corporation and to finance the project by selling bonds. He also asked repeatedly for an enactment granting municipalities the right to own and operate public utilities, but this too was ignored by Republican-dominated legislatures through 1928. Such was the water power situation when Roosevelt became Governor in January, 1929.

In his first inaugural address to a crowded legislative chamber, Roosevelt underscored the importance of water power to New York and the frustrating waste of electrical potential on State sites. Consistent with his campaign pledges, the Governor maintained that the State's water power belonged to all the people and that it was the duty of the legislature to see that this power was transformed into usable electrical energy and distributed at the lowest possible cost. "It is our power; and no inordinate profit must be allowed to those who act as the people's agents in bringing this power to their homes and workshops." The Governor then urged the citizenry to seriously consider how much of this project should be carried out by properly regulated private enterprises, how much undertaken by the State, and how much by some combination of the two.[4]

Reaction to Roosevelt's power policy was as varied as the political ideologies of his friends and opponents. Felix Frankfurter congratulated the Governor for placing the water power problem in its proper perspective, for it raised without a doubt the most far-reaching social and economic issue for the next decade.[5] Louis Waldman, defeated Socialist candidate for Governor, maintained that Roosevelt had repudiated his pre-election stand and warned that a compromise on short leases would be a virtual acceptance of Republican policies.[6]

Surprised that the Governor had devoted part of his inaugural address to water power, the Republicans, nevertheless, pointed out that he had not closed the door to discussion nor had he indicated that he was unalterably opposed to short leases of power sites under the provisions of the water power act, which act Governor Smith had always insisted should be repealed. John Knight, President pro tem of the Senate, went further to state that "Governor Roosevelt does not in any point of his discussion of water power . . . come out for State development and operation."[7]

No doubt recalling the effectiveness of President Woodrow Wilson's personal addresses to Congress, Roosevelt appeared before the legislature on March 12 to read a special message on water power development. He insisted that the State retain for all time the right to construct and own the dams on rivers bordering on, and within, New York. Power plants should be built by the State, and owned by it in perpetuity, never to be leased to private interests. The Governor hoped that in the construction of these dams and power houses, suitable arrangements could be made with private utilities for inexpensive transmission of electricity to home consumers. However, Roosevelt suspected that there might be some difficulty in making equitable arrangements, inasmuch as private power utilities were combining to become a monopoly within the State and therefore might insist on charging as much as the traffic could bear. The Chief Executive thereupon struck a new note in the water power struggle when he warned the private utilities that if they refused to transmit the electricity generated by the State to the consumer at reasonable rates, it might be necessary for the State to construct its own transmission lines.[8]

Specifically, the Governor urged the legislators to establish a power authority of five trustees who would report back within a year a definite plan for the construction of a dam and power site on the St. Lawrence and a specific contract. After receiving legislative approval, the trustees were to consult with the governments of the United States, Canada, and Ontario, concerning construction of the dam and power houses. The power authority would also be expected to confer with private utilities on a contract for the sale and transmission of electricity, insuring the final sale to consumers at the lowest rates possible. Realizing that the State would have to deal with a powerful monopoly, the Governor urged creation of a board of trustees composed of men like Charles Evans Hughes and Alfred E. Smith, who would attempt to negotiate all the necessary contracts before the State had invested a dollar.[9]

Although Republicans immediately charged that Roosevelt had merely revived former Governor Smith's power program, an essential difference was observable. Smith's plan would have had the Public Service Commission determine the rates to be charged by private utilities, whereas Roosevelt wanted his five trustees to determine them in the form of a contract. The Governor obviously distrusted the conservative-minded Public Service Commission dominated by Chairman William A. Prendergast.

The Republican legislators reacted no differently in 1929 than they had previously under Smith. By straight party votes, Republican leaders killed the proposed power bills in committee, preventing a general floor discussion. As the 1929 session drew to a close without water power legislation, Democratic spokesmen could, with justice, denounce the Republicans for being subservient to the water power interests which dominated their leadership.[10]

Yet the same might also be said for elements of the Democratic party in New York City. As the Seabury investigation was to disclose, a Tammany Mayor and subservient city legislators were not above secret agreements with utility interests, for such understandings usually meant padded pockets for the lawmakers and increased profits to the utilities.

Toward the end of June the Governor suddenly asked State Attorney General Hamilton Ward, a Republican, whether the proposed Niagara-Hudson Power Corporation—a $500,000,000 merger of the three great power systems of the State—was a violation of New York's antimonopoly laws. The Governor realized that if the St. Lawrence power project was eventually adopted and the State sought to sell electricity through a private utility, it would find itself dealing with a practical monopoly in determining rates to consumers. He feared not only unreasonable and unwarranted profits but also artificial restriction of the supply of electrical energy.[11]

In a lengthy reply to the Governor, Ward avoided a definitive response. Two weeks later the Governor asked Ward for a "definite opinion." The latter's second reply contended that the proposed merger did not constitute a violation of any State law.[12]

On July 4, 1929, Roosevelt addressed an enthusiastic audience at the dedication of Tammany Hall's newly constructed headquarters. From the flag-bedecked rostrum the Governor warned that it might soon become necessary to proclaim a new Declaration of Independence from the ever growing combinations of capital. He feared particularly the threat to people's liberties from such mergers as the Morgan power interests in New York.

Since the danger emanated from the development of a partnership between business and government, Roosevelt expressed the desire of preaching a new doctrine, a complete separation of government and business. He reminded his audience that the fight against business-controlled government at Albany had been made by Al Smith and himself for the last ten years, and that he was going to keep on with that fight. Pointing to the developing concentration of capital and power in the hands of a few individuals, Roosevelt concluded that these combinations were becoming more powerful in the influence they were building in the State and nation, an influence that someday would have to be met.[13]

The response to the Governor's address was generally favorable, especially since his words appealed to the great numbers of little businessmen. Roosevelt, however, was resorting to nineteenth-century solutions for twentieth-century problems. He was ignoring the simple fact, for example, that people would go on trading in chain stores throughout the State and nation.

Norman Thomas, long-time exponent of public power, who realized Roosevelt's potential threat to Socialist votes, sought to prove the Governor was not the vaunted liberal many pictured him but was actually talking language reminiscent of his famous cousin back in 1904. Thomas ridiculed the Governor's desire to separate government from business and to stop mergers, but not at the same time to discourage the growth of legitimate business, as an attempt to return to an earlier period of American capitalism. To separate government from business was "a funny thing to talk about before Tammany Hall and an impossible thing to carry out if the government must continually be busting trusts."[14]

Thomas conceded that the Governor was correct in fearing the dangers inherent in the Morgan power merger in New York State, a merger against which New York's inadequate regulatory system was powerless to fight. The Governor was also correct in thinking that the plan to lease State-developed power to private distributing companies would not work unless there was competition between the distributing companies. However, Thomas insisted that the Governor's plan was not the solution. The answer was to be found in Ontario, Canada, where low rates were secured through public distribution of power which had been publicly developed.[15]

The Governor made no reply to this challenging and valid criticism. Instead, he prepared to spend part of the summer journeying through upstate New York.

Sometime before leaving Albany, Roosevelt dispatched his personal secretary, Gurnsey Cross, with a confidential message for Canadian Prime Minister Mackenzie King. The message concerned his plans which would bring him to Lake Ontario and the Thousand Islands toward the end of July. While hoping to motor to Ottawa for a short visit with the Prime Minister, Roosevelt fully realized that

. . . if we meet, it must be in a wholly unofficial capacity on my part, for I would not presume in any way to violate the orderly procedure of intercourse between the Dominion Government and the Washington authorities!

Nevertheless, there are a number of matters which closely concern the State of New York and its neighbors, the Provinces of Quebec and Ontario; and at the same time the general policy of the Dominion and the United States Government is closely affiliated.[16]

Although the 1929 legislature had refused to accept his recommendations for State-owned water power sites along the St. Lawrence, Roosevelt was confident that he would eventually win out. Since success of the proposed venture depended, to a great extent, upon the cooperation of Dominion and Provincial authorities in Canada, he desired to smooth the way by meeting some of their officials. By the time the legislature established a St. Lawrence Power Authority, Roosevelt hoped that the international aspects would be settled and that construction could proceed at a rapid rate.[17]

In July, 1929, the Canadian press was overflowing with unfavorable references to possible increases in proposed American tariff revisions which would seriously affect Canadian trade. Along with the tariff discussion went a controversy over the St. Lawrence waterway and related power problems. In Parliament, Prime Minister Mackenzie King had taken the position that, pending final action by the United States, nothing should be said or done which might be construed as provocative of changes likely to be detrimental to Canadian interests. This attitude was misinterpreted by the Conservative opposition, which claimed that the Prime Minister was such a close friend of the United States that he would rather sacrifice Canadian interests than offend the neighboring republic.[18]

As a result of these developments the Canadian Prime Minister informed Roosevelt that it would be impossible to receive him at Ottawa, or elsewhere, without Canadians believing that the visit had an immediate relation to the St. Lawrence waterway. Fearing an unfortunate misunderstanding on the part of the

Canadian press, the Prime Minister postponed the meeting with Roosevelt while reminding the Governor that "politics in your State do not differ from our own politics in the degree to which resort is had to prejudice and deception, and that I have only to mention this possibility for you to see the political dangers of which, unfortunately, I am obliged at the moment to take more than ordinary account."[19]

Roosevelt appreciated the Prime Minister's predicament and assured him that he intended to make it very clear that the main object of his trip was to inspect State instutions and that the waterway and power questions would have nothing to do with his visit, "except the interest which I shall personally obtain from seeing the river with my own eyes."[20]

With the approach of autumn and cooling weather, sharp lines were again drawn for a renewal of the struggle between Roosevelt-led Democrats and utility-minded Republicans. One upstate political columnist believed that water power would dominate the State elections in 1930 and that only H. Edmund Machold of Watertown could possibly defeat Roosevelt's bid for re-election.[21] At that very moment Machold was busy effecting the superpower merger that was being financed by the Morgan interests.[22]

A reporter for the Buffalo *Times* commented that people all over the State had begun to sit up and take notice of the power fight. "We know that everything we publish here on power attracts much attention and receives wide-spread reader interest." One spokesman for the new Niagara-Hudson power combine had assured this reporter that Roosevelt had the popular side of the power question at the moment but that the power interests would explode his fallacies a little later on.[23]

Commenting on the future role of the new monopoly, the Governor agreed that Niagara-Hudson would soon start one of the most extensive publicity campaigns ever attempted. "They will make rates more uniform, contracts more simple and rates (in some cases) cheaper, during the next ten months, then tell the public 'See what a good boy I am.' Watch the process!"[24]

Frustrated by continued opposition of power interests to every constructive proposal made since 1919, Roosevelt made plans for his own frontal attack. Early in October, 1929, he directed Louis Howe to secure original electric bills, or photostatic copies, from comparable cities in New York and Ontario.[25]

When the 1930 legislature convened on January 1, the Chief Executive stiffened his position on water power. Not only did he demand that the ownership, development, and operation of the St. Lawrence power resources remain forever in the actual possession of the people of the State, or of some public agency representing them, but he wanted New York to finance a State-wide system of transmission lines. This had been Governor Smith's original contention, but from which he had subsequently receded. Roosevelt admonished the lawmakers to "stop once and for all the silly talk that the electricity available by developing the St. Lawrence is not needed or not usable in a practical way. We know that private companies are only too eager to proceed if the State were to abandon its rights."[26]

Rural and urban families, Roosevelt insisted, had been paying too much for their electricity and were unable to take advantage of the many labor-saving devices of modern invention. The variance of rates between communities was too great, and in some rural communities the cost was prohibitive. Until such time as regulation of public utilities became effective, it was urgent that relief be obtained by the development of the water power potential of the St. Lawrence River.[27]

With information secured for him by Louis Howe, the Governor was subsequently able to impress the lawmakers, and the public, with the fact that the people of New York were generally paying higher rates for electricity in their homes than were people in most other sections of the country and in Canada. Even within New York the prices charged had an absurdly wide range. Based on a monthly use of 250 kilowatt hours of electricity—an amount that would permit the occupants of an average four-room house or apartment to light their home and to use a flat iron, toaster, vacuum cleaner, electric fan, washing machine, radio, sewing machine, refrigerator, and electric range —a family living in Manhattan would pay $17.50 a month; in Brooklyn, only $13.40; in Staten Island, $11.55. In Buffalo, the family would pay $7.80; in Albany, $19.50; while only fifteen miles away in Schenectady they would pay $9.30.

If this family lived in Ontario, on the Canadian side of Niagara Falls, they would pay $2.79, but if they lived on the American side of the Falls they would pay $5.53. If they lived in Dunkirk, New York, a city owning its own municipal plant, they would pay $6.93, but in Oswego, which had a private plant, they would pay $11.20.[28]

For the first time in almost a decade, Republican leaders did not seek the floor of the Senate or Assembly to condemn a Democratic Governor's water power proposals. A new turn of events seemed foreshadowed by this development and by a letter which Roosevelt had received almost simultaneously from Floyd L. Carlisle, chairman of the board of directors of the Niagara-Hudson Power Corporation. Carlisle, an old acquaintance of the Governor, and Republican chieftains had spoken with Roosevelt in December concerning an amicable settlement of the St. Lawrence water power issue.[29] With the formation of Niagara-Hudson in 1929, Chairman Carlisle felt there were no longer any divergent points of view and varying interests which had previously existed in the public utilities upstate concerning the ownership of the "riparian rights" on the St. Lawrence. Carlisle's organization, representing the major upstate utilities, was prepared to cooperate with the best plan for the utilization of the power, and to assist in freeing the discussions from politics and of reducing them to their practical and business phases.[30]

The Republicans and their cohorts, the power interests, were definitely on the defensive by 1930, for public opinion had crystallized in support of the Governor. Many Republicans, including W. Kingsland Macy and the utility lobby, doubted the ability of the G.O.P. to defeat Roosevelt's bid for re-election in 1930 as long as water power remained an issue. In fact, in every

State where water power was made a dominant issue in the 1930 elections, victory went to the champions of public control—Gifford Pinchot was elected Governor of Pennsylvania; Philip LaFollette, Governor of Wisconsin; Thomas Walsh was re-elected to the United States Senate from Montana; Edward F. Costigan became the new Senator from Colorado; John H. Bankhead defeated J. Thomas Heflin in Alabama; and, of course, Roosevelt secured an overwhelming victory in New York.

The utilities, however, were not completely helpless. Granting legislative enactment of Roosevelt's water power proposals, they knew it would take many years before final arrangements could be made for the construction and operation of State-owned water power houses. In the nation's capital, meanwhile, the Morgan power interests could fall back upon a sympathetic Congress and President as long as they remained Republican. In addition, an international treaty had to be concluded between Canada and the United States before New York could proceed with construction of power houses along the St. Lawrence. With Roosevelt developing as Hoover's most formidable opponent for 1932, Carlisle could assume that President Hoover would view sympathetically the desires of New York Republicans and their allies in Niagara-Hudson.

Within two weeks after Roosevelt's annual message, Senator Warren K. Thayer and Assemblyman John M. Hackett, both Republicans, introduced a bill providing for a survey board of five commissioners appointed by Roosevelt to "devise and report a plan or plans for the development of hydro-electric power on the St. Lawrence River." If approved by the legislature, the final plans would be directed by a board of trustees.[31]

The following day Republican leaders were astounded to learn that Roosevelt had not only accepted their proposal but was hailing it as a great victory for Democrats. It is true that the Republicans had dumped the water power problem into the Governor's lap, but they had done so primarily to remove it as an issue in the forthcoming gubernatorial election. Although the Governor had stated repeatedly that he viewed public development and retention by the State of physical possession of the proposed plant on the St. Lawrence as the approved policy, with no deviation permissible, he was now approving the establishment of a commission which would study all proposals besides his own. Of course, Roosevelt felt that since he would be able to appoint the five members of the commission, without the need for Senate confirmation, he would get the type of report he wanted. But then there was the 1931 legislature to contend with, for they had to act upon the commission's recommendations. A Republican-dominated legislature, which was inevitable but for a political upheaval in New York, was not apt to give Roosevelt what he wanted in water power.[32]

Believing that this was a "red letter day" which would eventually insure cheap lighting and power for the people of New York, Roosevelt was overly exuberant when he wired former Governor Smith:

You will be happy to know that the Republican legislative leaders have introduced and come out in favor of an electric bill which seems to accept the great basic principle for which you and I have fought so long. There is no doubt it is a great victory.[33]

The Happy Warrior responded with "Happy Congratulations on your victory. It was a long battle and you should get great personal satisfaction from the outcome. All hands in the party rejoice with you."[34]

Walter Lippmann sent Roosevelt personal congratulations and interpreted the outcome as a complete triumph for the things he had been fighting to achieve. "More power to you," he concluded.[35]

From Felix Frankfurter, Governor Roosevelt received a heartwarming letter which reminded him that

All too often public men compromise essentials on a vital issue, accept stone for bread, and then comfort themselves with the metaphor that half a loaf is better than none. By holding out on your water power policy for New York, you have vindicated courage in government. You have also achieved the indispensable, correct first step in working out a socially sound water power policy.[36]

Frankfurter felt that Roosevelt would now be able to prove that the greatest natural resource owned by the State could be used predominantly for the public welfare and not for profit. Once New York proved that water power could be developed with due regard to the public interest, the unimaginative and selfish claims against State development would be quashed.

While Roosevelt adherents reacted joyously to the Republican "capitulation," Norman Thomas roared forth his dissatisfaction. According to the Socialist leader, this latest development proved his contention that electric utilities were more than willing to permit the State to use its credit for the construction of power houses. The utilities knew they would continue to control the distribution of electricity through their privately owned transmission lines where most of the profits were made. Thomas felt that there was no solution to the power problem aside from the problem of production and distribution of electric power, and he would not be satisfied until the State owned not only the power houses but the transmission lines which would bring the electricity directly into the homes of consumers. Until then, the utilities would continue to make their 8 percent, and more, profit on the inflated value of their watered stocks and capital.[37]

Disturbed by Thomas's reactions, the Governor displayed an alertness and open-mindedness which was rare among political figures when he wrote the Socialist spokesman, "entirely confidential and not intended for publication":

It has always been my belief that it is far more important to ascertain as fully as possible, and consider with an open mind, the criticism of those who do not agree with you on important public questions than it is to read the plaudits and encomiums of friends.

I am somewhat surprised to learn that you "bitterly attack" my power program. I was under the impression that both you and the party of which you are the acknowledged head in this state were largely in agreement with me as to the need of a better regulation of our public utilities and of the securing of cheaper electrical rates for our people, particularly our householders. For this reason I would very much appreciate a copy of your speech . . . if you have one available.[38]

Unable to locate a verbatim report of his address, the Socialist leader sent Roosevelt a summation in which he had urged the Governor to be more specific as to the transmission lines he would establish, the terms on which he would lease them, and whether he would give any preferential treatment to municipal distributing agencies. In a personal reply to Roosevelt's message, Thomas emphasized that his criticism was based on the conviction that the first duty of the State was to acquire public ownership of the whole power system as rapidly as possible. Thomas did well to point out that as a first step it was not only inadequate but dangerous not to give more attention to the distributing end.[39]

Before Roosevelt entered the White House he would agree with much that Thomas said on water power.

When the Governor signed the Thayer Water Power bill in March, 1930, he and his friends believed a new era had been inaugurated.[40] Five months later the members of the newly designated St. Lawrence Power Development Commission met with the Governor on the proposed site of the power project to begin their work.[41] During the months which followed the commission met with President Hoover and with officials of the Federal Power Commission and of the Hydro-Electric Power Commission of Ontario, Canada. While discussing the problem of cooperation between Federal and State authorities, President Hoover informed the St. Lawrence Commission that he could make no definite commitments until negotiations had been further developed between the United States and Canada.[42]

On January 15, 1931, the St. Lawrence Power Development Commission presented its conclusions to the Governor in the form of majority and minority reports. The commission unanimously found that a dam could be built across the St. Lawrence with absolute safety, and that the cost of construction would be $70,000,000 less than any previous estimate. The cost of the generation per horse power would be $10, in contrast to $25 for the equivalent by steam power. Both reports maintained that the policy of development should be to provide the maximum possible reduction in rates to domestic consumers, farmers, and small users of power.[43]

To insure fair electric rates and to avoid the waste of litigation in rate cases, the commission agreed with the Governor that rates should not be determined by the Public Service Commission but should be fixed by a contract based on a definite method of accounting and valuation.

On the vital question of transmission of power generated by the State-owned power house, the commission was confronted with the fact that the State's three largest holding companies of power corporations had merged to form the Niagara-Hudson Power Corporation. The State was, therefore, no longer in a position to bargain with competing companies for transmission of electricity on fair terms. The proposed power authority, which would assume responsibility for supervising construction of the power house and concluding arrangements for transmission of electricity generated, would be confronted with a monopoly on the other side of the bargaining table. The problem which then arose was whether equitable arrangements could be reached with Floyd Carlisle of Niagara-Hudson.

Both the majority and minority reports favored a contract with a private utility company for the delivery of power to consumers, if the company would collect only for the cost of the actual services rendered plus a reasonable profit. If this was impossible, the minority recommended that the power authority seek agreement with another major private company—which did not exist in New York State—or establish a private organization, through State sponsorship, for transmission of electricity to consumers. If no satisfactory arrangements could be made with utilities, the minority suggested, as a final alternative, that the power authority build its own transmission lines.

The majority was not as specific in suggesting alternative solutions for dealing with the monopolistic Niagara-Hudson. Desirous of retaining as many bargaining weapons as possible in the hands of the power authority, the majority concluded that "in the event of the inability of the trustees to make such a contract, they shall have such authority as it is necessary to make other disposition of power." [44]

The Governor's victory seemed complete. The commission had agreed with his fundamental tenets: that power could be developed cheaply; that the legislature should provide for a power authority to complete negotiations with the Federal government and the utilities; that the rates at which electricity was to be sold to small consumers should be fixed by prior contract; and that if such contracts were impossible of attainment, then the power authority was to resort to whatever measures it deemed necessary. [45]

Reaction to the commission's report varied from unswerving support of Roosevelt to raucous opposition. Throughout the proceedings of the St. Lawrence Commission, Professor James C. Bonbright of Columbia University had acted as confidential adviser to its chairman, Robert M. Haig. Familiar with the discussions which had led to the majority and minority reports, Professor Bonbright was worried that the power authority, if authorized to negotiate contracts with Carlisle of Niagara-Hudson, would yield to its desire to accomplish something definite by speedily concluding contracts with the utility spokesman. On the surface these contracts might appear to be quite favorable, but they could ultimately prove highly burdensome to the consumer. Consequently, Bonbright advised the Governor that any contracts which the proposed authority might enter into with Carlisle should be subjected to the fullest kind of public scrutiny and criticism. [46]

Bonbright had unsuccessfully sought to have the St. Lawrence Commission recognize that it was impossible to divorce their particular study from the general problem of rate regulation. He had urged that body to specify the type of contract which would be essential if the proposed power authority found itself relying on private companies for the transmission and distribution of electricity. Unfortunately, according to Bonbright, the commission thought otherwise because it believed that immediate announcement of any one form of contract would interfere with negotiations with Carlisle. The commission felt it was better strategy to allow Carlisle to suggest his own form of contract and then to show him, point by point, the features which were not satisfactory.[47]

Felix Frankfurter and Roosevelt agreed with Bonbright's criticisms of the commission's reports. Frankfurter suggested that the strength of the public position was not in "finessing or skillful maneuvering. The Carlisles and Ransoms cannot be beaten in that game. The public's case ought to rest on facts and arguments that can be frankly avowed." [48]

The Governor exhibited little modesty concerning his acumen as a political tactician when he argued:

One trouble with some of the Commission was that they thought they could play politics both with the Legislature and the Carlisle crowd. I told them to let me do the political fencing for them and, without taking undue credit to myself, I think I am a better trader in his kind of work than they are! As a matter of fact, I find the best kind of trading is to go after the objective in the simplest and clearest way.[49]

Edward Keating, the editor of *Labor*, a national journal, threw his weight behind the Governor to "block Mellon interests' effort to 'grab' the St. Lawrence Development project." The real issue, according to Keating, was public development versus Andrew Mellon's aluminum trust development. If private enterprise was permitted to develop the water power sites along the St. Lawrence, then Mellon would determine the electric rates in New York, and they would not be low. On the other hand, if the State or Federal government assumed control of the development of hydroelectric energy, then the people would share in the benefits through lowered prices. That was the issue in the conflict over the St. Lawrence power project, the power propagandists, the politicians, and some of the newspapers notwithstanding.[50]

On the other hand, the leading Republican farm journal in

New York viewed the St. Lawrence power project as having been a gold mine of political talk for years. It pictured former Governor Smith as having made the most of it in his time and Roosevelt having gone him one better by bringing the subject down to the broom and dishpan. According to this weekly, if the State had ever shown any efficiency in public undertakings it would be urged to undertake this project and go through with it to the doors of the consumers, but it had never shown capacity for anything of the kind.[51]

A major difficulty which would plague Roosevelt through 1932 remained that of transmission. With Niagara-Hudson a monopoly, the basic solution for the State was public construction of transmission lines. Carlisle's utility would never be put in its proper place by the simple action of setting up a few public agencies for the production of power. The great problem was to find out how best to develop a government-owned and government-controlled power industry. Nevertheless, it was incumbent upon all those who desired cheaper electricity to support public development of power on the St. Lawrence, but by no means in the belief that such development of itself would solve the major problem. Roosevelt had to learn to master the power trust, not to try to compete with it, or to outwit it in the making of contracts.

In March, 1931, the St. Lawrence Power Authority Bill, containing the Governor's basic objectives, was introduced in the Assembly by Republican Jasper W. Cornaire from Jefferson County.[52] After approval by the lower house, the Governor awaited action by the Senate. On April 2, the bill was suddenly emasculated upon the insistence of John Knight, President pro tem of the Senate and friend of utility spokesmen.

As adopted by the legislature the year previous, the original St. Lawrence Bill provided that the five members of the proposed power authority be appointed by the Governor. Knowing full well that Roosevelt would veto any alteration of this procedure, Senator Knight introduced amendments which, in addition to transferring responsibility of appointment to the Republican-dominated legislature, specifically named the members of the St. Lawrence Power Development Commission to the proposed power authority. Knight maintained that it was logical to place the power project in the hands of those who were with it from the start and who were best fitted to carry it out.[53]

The Governor immediately appealed to the people of the State over the heads of Republican leaders. He accused Senator Knight of contravening the law of 1930, of repudiating the unanimous recommendations of the St. Lawrence commissioners, and of rejecting the affirmative action of the Assembly which had accepted the Governor's appointive power. Denouncing this as typical Republican obstructionism, the Governor also blasted away at the utility interests for dictating the move.[54]

Public opinion is often not spontaneous but rather a planned and cultivated reaction, as in this instance when Roosevelt exhibited an unusual ability to build a groundswell of support for his policy. While the Governor was hurling broadsides at the Republicans, Samuel I. Rosenman and others on the Governor's staff kept telephone and telegraph wires buzzing with directives to key Democrats throughout the State. In "personal and confidential" messages, Rosenman requested that the Governor and legislators be swamped with "resolutions from civic groups and associations interested in water power approving the Governor's stand and disapproving the action of the Legislature. If you will send them here we will get the publicity on same." [55]

A mounting wave of protest against Senator Knight's amendment was immediate and overwhelming. Hundreds of supporting letters, resolutions, and telegrams swamped the Governor's office. Many who had consistently voted Republican were now thoroughly disgusted with their party's tactics. Chambers of Commerce from five communities in Republican St. Lawrence County publicly endorsed the Governor's stand.[56] The Chamber of Commerce nearest the projected power site reminded Roosevelt that he had convinced its members, on his visit the previous summer, that he was anxious to remove this problem from politics and that a method similar to that proposed in the Cornaire Bill was the only logical attitude in view of the conflicting ideas and the impossibility of reconciling them. After discussing the water power question with other Chambers of Commerce, and with prominent citizens in practically all of the towns north of Albany, the Massena Chamber of Commerce informed the Governor that it had found

. . . a decided public sentiment for a prompt settlement of this controversy and a feeling of confidence in the men you have named as commissioners and the recommendations they have made. It is our earnest desire and hope that in the appointment of the new power authority under the Cornaire Bill you will appoint men who are known to be in sympathy with and will endeavor to carry out the recommendations and policies contained in the majority report submitted to you by the Power Commission.[57]

Aware of the diverse response in support of the Governor's position, and with its only mainstay the utility lobby, Republican leaders realized that public opinion had surged against them. The final blow to Republican chieftains was the Governor's announcement that he would speak directly to the people by radio on April 7.

A few hours before the Governor began his scheduled radio address, Republican Senator Thayer rose on the Senate floor and moved that the Knight amendment be struck from the Cornaire proposal. In the midst of the heated debate which followed, Senator George R. Fearon, who was to become majority leader within a month, voiced the sentiments of the private utilities and of his party leadership when he maintained that the real proposition involved was whether the lawmakers wanted to put the State in the business of transmitting and distributing electrical energy, for that was what the Governor wanted. Roosevelt, he charged, would appoint men who would hamstring the majority report and who would not get a contract with the utility company for distribution of power because they wouldn't honestly try.[58]

Upon the conclusion of the debate two Republican Senators

joined Thayer and twenty-three Democrats to eliminate the amendment by a vote of twenty-six to twenty-three. In the final vote on the original Cornaire Bill, all forty-nine Senators were recorded in the affirmative.

The Governor did speak over the radio that day but utilized the opportunity for a stirring victory address. While granting the effective influence of a handful of political leaders, and of private corporations when they saw an opportunity to get something for nothing, Roosevelt contended that "stronger than all of these put together is the influence of Mr. and Mrs. Average Voter. It may take a good many years to translate this influence of the people of the State into terms of law, but public opinion, when it understands a policy and supports it, is bound to win in the long run." [59]

It was ironic, perhaps, for Roosevelt to have characterized public opinion as reacting spontaneously in the water power struggle, especially since he had sparked and planned the very reaction he finally received. This incident, however, revealed yet another aspect of Roosevelt's leadership—the ability to develop and activate public opinion.

Subsequently signed by the Governor, the Cornaire Bill provided for a Power Authority with the responsibility of developing the St. Lawrence River for commerce, navigation, and hydroelectric energy. The bed and waters of the river, within the borders of New York, and the power and power sites were to remain forever inalienable to the people of the State. In the process of developing power for domestic and rural consumers, the Authority was also to make available to authorized municipalities power at a reasonable cost. [60]

Roosevelt's success in the water power struggle had national implications for both conservatives and liberals. Senator Thomas J. Walsh, Democrat from Montana, indicated that this victory would not only aid water power development along the St. Lawrence but profoundly influence legislation and public thought on power problems. "The natural effect will be to dissipate whatever support the opposition to Muscle Shoals legislation has in the enlightened public opinion of the country." [61]

Speaking for conservatives, the Chicago *Journal of Commerce* bitterly assailed Roosevelt for his program of "subsidized socialism," and for taking the State into the business of manufacturing and transmitting power. Remarking that Franklin D. Roosevelt was Senator Burton K. Wheeler's choice for President of the United States, this business journal concluded that "Senator Wheeler is for the Governor because the Governor is for Socialism." [62]

The campaign lines were being drawn for 1932. This Chicago business journal, and those with a similar viewpoint, were mistaken in their characterization of Franklin D. Roosevelt. New York's Governor was neither a Socialist nor a radical. He was responsible, perhaps more than any other man, for stemming the tide of socialism in this country. His program brought the demise of much of what was left in the platform of the Socialist party on power. Like the British conservatives, Roosevelt believed that to preserve the finest features of democracy there must be at least periodic reform and revision.

After his election as Governor in 1928, Roosevelt had been advised by close associates to avail himself of experts in water power and related fields. That he made effective use of them is now recorded history. He was as amenable to trained experts as had been the elder LaFollette when Governor of Wisconsin. They had helped elevate the Badger State and LaFollette to the forefront of the political scene and they would do the same for Roosevelt.

In May, 1931, the Governor appointed Frank P. Walsh as chairman, and Delos M. Cosgrove, Professor James C. Bonbright, Morris L. Cooke, and Fred J. Freestone as the other trustees of the New York Power Authority. Leland Olds was designated executive secretary. In contrast to similar bodies in many other states, the integrity and independence of this commission from undue influence by utilities was, in part, illustrated by its persistent support of public power and subsequent records of some of its members. Bonbright remained with the Power Authority until 1946, becoming its vice-chairman and then chairman. In 1933, he served as the United States delegate to the World Power Conference at Stockholm, Sweden. Cooke was a member of the Power Authority until 1933, when he became chairman of the Mississippi Valley Committee of the Public Works Administration. Since then he has served as Administrator of the Rural Electrification Administration and technical consultant to the Office of Production Management, and he has been a frequent writer on the power issue. Leland Olds remained executive secretary to the Power Authority until 1939. For the next ten years he served as a member of the Federal Power Commission and as vice-chairman of the United States-St. Lawrence Advisory Commission. Frank P. Walsh, who had previously established a distinguished record as newspaperman, lawyer, and joint chairman of the War Labor Conference Board during World War I, remained chairman of the Power Authority until his death in 1939.

Following their appointment, the five trustees of the Power Authority initiated studies into the cost of transmitting and distributing St. Lawrence current, low cost rural electrification, the coordination of all power sources in the State, and a campaign to attract industry to northern New York. They approached the Federal-State problem with three basic concepts: that New York had vast property rights in the natural resources involved in the St. Lawrence project; that there were great social and economic interests of the people of New York involved; and that it was of prime importance that a full accord and understanding be reached between the United States government and the State of New York prior to negotiations with the Canadian government.

Beginning in June, 1931, the Power Authority made numerous attempts to secure official recognition from the Federal government of the interests of New York in the proposed treaty negotiations with Canada for the development of the St. Lawrence. Before New York could commence construction of a dam and power house on the St. Lawrence, Washington had to reach an accord with Canadian authorities. An added difficulty was the long-existing proposal for construction of a dam and lock project, to enable ships to sail up the St. Lawrence toward the Great Lakes.[63]

In a series of letters to Herbert Hoover, the Power Authority recalled to the President some phases of the history of the St. Lawrence project and of the interests of New York. In 1905, Secretary of War William Howard Taft had submitted to Congress a report from General Mackenzie, Chief of Engineers, U.S.A., upon a pending bill. The report contended that the Federal government had no possessory title to the water flowing in navigable streams, nor to the land comprising their bed and shores, and therefore Congress could grant no absolute authority to anyone to use and occupy such water and land for manufacturing and industrial purposes. The establishment, regulation, and control of matters pertaining to the comfort, convenience, and prosperity of the people came within the powers of the states, and the Supreme Court had held that the authority of a state over its navigable waters within its borders, and the shores and bed, were subject only to such action as Congress might take in the execution of its powers under the Constitution to regulate commerce among the several states.[64]

President Hoover was reminded that in 1926 the United States-St. Lawrence Commission, of which he was then chairman, had reported to President Coolidge: "On the American side the State of New York has a special interest in the power development of the International Section, and the coordination of these improvements with the State should be undertaken." [65]

As further indication of the Federal government's policy, Hoover was also reminded that as Secretary of Commerce he had said, in an address before the New Haven Chamber of Commerce on March 12, 1927, that the Federal administration desired to assist New York in bringing about the development of St. Lawrence power, and would gladly cooperate with any public or private agency approved by New York to undertake the American side of the water power development.[66]

In July, 1931, the Power Authority requested an early conference with President Hoover to hasten adoption of the proposed plans for a dam across the St. Lawrence. The Authority maintained that this project would provide work for tens of thousands of unemployed, release some five billion kilowatt hours of electricity annually to homes, farms, and industries, and open the interior of the nation to the commerce of the world through completion of the Great Lakes-St. Lawrence Waterway. The President's discouraging response maintained that an international agreement had to be entered into between the United States and Canada before any steps could be taken between the Federal government and the New York Power Authority.[67]

The Power Authority persisted in its efforts to have the Federal government recognize the special interests of New York in its negotiations with Canada. Unfortunately, President Hoover no longer adhered to some of the principles he had expounded while Secretary of Commerce. On August 1, 1931, the Power Authority again wrote the President, expressing the hope that suitable arrangements could be reached before negotiations commenced with Canadian representatives. A subsequent letter elicited a simple acknowledgment from the President's secretary. Immediately thereafter, Roosevelt transmitted to Hoover a letter from the New York Power Authority which emphasized the importance of New York's being represented in the direct negotiations about to commence between United States and Canadian authorities, concerning the St. Lawrence project, inasmuch as State-owned development was equally involved with the navigation plans of the Federal government. In an accompanying personal message, the Governor inquired of the President the status of the negotiations between the United States and Canada.[68]

Roosevelt's letter was referred to an Under Secretary of State who, despite persistent newspaper reports to the contrary, maintained that no negotiations of any kind were going on and that when the time came the interest of New York State would not be neglected.[69]

Viewing this as an inadequate response, and dissatisfied with the treatment accorded his State by the President and by Federal authorities, the Governor made it clear that he would push his State's power plan, and that conflict could be expected with the President's plan on the proposed St. Lawrence treaty. The Governor desired nothing less than a voice in the final determination of the pact, at least with reference to the interests of New York State.[70]

By the middle of October, the Canadian press quoted the Premier of the Province of Ontario to the effect that the Dominion of Canada and his Province had reached complete understanding with regard to their respective rights relative to the power development of the international section of the St. Lawrence River. Throughout his subsequent negotiations with Canada, President Hoover refused to accord the State of New York the same recognition granted Ontario by the Canadian government in Ottawa.

Finally, in response to insistent demands by Chairman Walsh, President Hoover consented to a conference between Power Authority spokesmen and Secretary of State Henry L. Stimson. In late October, 1931, Walsh and Cosgrove met with Stimson. They presented the Secretary with a written memorandum from the Power Authority which set forth four points as "definitely settled": that the Federal government had paramount authority in the improvement of commerce and navigation along the river; that New York owned the water and adjoining land on the American side; that disposition of the water power was a domestic question; and that New York was to pay toward the cost of the project only what might be fairly allocated to the production of power on the American side.[72]

After agreeing to periodic conferences in the future, and promising to reply to the memorandum at a later date, Stimson stated there had been no negotiations whatsover between the United States and Canada. According to Walsh, Stimson saw no reason why there should not be an agreement with New York State before even a tentative agreement was reached with Canada. While not committing himself as to the rights of New York to the power, Stimson thought it desirable that there should be an agreement with New York that by paying its share of the cost, the State would have the disposal of the power. The Secretary preferred such an agreement to a law suit.[73]

Within a week the Secretary of State replied to the lengthy memorandum of the Power Authority. As part of a discouraging communication, Stimson suggested that it would be unnecessary, if not unwise, to attempt to arrive at any agreement or definitive adjustment with New York until at least substantial progress had been made toward the conclusion of a treaty with Canada. President Hoover had thus rejected New York's plea for an adjustment of the St. Lawrence power issue prior to negotiations with Canada. Of prime importance, however, was the sentence in which Stimson stated:

Whatever the rights of the State of New York may be in respect to any electric power developed by the navigation project on the river along the international boundary, utilization of that electric power must in the end depend upon the authority and permission of the Federal Goverment.[74]

This statement appeared to claim that after the improvement of navigation and commerce along the river and the protection of traffic upon it, the Federal government possessed additional authority over the development and disposal of the electrical energy to be generated.

Replying for the Power Authority, Chairman Walsh informed Secretary Stimson that the assumption of such authority by the Federal government would amount to a denial of the "soverign and proprietary interest of the State" in the waters and lands of the St. Lawrence River lying within its boundaries, and of its right to develop and dispose of its hydroelectric power. Walsh referred to a legal definition of the rights of the State in the St. Lawrence River, as expressed six years earlier by Charles Evans Hughes in the latter's capacity as special counsel to the State of New York, and before he had become Chief Justice of the Supreme Court. At that time Hughes had said that it was appropriate that there be supervision of construction of the project works and suitable provision for the approval of original plans and alterations, but so far as Federal authority was directed to the protection of navigation and the enforcement of Federal right, that supervision and control rested with New York State. In case of any conflict of views with respect to such construction, and where the protection of navigation and the enforcement of Federal right were not involved, the determination of the State had to control.[75]

For the next six months the Power Authority held periodic conferences with the State Department in attempts to settle these questions. Finally, it became evident to the Power Authority that the Federal administration had no sincere intention of reaching a definitive agreement with New York prior to the signing of an international treaty with Canada.[76]

On June 7, 1932, the Power Authority was suddenly advised by the State Department that the policy of the Federal government in St. Lawrence matters would thereafter be decided by President Hoover, and that a treaty between Canada and the United States would be signed in July. Immediately, the Power Authority reminded Secretary Stimson of the oral agreements which had already been reached with representatives of his department, and requested an early conference to settle the issue of financing the power project.[77]

While the Power Authority received no response from the Secretary of State for an entire month, Canada and the Province of Ontario reached substantial agreement on major details relating to plans, costs, and terms of payment for the Canadian part of the St. Lawrence project.

Throughout its negotiations with Power Authority spokesmen, the State Department had assured them that no treaty would be signed before agreement had been reached with New York. State Department spokesmen had also given Walsh and Cosgrove definite pledges that the final conferences would not be withheld until the last moment and that ample opportunity would be given the Power Authority to arrive at a considered judgment.[78]

Despite these assurances, Chairman Walsh had come to the conclusion that Hoover had purposely delayed the signing of the treaty with Canada, besides refusing to permit New York to participate in the treaty negotiations, until after the respective 1932 national conventions had nominated their obvious candidates, Hoover and Roosevelt. Walsh believed that the claim could then be made by Hoover that the treaty was under way, that the Federal government and New York were having harmonious negotiations, and that an accord would doubtless be reached between the two governments, thus eliminating the power question as an issue in the 1932 campaign. The prolonged delay, the insistent shrouding of negotiations in secrecy, and the Federal government's withholding of their figures, in contrast to New York's representatives, aroused in Walsh the suspicion that it was Hoover's plan to delay submission of the treaty to as late a date as possible, and to present New York with a cost allocation which would make it futile for the State to use its great resource in the St. Lawrence to lower electric rates to domestic consumers and to extend rural electrification.[79]

Having learned unofficially, on July 8, 1932, that the St. Lawrence treaty would be signed in a matter of days, and still without response from Stimson to their month-old letter, the Power Authority suddenly dropped the entire problem into the lap of the Governor. Roosevelt immediately wired President Hoover requesting a conference, so that agreement might be reached on the respective shares of the cost of the St. Lawrence project to facilitate early submission of the treaty to the Senate.[80]

The President's reply indicated progress on the treaty, but declined to enter into conference with New York until the treaty was not only consummated but also approved by the Senate. The President based his reasoning on the fact that the treaty-making power of the United States rested with the Federal government and that the proposed treaty with Canada reserved all questions concerning the interests of the State of New York for purely domestic action.[81]

President Hoover had misinterpreted Roosevelt's communication, for the reasoning behind the Governor's request for an early conference had nothing to do with questioning the treaty-making power of the Federal government. The proposed treaty could not be divorced from any arrangement between New York State and the Federal government for the disposition of water power. The soundness and economy of the engineering plans for the location and construction of the dams and channels were the determining factors as to whether New York State could produce the promised cheap electricity. It was therefore logical that Roosevelt and the New York Power Authority know of the developing agreements between Canada and the United States before the consummation of negotiations by treaty.[82]

The President's statement that "if the treaty is consummated and ratified, I shall be glad to consult with you and other Governors," [83] closed the door of the Federal administration to any further consideration of New York's rights in the St. Lawrence project until the treaty was concluded. The President's position directly violated pledges given the Power Authority by Secretary of State Stimson, and contradicted a statement by Hoover in 1926 when, as chairman of the United States-St. Lawrence Commission, he transmitted that body's conclusions on the engineering report. Point four of his summary of conclusions stated that negotiations should be entered into with Canada in an endeavor to arrive at an agreement on the St. Lawrence seaway. In such negotiations, Hoover maintained that "the United States should recognize the proper relations of New York to the power development in the International Section." [84]

The day following the President's reply to Roosevelt, Senators George W. Norris, Robert M. LaFollette, Jr., and Edward P. Costigan endorsed the Governor's move as a fine one. Norris maintained that the strongest points for a reply from the Governor were that President Hoover had taken a highly technical position and that the Governor's real proposal was to eliminate red tape; and that Hoover's position in refusing to discuss an understanding with New York before the treaty was signed was, in fact, a definite breaking of the State Department's pledges to the Power Authority. LaFollette suggested that if the treaty was signed before Congress adjourned and was not sent to Congress, Senator William E. Borah might be willing to write President Hoover asking for the treaty in order that it be referred to the Foreign Relations Committee. He offered to recommend this move to Senator Borah. However, the three Senators apparently felt strongly that as the power question was not really in the treaty, Roosevelt ought not to put himself in the position of delaying ratification. New York's fight, they felt, should be made when it came to the question of legislation providing for the development.[85]

On July 18, 1932, the St. Lawrence treaty was signed by American and Canadian representatives. Hoover's defeat in the November elections resulted in a shelving of the treaty by Congress. Not until 1954, however, was a St. Lawrence treaty approved by the United States, despite earlier pleas by Presidents Roosevelt and Truman.

In an interim report to the Governor, early in 1932, the Power Authority underscored the difficulty of attempting to negotiate contracts for the disposition of St. Lawrence power. Niagara-Hudson now owned basically all of the transmission and distribution lines in central New York and, in addition, was financially allied with the Consolidated Gas Company which dominated the utilities in the New York City area.[86]

The Power Authority thereupon urged the Governor to recommend legislation which would permit municipalities, with the consent of their citizens, to engage in the distribution of electricity. In February, 1932, the Governor included these recommendations in a special message to the legislature. Earlier, the Governor had renewed his request that the legislature authorize municipalities of the State to form public utility districts, with the consent of their voters, for the purpose of generating, distributing, and selling electricity.[87] The Republican leadership, however, rejected the Governor's pleas and closed its legislative books to any further enactments in the field of power development, as long as Roosevelt remained their Chief Executive.

As Roosevelt prepared to transfer his activity to the nation's capital, Carlisle's Niagara-Hudson was seemingly the victor in New York's power struggle. However, the obstructionist, short-sighted tactics of Carlisle and his Republican cohorts in Albany and Washington insured the setbacks they would receive in years to come. By frustrating Roosevelt's attempts to secure cheap and plentiful electric power on the State level, utility spokesmen educated the Governor to the need for far-reaching Federal, state, and local cooperation on the water power issue.

In May, 1933, after years of valiant struggle by Senator George W. Norris, Congress finally provided for, and President Roosevelt approved, the creation of the Tennessee Valley Authority to harness the Tennessee River. The twenty-odd multipurpose dams which now dot this seven-state area no longer permit floods, make navigation feasible twelve months of the year, manufacture nitrates, and generate electricity for this region's great industries.

The TVA built transmission lines and sold its surplus electricity to towns and cooperatives in the seven-state region, and to private power companies by contracts which embodied provisions for low retail rates for small and large consumers. TVA, as a yardstick, has been instrumental in stimulating private utilities to lower their rates to levels well below the country's previous averages.[88]

In 1935, Congress established the Rural Electrification Administration to loan government money for the construction of power plants and transmission lines in the farming regions. Within a few years the REA had brought electricity to the homes of hundreds of thousands of rural folks.

From early in his public career Roosevelt had opposed the unlimited acquisition of State-owned water power sites by private utilities. In the process of his struggles with Republican-dominated legislatures, he helped educate a majority of the public to support the development of major water power resources by agencies of the government as the inalienable possession of the people; the marketing of power from such public developments, if possible, through private agencies under contracts; and the availability of public transmission and distribution as an alternative if the companies refused to make contracts favorable to the public.

Roosevelt, however, temporized in 1930 when he receded from his previously stated policy and accepted a Republican proposal for a survey commission. Although the commission's report, and subsequent legislative action, endorsed Roosevelt's basic water power proposals, the Governor was frustrated by a President who repudiated previous commitments on the St. Lawrence waterway issue.

Roosevelt, as he learned with the passing years, had to master the power trust, not try to compete with it or try to outwit it in the making of contracts. Carlisle's Niagara-Hudson would never be put in its place by the mere construction of a few State-owned power houses. Only a yardstick in the form of a government-owned, and government-controlled, power industry such as the TVA, supplemented by an effective independent regulatory commission, could stimulate private utilities to reduce their high rates, improve their services, and bring electric power to the rural areas. Ironically, Roosevelt offered only a cautious endorsement of Senator Norris's proposal for a Tennesse Valley Authority while Governor.

Despite his inability to secure his water power objectives during his governorship, because of Republican opposition in Albany and Washington, Roosevelt had opportunity to exhibit many of the traits of leadership with which the nation generally became familiar during his presidency. He developed an educated public opinion by his radio and public addresses, and then activated it, when necessary, by means of organized campaigns.

The water power struggle also indicated that private utilities, as a power formation, still had access to legislators in Albany, although the future prospects of such access looked dim, especially after the November, 1932, elections. Whenever the occasion demanded, however, Roosevelt used the utilities as a "whipping post." This tactic endeared him even more to the people, for the issue of high electric rates affected the pocketbook of the average voter in New York and elsewhere throughout the nation.

The Federal-State squabble which developed between New York and the national administration over the power issue, became immersed in the 1932 national elections. Although the St. Lawrence treaty was obviously a Federal responsibility, President Hoover should have consulted New York during the negotiations, for even he had admitted, years before, that the Empire State had special interests in the matter of developing the power potential along the St. Lawrence. Certainly, New York merited no less respect from Washington than that accorded the Province of Ontario by the Canadian government.

The State Power Authority served Roosevelt well, for this group of experts and independent minds was used by the Governor to develop his power program for New York, and later for the nation, as it endeavored to attain Roosevelt's original objectives—cheap and plentiful power for the people.

Finally, Roosevelt was not a Socialist. While business journals and Republican spokesmen for utilities condemned Roosevelt for his seeming "radicalism," Socialist spokesmen were equally as vociferous in their criticism of the Governor for adopting watered-down versions of his original proposals, and for trying to compete with or outwit the power trust instead of learning to master it. Whereas the Socialists, led by Norman Thomas, demanded outright government ownership of all the utilities, from power stations through distributing agencies, Roosevelt made clear his opposition to government ownership or operation of all utilities. He felt that as a general rule the development of utilities should remain, with certain exceptions, a function for private initiative and private capital.[89] In fact, Roosevelt's water power policy, enunciated during a critical period in our nation's history, did much to undermine the appeal of Socialists and contributed to their decline on the American political scene.

XI

"*A REASONABLE RETURN*"

THE REGULATION of businesses legally recognized as being affected with a public interest has had a long and stormy history in New York. One of the major problems confronting regulatory bodies has been the determination of the extent of coverage included in the term "affected with a public interest."

During the early part of the nineteenth century, states exercised supreme authority within their boundaries by means of special charters to local utilities. This was followed by cities granting local franchises, under the influence of the home rule movement. Not until the first decade of the twentieth century were state public service or railroad commissions created with varying degrees of authority.

During the twentieth century New York and Wisconsin led the states in establishing public service commissions with broad authority and regulatory power over local as well as interlocality operations. Prior to 1907, the New York legislature had sought to supervise utilities by stating annual maximum rates. This unscientific system, which insured logrolling and corruption, was corrected when, following the revelations of the insurance investigation, Governor Charles Evans Hughes fought valiantly to secure legislative approval for a public service commission to supervise the activities of utility companies.[1]

During the intervening years between 1907 and 1928 the commission came to consider itself more and more a court between the public on one side and the utility companies on the other. After he became Governor, Roosevelt was plagued with endless complaints concerning the partiality of the Public

Service Commission toward private utilities. Severest criticism was reserved for Chairman William A. Prendergast, who had been appointed in 1921 by Republican Governor Nathan L. Miller. Commissioner George R. Van Namee, more recently appointed by his close friend Governor Smith, was likewise condemned for a blatant pro-utility attitude. The New York *World* and the City Club of New York joined in accusing the majority of the five-man commission with subservience to utility holding corporations.[2]

The Public Service Commission was charged with permitting purchases and consolidations of power ,companies at prices greatly in excess of book value and allowing bankers to take excessive commissions. Especially disturbing was the threat of utility companies to include the inflated values of merged companies in their rate base, and the excessive figure of an 8 percent return permitted utilities by the commission.[3] Fearing eventual domination by the Mellon-Morgan combination, which was then in the process of acquiring control of the major power interests of the State, the Public Committee on Power, and the City Club, stressed the urgent need for a Moreland investigation of the P.S.C., insisted that the personnel of the commission be improved by future appointments, and suggested that a People's Counsel be appointed to put a little aggressiveness into the commission.[4]

The New York *World* devoted four editorial columns in one issue to the "Breakdown of the Public Service Commission," when it held that the commission had consistently delayed the determination of rate cases. It therefore requested a thorough investigation of holding companies and a revision of the antiquated Public Service Commission Law of 1907.[5]

In taking up the cry for an investigation of the Public Service Commission, the *World's* criticisms appeared contradictory when it recommended that ex-Governors Hughes, Miller, and Smith be appointed to a commission to investigate the entire subject of public utility regulation. Charles Evans Hughes was attorney for one of the worst utilities in New York City, the Interborough Rapid Transit Company. This subway and elevated line was contesting the principle of regulation in the seven-cent case before the Supreme Court. Nathan L. Miller, who had appointed utility-minded Prendergast to the P.S.C. in 1921, was attorney for the steel trust and for another of New York's subway systems. Alfred E. Smith had not improved the complement of the P.S.C. with his appointment of George R. Van Namee.

Commissioner Van Namee challenged the validity of the charges which had been leveled against the P.S.C. by the New York *World*, particularly that relating to delays in rate cases. He maintained that most difficulties in regulations could be laid at the doors of the United States Supreme Court, for the commission always had to keep in mind that it was a fact-finding body and had to be governed by the decisions of the courts. It was wrong and stupid for the commission to make decisions which could not be supported by law. If the Supreme Court would only define "fair value," then, according to Van Namee, it would help solve the problem of rate making.[6]

In his inaugural address in January, 1929, Roosevelt took cognizance of his conservative commission when he warned against too hasty asumption that mere regulation by public service commissions was, in itself, a sure guarantee of protection of the interest of the consumer.[7]

Following a conference in his office on February 13, 1929, with Morris L. Ernst, spokesman for the Public Committee on Power, the Governor urged the lawmakers to authorize a small, nonpartisan commission to make a thorough study of the whole subject of the public utility field. Contending that the existing public service commission laws needed revision to insure more efficient and just supervision and regulation of public service corporations, Roosevelt suggested that the study encompass the history of regulation in New York, the reasons for its breakdown in recent years, and the application of the principle of contract approval by a public body as distinguished from straight regulation.[8] In an attempt to circumvent his utility-minded P.S.C. and facilitate eventual establishment of a State power authority, Roosevelt was now advocating contractual agreements with utilities.

On April 16, 1929, the Governor reluctantly approved legislation creating a nine-man Commission on Revision of the Public Service Commission Laws, for it was to be composed of six Republican legislators and only three Roosevelt appointees.[9] While approving the bill, Roosevelt insisted that the theory of twenty years ago that the return to public service corporations should not exceed a fair profit on the money actually invested was constantly and flagrantly violated. Some method had to be found to return to the original principle.[10]

The Governor's remarks were shortly thereafter challenged by Commission Chairman Prendergast, who contended that the highest courts had decided that the return should be based on a valuation of property used and reckoned on "present-day values." He claimed that the theory of valuation and rate making held by the Governor was unsupported.[11]

Elaborating on this theme in subsequent months, Prendergast insisted that the all-important question in the utility controversy was that of valuation upon which the rate returns were computed. This valuation, he maintained, had to be based on the present value or reproduction cost of the plant, not on what it cost at the time the plant was originally built. The value of money changed and therefore the investment in money and in property had to be permitted to earn a return sufficient to keep the purchasing value of the interest at least constant.[12]

As Commissioner Van Namee had already pointed out, a major problem which confronted public service commissions was that Supreme Court decisions on the question of valuation had not been very helpful in determining a definitive measuring rod. The *Smyth* v. *Ames* decision of 1898, which was invoked in the majority of judicial decisions on rate cases, found that almost every possible index to value should or might be taken into account in the determination of the valuation of a utility for rate-making purposes. Throughout this period, the courts were unwilling to express any clear-cut preferences among the various indexes, urging instead that all the factors affecting value be taken into account, particularly evidences of historical cost on the one hand and reproduction cost on the other.

While refraining from a direct reply to Prendergast's attack, Roosevelt continued to think and speak along lines of comparatively new paths in the regulation of public utilities. He felt the whole question revolved around the issue whether a public utility had the right to make any profit that it could, and whether there was any real distinction between a public utility company and a purely private business. He lamented the fact that the situation had changed radically from that of twenty-five years before when

The basic theory of Charles Evans Hughes and others at that time was that people who invest in public utility common stock should do so with two definite thoughts in mind; first, and through public regulation, cut-throat competition will be eliminated and dividends on their stock will be reasonably assured up to a reasonable amount, i.e., about eight per cent; and secondly, that in return for this freedom from cut-throat competition they must not expect to get more than a reasonable return on the investment, and that savings in operating costs and ability to earn more than the eight per cent should rightfully come back to the consumers in the form of reduced rates.[13]

To see that their interests were well represented and to make sure that no "harmful legislation" was passed, the utilities maintained an effective lobby in Albany. This lobby included not only utility spokesmen who testified before legislative committees but also at least one very important legislator who was receiving retainers from private utilities.

During an investigation by the Federal Trade Commission in 1934, it was disclosed that State Senator Warren T. Thayer was in the direct pay of the Associated Gas and Electric Company of New York. It should be remembered that Senator Thayer was chairman of the Committee on Public Service of the Senate, through which all bills on utilities had to pass. In a damaging letter dated March 28, 1927, Senator Thayer informed the vice-president of the Associated Gas and Electric Company:

In keeping with your instructions of March 22, regarding my expense account . . . I herewith hand you bill as suggested.

The Legislature adjourned last Friday and I have now returned to Chateaugay and will be here most of the summer. If at any time I can be of further service to you, please do not hesitate to call upon me. I hope my work during the last session was satisfactory to your company; not so much for the new legislation enacted, but from the fact that many detrimental bills which were introduced we were able to kill in my committee.[14]

Since the chairmen of legislative committees in Albany had virtually dictatorial power, it is now quite understandable why Governors Smith, Roosevelt, and Lehman had such difficulty in getting proposed utility legislation out of the Committee on Public Service. In addition, Senator Thayer was an important member of the Commission on Revision of the Public Service Commission Laws appointed in 1929.

Confronting the group which was to investigate the Public Service Commission, therefore, was the issue of rate bases. But more significant, one might conjecture that this vital question would never receive the fair and balanced hearing it merited because of the direct lines of communication the utilities had with Republican legislators.[15]

Prior to public hearings, the three commissioners appointed by Roosevelt—Frank P. Walsh, James C. Bonbright, and David C. Adie—met with the Governor to discuss the problems which would face them as a minority, and to attempt to delineate the scope of the commission's work. The Chief Executive touched on a significant issue for the future when he contended that the special commission ought to examine the possibility of public competition with private utilities, at least as a yardstick.[16] The Governor also suggested that the three minority members agree on something strong about rural electrification in the final report, for the principal fight on the question of electrical power was on behalf of the household and farm consumer inasmuch as the rates to the very large consumers of industrial power were about as low as they could be.[17]

Unfortunately, the commission's Republican majority decreed from the start that the problem of St. Lawrence power was not within its jurisdiction. This meant that any attempt by Bonbright, Adie, and Walsh to go into the connection between the St. Lawrence River and public utility control was foredoomed to failure.[18]

By the end of 1929, the minority members of the Commission on Revision felt they had sufficient information to sustain the charges previously leveled against the Public Service Commission. The more dominant members of the P.S.C. were described as "utility-minded," particularly Prendergast and Van Namee. George R. Lunn was pictured as having his heart in the right place but being hopelessly ignorant on the technique of public service regulation and unable to occupy the role which Joseph B. Eastman played on the Interstate Commerce Commission. The counsel for the Public Service Commission, Charles G. Blakeslee, meant well, but the minority felt he was too willing to accept defeat in a lower court and was reluctant to resort to the courts for fear of defeat. Unfortunately, he did not pursue a vigorous policy required of a counsel for a public service commission.[19]

The testimony of Commissioners Prendergast, Van Namee, and William R. Pooley was to the general effect that the work of the Public Service Commission had been highly efficient and that the rates of public utility companies throughout the State were, on the whole, reasonable. The Commissioners used the phraseology "quasi-judicial" and "fact-finding" when describing the responsibilities of the P.S.C.,[20] perhaps as a cloak or mask on behalf of private power interests, rather than expose themselves for their real role as defenders of private utilities. "Judicial" was a more neutral term, although in actuality the P.S.C. had been an active arbiter in recent years on behalf of private utility interests.

According to Bonbright the evidence showed that the P.S.C. lacked the data as to the physical valuation of utilities which was necessary in order to determine whether a rate was reasonable in accordance with the principles set forth by the courts, and to which the commission said that it adhered. While discussing this question with Senator John Knight, Bonbright asked him why the members of the P.S.C. were not more frank in admitting that their work had been handicapped by lack of an adequate engineering and accounting staff. The Senate leader replied that Prendergast and the others hardly dared bring forth this excuse for they had previously made no strenuous efforts to secure adequate appropriations for their staff.[21] Here again, by neglecting to establish strong staff aids in the engineering and accounting divisions, the P.S.C. was, at the least, preventing enforcement of a policy which might prove harmful to utilities. The strategy of the utilities in New York State, planned or otherwise, could not have been improved upon, according to disclosures before the Commission on Revision. A majority of the P.S.C. was sympathetic to the utilities; the stress on the role of the P.S.C. as a "quasi-judicial" and "fact-finding" body, and the weakness of the working staff of the P.S.C., all but made for some sort of "subtle sabotage."

In its decision in *Smith* v. *Illinois Bell Telephone Co.*, early in 1930, the United States Supreme Court requested a lower tribunal to make a specific finding as to whether the fees charged to operating companies for services bore a reasonable relation to the cost to the holding company of furnishing these services. When Chairman Prendergast seemed inclined to delay putting the decision into effect in regard to new rates, Roosevelt wrote "a pretty stiff letter" to the commission demanding action. This clear-cut conflict led Prendergast to resign from the P.S.C. in February, 1930, despite the fact that his term had another year to run. Prendergast explained to the press that Roosevelt had certain ideas relative to the regulation of public utilities with which he was in complete disagreement. Among other things Prendergast did not feel that the Public Service Commission, with its "quasi-judicial" functions, should be influenced in the exercise of those functions by the Executive or any other State agency.[22]

Here was a new line of strategy—Prendergast was using the

claim of "independence" as an attack against any outside pressure from Roosevelt, and from other exponents of stricter utility regulations, on the P.S.C.

Roosevelt made a shrewd and strategic move when he designated Milo R. Maltbie, an independent in politics, as the successor to Prendergast. Maltbie, with a nation-wide reputation as a public utility expert, had been appointed by Governor Charles Evans Hughes to one of the two original Public Service Commissions, on which he had served from 1907 to 1915. At that time, Maltbie was regarded as having decidedly progressive tendencies and, although usually outvoted by his colleagues, was on the side of the public and against the arguments of the public utility corporations on most controversial matters that came before this commission.

Since 1915 Maltbie was frequently retained by New York City and other municipalities throughout the country as an expert on public utilities in rate cases. When appointed to the P.S.C. by Roosevelt, he stated that he agreed with the Governor that the commission should not be merely a quasi-judicial body but should take the initiative in protecting the interests of the public.[23]

A few days after Prendergast resigned, the Commission on Revision of the Public Service Commission Laws filed majority and minority reports. Both reports concluded that the virtual breakdown of public utility regulation in New York State was due primarily to the complicated and outworn valuation procedure. The Republican majority, however, was completely opposed to the minority contention that the Public Service Commission should not act merely as a quasi-judicial body but should vigorously pursue a program of securing the least expensive service for the State.[24]

Although denying that public utility regulation had been a complete failure, the majority admitted that by becoming too wrapped up in what had been termed its quasi-judicial function, the P.S.C. had neglected its primary duty to protect the public against invasion of its rights by public utility corporations.

Besides charging the P.S.C. with laxness in the enforcement of the law and pronounced leanings toward public utility corporations, the minority disagreed with the majority's recommendation with regard to the valuation of utility properties for rate making. The majority would have enabled the P.S.C. to arrive at agreements with corporations with regard to rate bases, such valuations, with changes to cover additional investments, to be embodied in contracts which would remain in force for periods not to exceed ten years. The majority also recommended an immediate valuation within three years of the properties of all public utility corporations in the State, with the exception of steam railroads and trolley roads.

After suggesting that the staff of the P.S.C. be increased, and additional funds appropriated, the majority contended that many of the shortcomings noted were due to the inadequacy of staff and added duties.[25]

The minority of Bonbright, Walsh, and Adie stated without equivocation that effective regulation of public utilities in New York had broken down and that the consumer had "been left to the exploitation of the monopolistic private companies which control the public services." Though the Public Service Commission Laws had been designed primarily to protect the interest of the public through good service and reasonable rates, these objectives had not been attained. The P.S.C. had accepted a judicial rather than an administrative point of view, which helped insure its failure. The minority placed the prime responsibility for ineffective regulation upon the prevailing legal system of rate making on the basis of valuation of property which was subject to review both as to law and as to facts by the Federal courts.

The minority charged further that the P.S.C. had sanctioned rates which they had subsequently been unable to justify economically. Fearing court reversals, the P.S.C. had virtually surrendered to utility companies the right to charge whatever rates the conditions of their business and the monopoly character of their enterprise could support. The utility companies had resorted to the reproduction cost theory to undermine regulation by means of overcapitalization. The minority further singled out the Niagara-Hudson Power Corporation, which controlled 54.6 percent of all electrical energy sold in the State, the Consolidated Gas Company, which controlled 34.8 percent of the sale of electricity, and the Associated Gas and Electric Company, which sold 7.6 percent of the electricity of the State, for breaking down effective regulation by circumventing and undermining the regulatory machinery in order to secure larger profits at the expense of consumers.[26]

Bonbright, Walsh, and Adie approached the crux of the matter when they insisted that truly effective regulation would be impossible as long as there prevailed in New York the rule that the so-called value of property, as determined by the courts, was the basis of rate control. So long as this rule persisted, no amount of administrative reform, no enlargement of the commission's staff, and no enhancement of its statutory powers could do more than palliate the existing evil.[27]

Walsh agreed with Bonbright that in order to overcome possible constitutional objections by the utilities to the application of any different standard which might be set forth by the legislature, the State ought to adopt a modified prudent investment rate base. To give companies an incentive to improve their efficiency, Bonbright suggested a flexibility in the rate of return whereby the more efficient companies would be permitted to earn more than the less efficient ones.[28]

In its report, the minority proposed that upon the adoption of a prudent investment rate base the companies be invited to contract with the State government for a specified length of time. Bonbright had previously informed Roosevelt that, fearing the reaction of the courts on this matter, he had discussed the problem with Judge Learned Hand. The renowned jurist had informed the Columbia professor that he was inclined to feel that if the contract were for a reasonable period of time rather than perpetual it would pass the scrutiny of the courts.[29]

Almost a decade earlier Supreme Court Justice Louis D.

Brandeis had argued that in order to give public utility capital its due constitutional protection the rate base had to be definite, stable, and readily ascertainable; that the percentage to be earned on the rate base had to be measured by the cost, or charge, of the capital employed in the enterprise. Despite the Supreme Court's preference for the reproduction cost theory, Brandeis insisted, in the Southwestern Bell Telephone Company decision in 1923:

Capital honestly and prudently invested must, under normal conditions, be taken as the controlling factor in fixing the basis for computing fair and reasonable rates. The adoption of the amount prudently invested as the rate base, and the amount of the capital charge as the measure of the rate of return would give definiteness to these two factors.[30]

Whereas in the *Smyth* v. *Ames* case in 1898, it had been difficult, if not impossible, to ascertain what it cost in money to establish the utility, or what income had been earned by it, or how the income had been expended, Brandeis contended that the situation had been greatly altered by 1923. These amounts were now readily ascertainable in respect to a rapidly increasing proportion of the utilities. It was, therefore, feasible to adopt, as the measure of a compensatory rate, the annual cost, or charge, of the capital prudently invested in the utility.[31]

In addition to the prudent investment principle, the minority of the Commission on Revision recommended appointment of a People's Counsel to act in behalf of the public; suggested greater publicity of P.S.C. activities; favored control by the commission over utility expenditures; and endorsed municipal operation of, or competition with, utilities, as a threat on one hand, and a remedy on the other, if utility regulation continued to falter.[32]

Throughout the hearings of the Commission on Revision, Felix Frankfurter had corresponded with Bonbright and Walsh. After reading the majority and minority reports, Frankfurter concluded that the minority had made the most important contribution to the solution of modern problems of utility regulation. The majority report, on the other hand, had shrunk from the conclusions of its own analysis and suffered from the "timidity of excessive conservatism and partisan alignment." Lamenting the viewpoint of the majority of the Supreme Court on utility valuation, Frankfurter maintained:

It is perfectly idle to find such tyrannous authority in the dicta of the Supreme Court in regard to valuation, or at least to have such fear of these dicta as is manifested by the [majority] report. One may be considerably confident that we have reached the peak of the Supreme Court's reactionary attitude and that the next ten years will find the court going over gradually into a more liberal attitude. Moreover, with the drop in commodity prices, the utilities themselves will want to slide over to the "prudent investment" basis. I have not a little basis for so thinking.[33]

Two weeks later, Frankfurter visited the Governor at the Executive Mansion to discuss the report of the Commission on Revision. It was the former's contention that in his message to the legislature the Governor should not support any form of a voluntary contract bill, for that would be futile. Worse still, the Governor would be throwing away the vital political issue of adequate utility regulation. Should Roosevelt insist on supporting the idea of voluntary contracts, the Republicans might then say with glee that they and the Governor were in harmony. Differences in detail, contended the law professor, could not be dramatized for the man in the street, and the alternative or additional proposal for a new scheme of valuation would be treated by the Republicans as so much eyewash.

Frankfurter did not believe that the constitutional difficulties raised by some close associates of the Governor were sufficiently valid or serious. If the Governor persisted in considering them as serious then it was his responsibility to attack them with the same kind of educational campaign he had instituted in the past. Frankfurter insisted that some of Roosevelt's associates took "the *words* of the Supreme Court all too seriously—much more seriously than the Supreme Court takes its own language." Frankfurter concluded by advising the Governor to avoid the slightest attack on, or criticism of, the Court. "You can take the offensive by saying that your policy is grounded in justice and in good economics, and let the other side prove that that which is good economics and socially just is unconstitutional."[34]

The Governor adhered to Frankfurter's advice by informing the people of the urgent need for a new system of determining the valuation of utilities, without involving Supreme Court decisions. In particular, Roosevelt urged adoption of the prudent investment principle, insisting it was economically and socially right to establish a new system of utility valuation since it would benefit the great mass of people. Roosevelt maintained that its adoption would halt the activities of utilities in watering their stock and then determining rates to consumers on the basis of overcapitalization of their organizations.[35]

The Governor insisted that there were two methods by which reasonable rates for electricity could be restored to the people. One was to grant municipalities the right to establish their own power plants and distribute the electricity to their community; the other was to give the Public Service Commission a definite rule for valuation and make it obligatory on the commission to fix rates in accordance with this definitely set standard and no other.[36]

In the legislature, meanwhile, thirty-four bills were introduced containing the majority and minority recommendations of the Commission on Revision. The four bills based on the minority report were rejected outright. After considerable modification twenty-six of the majority-proposed bills were adopted. A preponderance of these bills, however, were insignificant, dealing mainly with language and minor changes in the procedure of the Public Service Commission. One bill gave the commission authority over holding companies; another sought to extend rural electrification; a third proposed a People's Counsel in the office of the State's Attorney General; while a fourth would create a Bureau of Valuation and Research. With the exception of the proposal for a People's Counsel,[37] all were approved by the Governor.[38]

Two other majority measures which sought to regulate private water companies and the practice of sub-metering electric lights to tenants of large buildings were inexplicably lost in the rush of bills between the Senate and Assembly on the final night of the legislative session, moving Roosevelt to wish that he could someday learn the true story of where and how these bills got lost.

The power of the utility lobby was never more effectively displayed, at least publicly, than in the days following introduction of the valuation and contract bills. The majority's valuation bill would have authorized the P.S.C. to valuate all utility companies so as to enable the commission to determine a level of rates which would insure a fair profit to utilities.[39] The Governor had opposed this bill from the start because it failed to set up standards by which the valuation of the utilities could be determined. The contract bill provided for voluntary contracts between the P.S.C. and utilities, on valuation, for ten-year periods.

More than fifty officials and lawyers of all the important electric, gas, railway, and telephone companies in the State, representing several billion dollars of valuation, suddenly descended upon Republican leaders in Albany to voice general opposition to these proposals. Only five of the minor bills introduced by the commission's majority escaped the blistering attack of the utility spokesmen. William L. Ransom, counsel for the Consolidated Gas Company, voiced the sentiments of his fellow-lobbyists when he described the majority bills as dangerous, crippling, arbitrary, and destructive. He contended that the measure providing for an evaluation of all utility properties would be useless, while that authorizing ten-year voluntary contracts stabilizing valuations and rates would drive investors to other states.

The bill extending the control of the P.S.C. over holding companies would, from Ransom's viewpoint, invade private affairs and make public utilities a proscribed class. Even the aparently innocent proposal to create a bureau of valuation and research was condemned by Ransom as part of a program "furthering burdening the taxpayers along the lines which would make state regulation unfair, arbitrary and unmindful that investors in public utilities are not public enemies."

No words were sufficiently harsh for the minority proposals of Walsh, Adie and Bonbright. The general counsel for the Niagara-Hudson Power Corporation described them as "fanciful, professorial schemes," while his counterpart in the New York Telephone Company added that this was a government of law, not of pseudo economists.[40]

Shortly after utility spokesmen had made their positions quite clear, the Republican members of the Committee on Public Service, under the chairmanship of the agent of the Associated Gas and Electric Company, Senator Warren T. Thayer, fell over themselves in drastically amending the Republican majority proposals of the Commission on Revision. So well did the Republicans do their work that the proposer of the original valuation bill refused to vote for it in its final form. It was passed during the last hours of the legislative session in a form that was not even printed, so that few of the legislators who voted for it knew its contents. The valuation bill became meaningless, for it was made wholly discretionary and would have perpetuated a system of regulation which did not regulate. It received the Governor's veto with a slashing memorandum.[41]

The contract bill was similarly emasculated until the original proposer could, likewise, not support this final measure which provided merely for optional contracts between municipalities and the utilities which served them. This bill was not based on any recommendations from either the majority or minority members of the Commission on Revision. It was never considered by the legislative committees or by the members of the legislature and was, according to Roosevelt, a complete evasion of the issue.[42] The utility legislators had done their work well.

In complete disgust, Roosevelt summed up his reactions with the comment, ". . . the mountain labored and brought forth a mouse," and this in spite of the fact that nearly one hundred thousand dollars was spent trying to provide some really useful legislation.[43]

All was not in vain, however, for the minority report and the Governor's supporting statements to the press and over the radio did much to educate the public. Here again, Roosevelt took fullest advantage of the public debate raging over utility regulation and electric power.

Felix Frankfurter was very definite in his feelings that the Governor's vetoes were a superb set of documents in which he had crystallized the central difficulties in regard to regulation and the means for their correction. Frankfurter maintained that by his action on these bills, and through his speeches, Roosevelt had been "the most powerful single influence in bringing the serious public interest behind present tendencies in utility management before the public. And there is no better issue on which to stake a popular fight."[44]

Frankfurter was correct in his conclusions, for Roosevelt's tactics helped prepare the people of the State and nation to support decisive measures in the field of utility regulation after March, 1933. It was a struggle which brought Roosevelt unusual public support, for later that same year he was re-elected Governor by a record-breaking plurality. Despite the efforts of Mark Sullivan and others, water power and utility regulation were important campaign issues.

National interest in the conflict between New York's Governor and the State's public utilities blossomed with the passing months. Increasing numbers of Democrats turned hopeful eyes toward Albany with the approach of another presidential election. While conservative Democrats tended to shy away from Roosevelt, many liberal Republicans found themselves attracted by his activities and objectives.

In the State of Washington a referendum was to be held on the issue of municipally-owned hydroelectric power. Although municipalities could have municipal plants, the country districts not only were denied that right but could not purchase electricity from a municipally-owned plant. United States Senator

Clarence C. Dill of Washington appealed to Roosevelt to endorse a State-proposed bill authorizing people in country districts to hold special elections to form public utility districts.

In contrast to other occasions when he refused to commit himself on controversial issues which did not directly involve New York, Roosevelt did take a clear-cut stand.[45] He informed Senator Dill that he wholeheartedly endorsed efforts to grant rural areas the right to set up public utility districts to purchase electricity from municipally-owned power plants. At the same time, he informed the Senator that he was infuriated by the "loose talk that municipal, county, or district supplying of electricity is socialistic! If that is the case, it is also socialistic for a city to own and operate its own water supply, or its own sewage disposal. Some day the utility companies may cry 'wolf' just once too often."[46]

In Iowa, local Democrats attending the Butler County convention in June, 1930, concluded that the most pressing question of the hour was whether the "public utilities shall rule the people or whether the people shall rule the public utilities, and we commend the stand taken by Governor Franklin D. Roosevelt of New York against the rule and control of the public utility trusts."[47]

From a correspondent in New Market, Virginia, Roosevelt learned that Southerners, regardless of party, were watching every movement he made in the fight against the utilities and power interests.[48] In Sheffield, Alabama, the American Legion post appealed to Roosevelt to do all in his power to publicize and support the campaign for government development of a power plant at nearby Muscle Shoals.[49]

Not every letter sent the Governor was a laudatory message. There were those who, though very much in the minority, appealed to him to desist in his conflict with the utilities. After praising Coolidge's administration for proving that a "Hands Off Business Policy" would always succeed, one Arkansas citizen informed Roosevelt:

. . . I am one of the thousands of widows who have put money into stocks such as the Consolidated Gas Company of New York.

So, please when you attack that company, remember that you are attacking the interests of thousands of widows who must invest in bonds and stocks such as these.

Yours for a democratic party that is high principled, and not a mere opportunist party as it has been of late.[50]

While Governor Roosevelt continued his running conflict with the power interests, Chairman Maltbie instituted an era of stricter utility regulation by the P.S.C. The commission assumed an active part in every court case involving the interests of the public to insure that all arguments in favor of the orders of the P.S.C. were presented. Where necessary, the body was willing to present testimony. In contrast to previous years, the commission acted aggressively and forcefully to maintain its orders and not permit cases to go by default.

While granting the New York Telephone Company an increase in its business rates in May, 1930, the commission not only rejected the pleas of the company for increased home rates but put the charges of 900,000 home phone users at slightly under the previous schedule. The commission also ordered the telephone company to reduce its valuation by some $35,000,000, lowering at the same time its revenue by approximately $900,000. The company was censured for its business activities, particularly for permitting a rise in operating expenses.[51]

During the six-month period from April 1, to September 30, 1930, after Maltbie had become chairman, the number of informal complaints handled by the New York office of the Public Service Commission was 4,006, compared with 2,676 dealt with during a corresponding period in 1929—an increase of 50 percent.[52] During the nine years that Prendergast was chairman, from 1921 to 1929, the Public Service Commission initiated 244 formal cases upon its own motion—an average of twenty-seven per year. In 1930, the year Maltbie became chairman, 265 cases were initiated by the commission, and in 1931, 329 cases. Thus, in each of these last two years, the commission began upon its own motion more proceedings than had been initiated in all of the nine preceding years.[53]

Another indication of the commission's change of policy was its order, in 1931, directing some utilities in the New York City area to reduce their rates immediately, This ruling meant a total annual savings to consumers of some $5,500,000, of which $2,400,000 applied to residential consumers of the Brooklyn Edison Company, a very large proportion in view of the size of the company. The proceedings which brought about these reductions had been initiated by the commission.[54]

Roosevelt insisted that it was the duty of a regulatory commission not only to verify rates actually charged consumers but also to go to the root of the question of capitalization and valuation. Although he had no desire to prevent legitimate investment capital from earning a reasonable return, he felt that the government must insure that this reasonable return, and the actual value of the invested capital, did not automatically double and treble, as had happened in some instances.[55] He sought, through regulation and the threat of State development and distribution of electric power, to influence utilities to revise their business methods. Lower rates would then result from squeezing water out of stocks and from dissolving overcapitalization of utilities and holding companies.

Following Roosevelt's overwhelming victory in the 1930 elections, the Chicago *Journal of Commerce* had reminded its readers that the Governor's ideas on power control were moderate and had aroused little opposition except among reactionaries. This business journal insisted that Roosevelt had gone only so far as to demand state development, though not state operation, of water power, and that he might not fulfill the expectation of radicals in and out of Congress who counted on him to support legislation designed to promote public control of utilities. Utility control in many states, concluded this editorial, was still relatively ineffective.[56] Even the Governor felt obliged to assure one Wall Street business leader that there was nothing radical or dangerous in his attitude and that his stand was understood and backed by a large number of bankers and others in New York who did not want to see the utility question thrown into the field of "socialistic politics."[57]

In his annual message to the 1931 legislature, the Governor again urged adoption of the minority recommendations of the Commission on Revision of the Public Service Commission Laws. When the lawmakers had taken no action by the eve of adjournment, Roosevelt reminded the legislators that housewives were looking to Albany for relief from the high rates of electricity. Exorbitant electric charges deprived them of the use of newly developed products of scientific research which would release the average homemaker from many household drudgeries.[58] Except for placing bus lines and private water companies under the supervision of the P.S.C., Senator Thayer and the Republican-dominated legislature rejected not only the strong minority but the very weak majority recommendations of the Commission on Revision. Despite new problems arising from developing mergers, holding companies, and other devices initiated by utility companies, Republican leaders refused to give the P.S.C. strong teeth with which to regulate these gigantic combines.

Thomas F. Woodlock, columnist for the *Wall Street Journal*, voiced the sentiment of utility leaders when he maintained that, in fostering his prudent investment theory, Roosevelt was preaching a doctrine condemned by the Supreme Court and by considerations of elementary justice. He held the Governor's viewpoint on prudent investment profoundly discouraging. Being a member of the bar, the Governor should have known what the Supreme Court meant when it held that it was the property devoted to the public service, and not the original cost thereof, of which the owners might not be deprived. "He is a fair-minded man who knows that the wage of labor and management must go up when prices go up. He knows that 'return' is but the wage of capital and that if that wage does not go up when prices go up the value of that capital is decreased." Woodlock contended further that the Supreme Court had already ruled that imposition of the prudent investment concept upon the property of public utilities, after a tremendous rise in prices, was plain confiscation.[59]

A critical admirer of Woodlock immediately took issue with the columnist. Feeling that Woodlock had been somewhat unfair to the Governor, the reader maintained that Roosevelt was very much conversant with the rulings of the Supreme Court on this issue, but that his support of prudent investment was not based exclusively on legalistic reasoning. He was appealing to the utilities as a hardheaded business proposition to be content with a fair return on their prudent monetary investment, or else put up with governmentally operated competition.

An excellent portrayal of Roosevelt's concept of the economic state was presented by this same correspondent who maintained that the Governor had not

. . . indicated his disbelief in capitalistic society or private initiative. On the contrary, he would have capital train itself into better condition by reducing unnecessary profits and improving its relations with the public. His position on public utilities is but a phase of this general viewpoint. Personally, I do not believe that Governor Roosevelt is a red. I do not believe he is even a blushing pink. I believe he has far more regard for capitalistic society than those who would stand idly by and see it commit suicide. I believe that the capitalistic ship of state would be far better in the hands of a skipper such as Roosevelt, who can really see shoals and bars, and fears not to discipline his own crew than under the leadership of certain political navigators who persist in taking their bearings through rose colored binoculars.[60]

Franklin D. Roosevelt did not advocate disobedience to the mandates of the Supreme Court. He did recognize, however, the inability of the Court, and of independent regulatory commissions on the whole, to prevent greedy utilities from committing financial suicide. Throughout his governorship, Roosevelt persisted in his disagreement with utility spokesmen who contended that the Supreme Court was the final tribunal in the administration of commercial affairs. Public opinion, with the power of purchase, which was more drastic than the enforcement powers of the bar, was a greater court than the supreme judiciary in Washington.

Roosevelt knew full well that just so long as the cost of labor and materials went up, all utility companies would favor the reproduction cost theory, but as soon as it looked as if the cost of labor and material would go down over a long period of years, they would abandon the reproduction cost investment theory. In other words, industry didn't care which theory was right; they would be for whichever theory gave them the largest capital increase.[61] The year Roosevelt took office as President of the United States, the Supreme Court veered in the direction of accepting the prudent investment theory enunciated earlier by Justice Brandeis.[62] By 1937, after eight years of decreasing prices, utility spokesmen were also publicly supporting the prudent investment theory.[63]

During his last year as Governor of the Empire State, Roosevelt pleaded in vain for enactment of legislation rejected previously by Republican lawmakers. The legislators ignored his request for a statute authorizing municipalities of the State to form public utility districts, with the consent of the voters, for the purpose of generating, distributing, and selling electricity.[64] A few days before the conclusion of the legislative session the Governor reminded the lawmakers that despite the change in the purchasing price of the dollar in the third year of the great depression, there was no voluntary State-wide or nation-wide effort by utility companies to cut their rates proportionately to the cuts being made in other commodities. The best way to bring about reduction in rates, according to Roosevelt, was to give the Public Service Commission more adequate powers.[65] Unfortunately, the vision of the dominating chairman of the Senate Committee on Public Service could only encompass the wishes of the utilities, and therefore no important legislation was adopted which might hinder Niagara-Hudson or Associated Gas and Electric.

Aware that much of the electricity generated in the United States crossed state borders,[66] that regulation by commissions in New York and other states had serious shortcomings because of the influence of private utilities, and educated by Republicans to a realization that much-needed legislation in the regulation of public utilities would not be easily achieved on the state level, Roosevelt concluded by 1932 that electrical development and distribution was primarily a national problem.[67]

Stricter utility regulation became a crucial campaign issue during the 1932 presidential race. In Portland, Oregon, Roosevelt reminded his listeners that as Governor of New York he had consistently maintained that the Public Service Commission, as the agent of the legislature, had and was to continue to have a definitely delegated authority and duty to act as the agent of the public themselves; that it was not a mere arbitrator between the people and the public utilities but was created for the purpose of seeing that the public utilities did two things: first, give adequate service, and second, charge reasonable rates.[68]

Two years after Roosevelt took office as President, Congress adopted the Public Utility Act which gave the Federal Power Commission broad authority over electrical utilities engaged in wholesale transactions in interstate commerce. It authorized the Securities and Exchange Commission to prescribe a uniform system of accounts and to approve plans for reorganization for all transfers of ownership and for the financial policies of holding companies subject to its jurisdiction.

Before assuming office as Governor in January, 1929, Roosevelt was aware that New York's Public Service Commission was neither an aggressive regulatory body nor independent of utility influence. In his first inaugural address he exhibited this awareness when he indicated that mere regulation was not, in itself, certain guarantee of the protection of consumers. With this background Roosevelt recommended, and the lawmakers provided for, a study of the breakdown of utility regulation.

While the Commission on Revision was undertaking its survey, Roosevelt publicized his belief that utilities ought to get a fair return only on money actually invested, which was immediately challenged by P.S.C. Chairman Prendergast who maintained that valuation should be based on the present value or reproduction cost of the utility plant.

Shortly after Prendergast resigned in 1930, the Commission on Revision concluded that the Public Service Commission had not fulfilled its job. The Republican majority contended that it had become too wrapped up in its quasi-judicial functions and suggested, as a solution, contracts between the P.S.C. and utilities on rate bases, for ten-year periods. The minority's basic solution was adoption of the prudent investment principle, the percentage to be earned on the rate base to be measured by the annual cost, or charge, of the capital employed with the enterprise.

Following vigorous condemnation by their friends in the utility lobby, the Republican leadership drastically revised their originally weak proposals to make them meaningless.

Roosevelt may have lost this particular battle with the utilities and with a Republican-dominated legislature, but he went on to all but win the war after becoming President. The utilities afforded Roosevelt, while Governor and then as President, an excellent platform on which to mold and then activate public opinion in support of his proposals. Roosevelt took fullest advantage of this opportunity.

Before Roosevelt left the governorship, the Public Service Commission veered in the direction of acting as a truly independent regulatory body under the leadership of Milo R. Maltbie.

The story of Roosevelt and utility regulation, then, revolves around his attempt to cope with increasingly elaborate and protracted procedures devised by utility spokesmen to delay or circumvent the efforts of regulatory bodies. With Niagara-Hudson having reached a status in New York substantially free from competition, it sought, by the establishment of elaborate techniques, to secure the arbitrary control of cost and rates.

The "independence" of state regulatory agencies, according to one authority, "is more myth than reality."[69] The danger lay in lulling the people into a false confidence in independent regulatory commissions and in diverting their attention from the influence of private utilities on these commissions. Until such a time as utility commissions include more effective representation of the average consumer, and as long as the general public remains ignorant of the forces at work on the utility commissions and how to cope with them, these commissions will not be truly independent nor regulatory.

XII

"HONEST GRAFT"

AFTER WEEKS of maneuvering among Republican leaders, the State legislature finally ratified the Hofstadter-Story concurrent resolution in March, 1931. Adopted over the violent opposition of Democrats, this resolution provided for a joint legislative inquiry into the administration and conduct of the various departments of the government of New York City and of State and local courts within its geographical area. It was understood beforehand that Samuel Seabury would be the counsel for this committee, which was under the chairmanship of Republican Samuel H. Hofstadter of New York City.[1]

The busiest man in New York appeared to be Seabury, the independent Democrat. This tireless and fearless six-footer was in the process of concluding his damaging investigation into the Tammany-dominated Magistrates' Courts, was looking into charges leveled by the City Club of New York against elderly District Attorney Crain of New York County, and was now expected to initiate and carry through a thoroughgoing inquiry into alleged graft and corruption in the governmental structure of New York City.

This marked the beginning of the end for wise-cracking Jimmy Walker as public officeholder. It also signaled the advent of a serious cleavage between Tammany Hall and Governor Roosevelt which would spill over onto the floor of the Democratic national convention in Chicago the following year.

James J. Walker's story was not atypical of Tammany officeholders. He had come to the mayoralty of New York City through steady promotion at the hands of Tammany colleagues.

His father had been a Tammany alderman, assemblyman, and leader of the old Ninth Ward. At Albany, where he served for fifteen years in the legislature, Walker revealed two qualities necessary for political success. He always voted with the machine and he made a host of warm personal friends. He dressed boldly, drank gaily, and fought for the freedom of sports. His party chose him as leader in the Senate, from which post Tammany promoted him to City Hall, with the potent help of Alfred E. Smith.

After the stupidities of Mayor John F. Hylan's administration, the city's electorate and Tammany Hall gave a sigh of relief when a personable and plausible mayor moved into City Hall. In contrast to Hylan, who had neither intelligence nor charm, New York now had a colorful figure and Tammany had a man who would obey orders.

Walker threw all caution to the winds in appointing Tammany district leaders and in rewarding his personal friends. In his administration eighty-five district leaders — the real political rulers of New York—sat in comfortable chairs with their feet on large desks and drew an average salary of $7,300 a year. The mayor, meanwhile, directed subservient lawmakers to boost his own salary to $40,000.

Despite its limitations, the magistrates' investigation under Seabury had been lively and productive. By the time it was concluded two magistrates had been removed, three had resigned under fire, a half dozen police officers were convicted in connection with extortion practices of the vice squad, and the latter agency itself was completely revamped.[2]

Since the beginning of 1931, public pressure for a thorough housecleaning of the city's political stables had reached a crescendo. The City Club of New York filed specific charges with Roosevelt demanding the removal of bumbling District Attorney Thomas T. C. Crain of New York County.[3] After being appointed by the Governor to look into these ouster charges,[4] Seabury eventually sustained four of the original twenty-seven counts against Crain when he disclosed that the

District Attorney had been unable to halt any of the major rackets plaguing New York's shopkeepers, union members, and the body politic. However, he held that Crain's removal from office was not legally justified.[5]

On March 17, 1931, formal charges requesting the removal of Walker as mayor were forwarded to the Governor by two civic leaders, Reverend John Haynes Holmes and Rabbi Stephen S. Wise, for the City Affairs Committee. These courageous clergymen charged the mayor with failing to administer the City government properly in the interests of the people; ignoring conditions of inefficiency and corruption; appointing unworthy men to public office; and conducting the office of mayor in such an incompetent, inefficient, and futile manner that the local machinery of government had failed to function properly and the administration of the City had been brought into disrepute.[6]

In reply to the charges, Walker submitted a rambling 15,000 word rebuttal, not given under oath, and marked by superficiality, important omissions, and reckless and false charges against Holmes and Wise.[7] Refusing to subject the evidence to cross-examination, or to appoint a commissioner to take evidence as he had done in the Crain case, Roosevelt informed the spokesmen for the City Affairs Committee that he did not find sufficient justification in their charges for removal or for further investigation.[8]

Earlier that same year, however, Roosevelt had been sufficiently disturbed by Walker to send William Randolph Hearst a number of messages in which he had expressed the feeling that "our little Mayor can save much trouble in the future by getting on the job, cleaning his own house and stopping wisecracks. If he does not do all this he can have only himself to blame if he gets into trouble."[9]

Tammany's acid reactions to Roosevelt, and the obstructionist tactics of its spokesmen at the Hofstadter Committee hearings, underscored that organization's mental impoverishment. Tammany's opposition to the Governor also helped sway national

Democratic sentiment toward Roosevelt with the approach of the presidential nominating convention.

Stunned by the legislative decision for an exhaustive inquiry, particularly under Seabury,[10] Tammany counterattacked blindly and emotionally. The Housing Commissioner, for example, suddenly ordered the Tenement House Bureau to transfer fifty-four of its employees.[11] In one of the biggest shakeups in police history, the Police Commissioner replaced his entire vice squad and barred the use of informers.[12] Was Tammany really trying to clean house?

Failing to halt the investigation by legal maneuvers within the Hofstadter Committee, Democratic members denounced the proposed hearings as a "Spanish Inquisition,"[13] and eventually accused Seabury of a political plot with Republican leaders W. Kingsland Macy and George Z. Medalie.[14]

With an appropriation of one-half million dollars, and the widest powers accorded any similar legislative body in recent history, the inquiry got under way in June, 1931, with private hearings by Seabury's youthful staff. While plowing through checkbooks, bank accounts, payrolls, ledgers, and other financial records dealing with Tammany officeholders, these young attorneys secured amazing information which could not be refuted on the witness stand. Testimony taken publicly and privately during the next fourteen months totaled some 69,000 pages.

Taking their cue from its Democratic members when called to testify before the Hofstadter Committee, Tammany officeholders and ward-heelers showed that they too could resort to obstructionist tactics as they refused to answer questions or to waive immunity.[15] When veterinarian William F. Doyle, who had great influence with the Appeals Board of New York City, was fined for being in contempt of the Hofstadter Committee, Tammany Boss Curry secured a stay of sentence after secretly phoning a Tammany judge who was vacationing in nothern New York. In the process of admitting having made the call, Boss Curry denounced the Hofstadter investigation as a "crucifixion" of Tammany.[16] On appeal of the Doyle case to the

Court of Appeals, Chief Judge Benjamin Cardozo, speaking for the majority, ruled that the investigating committee had no power to give witnesses amnesty. In the opinion of the learned Chief Judge, however, he suggested that the remedy for this situation was a statute authorizing the joint legislative committee to grant such immunity. On the request of Seabury and the Hofstadter Committee, Governor Roosevelt convened a special session of the legislature toward the end of August, 1931, and over the violent opposition of Tammany, approved legislation developed by Seabury which empowered the joint legislative committee, in proper cases, to grant immunity to witnesses.[17] During the weeks and months which followed, the committee counsel publicized the real cancerous growth of graft and corruption in New York City.

Big-time gamblers had been operating freely and safely in a number of major Tammany clubhouses, including that of Sheriff Thomas M. Farley of New York County.[18] When former Tammany Boss George Olvany was questioned concerning his splitting of fees for cases before the Appeals Board, he refused to reply, pleading that these transactions had been confidential.[19] It was subsequently disclosed that Olvany's income, while Tammany leader, had been some $2,000,000.[20] Even Republican candidates for political office in New York City were involved with Tammany in its activities before the Appeals Board.[21]

Thomas M. Farley, Sheriff of New York County, was found to have made bank deposits of $360,000 in a seven-year period during which his salary and the other legitimate income totaled $90,000. When asked to explain the source of the remaining $270,000, the Sheriff told of a "wonderful tin box" that he kept at home and drew on occasionally to fatten his bank account.[22] At the request of Seabury, and following hearings in the chambers of the State Executive, Farley was removed from office by Roosevelt because he could not satisfactorily explain "the sources of a large portion of the sums of money involved," and because he had not complied "with the spirit or the letter of the rule which should guide public officers."[23]

First Deputy City Clerk James J. McCormick, who presided over wedding ceremonies in the marriage clerk's office, accumulated over a quarter of a million dollars during a period of six years when his annual salary was only $8,500. McCormick had made it quite clear to thousands of prospective grooms that he expected to be handed some gift money. He subsequently found himself in difficulty with the Federal government for not having reported this income.[24]

Thus far, sophisticated, night-clubbing Jimmy Walker had been embarrassed to the extent that some of his subordinates had been "caught with the goods." Seabury and his aggressive staff, however, prepared to deal with the incompetency, inefficiency, and futility of the mayor himself.

Until Jimmy Walker took the stand in his own defense, millions of New Yorkers refused to believe that he was personally guilty of any wrongdoing. Although Seabury had never produced an indictable offense committed by the mayor, the months of investigation had nevertheless revealed gross improprieties on the part of dapper Jimmy. There was the Equitable Bus Company which had sought a monopoly of the City's bus transportation, with Walker's ardent support, despite the fact that it had no financing, no experience, or any other qualification.[25] If Walker had had his way the city would have lost millions of dollars as windfall profits to his friends and their associates.

Then there were "beneficences" from a number of interested friends and businessmen. Paul Block, the newspaper publisher, split his profits from certain stock transactions with the mayor, the latter receiving $246,692 despite the fact that he had not invested a penny. J. A. Sisto, who represented a taxicab holding company which had a financial interest in limiting the number of taxicabs on the streets of New York, gave the mayor $26,535 in various bonds.[26]

The mayor had also neglected his official duty when he permitted his corporation counsel to designate doctors in city compensation cases who split tens of thousands of dollars in fees with the mayor's brother, also a doctor.[27]

The most damaging evidence in the case revolved around the mysterious disappearance of Russell T. Sherwood and his refusal to return to New York to appear before the Hofstadter Committee. Sherwood, a $60 a week bookkeeper in Walker's old law firm, had become informal financial agent for the mayor. During Walker's first year in office, Sherwood's personal bank account rose suddenly to $98,000. Five years later, when Seabury staff members examined his books, Sherwood, or someone else, had deposited to Sherwood's account $961,000, of which over $700,000 had been in cash. Out of this account Sherwood paid many of the mayor's personal and family bills.[28]

This was the background when Jimmy Walker was called to the stand on May 25, 1932, in a courtroom which normally seated 300 but into which 700 had jammed. Despite distractions from hot, partisan crowds which cheered and hissed, and obstructionist tactics by Senator McNaboe and other Democratic committee members, Seabury was able to present damaging evidence against the mayor during two days of endless questioning. Although he fought back with quips and angry retorts and streams of political oratory, Walker could not undo the harm done him by cold facts and figures offered in testimony by Seabury from official reports of the Transportation Board and the City's Board of Estimate.

Walker admitted receiving bonds from Sisto but denied that he had worked for a decrease in the number of cabs. He admitted getting a letter of credit from the Equitable agent, J. Allan Smith, but said that it was merely an accommodation and that the money had been supplied by himself and his friends. Walker said he just didn't know why this same Smith later made good on a $3,000 overdraft by the mayor. He denied all responsibility for Sherwood's disappearance and any knowledge of the funds Sherwood had accumulated.[29]

Concluding his second day of testimony, Walker derided the charges which had been generally leveled against him by committee disclosures, rebuked the Hofstadter inquiry as destructive, scoffed at any secret fund, and expressed the hope that the committee could "prove mine"—the $263,838 withdrawal from Sherwood's account. Walker blamed the archaic charter for the City's ills and urged its complete overhauling. He also asserted that the inquiry had broken the morale of the administration and had helped to undermine City securities.[30]

When Walker stepped down from the witness stand after two days of ordeal at the hands of the white-haired Seabury, the New York *Post* commented that "from any standpoint of real intelligence he scored a failure so deep as to make one's flesh creep."[31]

Tammany was pleased by Walker's showing, feeling that the dapper mayor had come off best with Seabury. Unfortunately for Jimmy, his thrusts, under a judicial scanning of the record, looked more like evasions.

Seabury's questioning of Walker and the mayor's replies were topics for heated discussion throughout the nation. This was a presidential year and all eyes were turned on Albany. Would Roosevelt, who was in the front race for the Democratic presidential nomination, take a forthright stand on the Seabury disclosures, or would he seek to straddle the issue?

Within a few days after being rebuked by Roosevelt for his delay in taking a definite stand on the mayor's testimony, Seabury put the complete Walker data in the hands of the Governor.[32] The committee counsel termed the mayor "unfit" and charged him with acting on improper and illegal considerations. Malfeasance was alleged. Seabury also cited the Equitable bus deal, the mayor's link to Sherwood, and beneficences received from Block and Sisto as being contrary to the dignity of the office.[33] The Governor accepted Seabury's message, which accompanied the eight volumes of committee records, as a formal letter of complaint against Walker.

Following a request from the Governor to answer the Seabury allegations, Walker delayed his reply until after the national Democratic convention had selected Roosevelt as its presidential nominee. In a lengthy brief the mayor charged that the Seabury investigation was the result of a political plot against him and complained that he was the victim of a campaign of calumny to aid the faltering Hoover regime. He defended the Equitable deal; declared that the men who had given him cash had received no favors; and denied that Sherwood had been his agent.[34]

In rebuttal, Seabury held that the mayor's defense was based on evasion and falsification, and declared that the mayor was not worthy of belief. The committee counsel deplored the sorry sight of legal maneuvering, for Walker's honor as mayor was impugned. He again stressed the Sherwood case and concluded that the Equitable bus deal alone justified the mayor's removal.[35]

Faced with the overwhelming task of initiating a presidential campaign, with the election only three months off, Roosevelt broke the calm of an August weekend when he designated James J. Walker as the first mayor of New York City to receive a public hearing by a Governor concerning his fitness to continue in office.[36]

Almost four years to the day he had nominated Roosevelt for Governor, Walker was fighting for his political life in the same cherry-paneled executive chamber where former Sheriff Farley had been interrogated only a few months previously. It was a charged atmosphere, for at stake was not only Walker's political future but, to an extent, the 1932 presidential race. Any indication of weakness or temerity on the part of the Governor would lose him tens of thousands of anti-Tammany votes throughout the nation. On the other hand, Walker's removal might well result in a vindictive campaign by Tammany against their national candidate—not an unfamiliar role for New York City's Democracy.

The Governor's examination of Walker was judicious and searching. He required the mayor to answer for all his acts during his first, as well as his second, term of office.[37] Finding himself on the defensive before the Governor's sharp and persistent inquiries, Walker frequently turned to his counsel, John Curtin, in an effort to prod him on into clashes with the sharp-witted

Roosevelt. When Walker sought to shield his private financial deals with Sherwood from the bright glare of public record, the unruffled Governor warned him to answer the questions, citing the Farley case as an example.[38] When Walker's counsel requested a dismissal of the charges against the mayor, the Governor refused, with the retort that it would take more than the mayor's own denials of wrongdoing to clear him of the "inference and innuendo" in counsel Seabury's fifteen conclusions that the mayor was unfit to remain in office.[39]

Fearing the worst after days of piercing interrogation by Roosevelt, Walker's counsel resorted to the courts in an attempt to stay the Governor's hearings on the basis that the Chief Executive had no constitutional right to remove the mayor.[40]

Three days after State Supreme Court Justice Ellis J. Staley upheld the Governor's power of removal,[41] James J. Walker threw the biggest bombshell into the political cauldron when he suddenly announced his resignation as mayor to an astonished public. Without justification, Walker maintained that he had been forced to resign because the trial before the Governor had become a travesty on justice and that the verdict would have been based on political expediency. The dapper Tammany leader promised to seek public vindication by running for mayor at the special election, at which time he would appeal to the fair judgment of the people.[42]

Tammany, of course, was bitter. Democratic leaders in four of the five counties of New York City threatened to avenge Walker by opposing Lehman's nomination for Governor at the State convention, and by knifing Roosevelt at the polls in November. Although terribly frustrated because he had been denied the presidential nomination, Al Smith made it clear that he would not support Walker in the special election nor would he permit the knifing of Lehman at the State convention. Newspaper publisher Hearst, who had been close to Walker in recent years, also warned the former mayor that his avowed candidacy would be viewed as a hostile move against the party's presidential candidate.[43]

Tammany did not knife Roosevelt at the polls but came close to denying Lehman the gubernatorial nomination.[44] They were successful, however, in handing Roosevelt a personal affront, which he never forgot nor forgave, when they denied youthful Samuel I. Rosenman the nomination to fill out the unexpired balance of a Supreme Court vacancy to which Roosevelt had appointed him earlier that year. Instead, Tammany leaders dictated the choice of Republican Senator Hofstadter for the post. The ways of Tammany have always been many and curious.

Following Roosevelt's ascendancy to the governorship of the Empire State in 1929, the clamor for a thorough investigation of New York City affairs, and for Walker's removal, rose to a higher and higher pitch. Roosevelt, however, refused to resort to a city-wide inquiry. His usual reply to such requests was that "where the local inquisitorial machine is being properly used for investigating purposes," it was neither "the duty nor the right of the Governor to interfere."[45]

Roosevelt neglected to acknowledge publicly that the wholesale corruption which characterized New York City under Mayor Walker could not have taken place if the "local inquisitorial machinery" had been "properly used for investigating purposes" to ferret out crime wherever it might be found. The local inquisitorial machinery in New York City was manned by assistants, clerks, and investigators who were part of the Tammany machine, whose misdeeds they were supposed to investigate. The personnel of the local prosecuting offices owed their jobs to Tammany. Was it therefore reasonable to suppose that such personnel would bite the hand that fed it?

Friendly local prosecuting officers had many ways of serving the local political machine and its henchmen, without always appearing to refuse or to fail to carry out the duty imposed upon them by law. Where public appearance absolutely required, they went through the motions of a prosecution. The matter affecting a favored son was submitted to a grand jury but no indictment was found. Or, if an indictment became necessary to appease popular clamor, a young and comparatively inexperienced assistant was selected to try the case. With rare exception he was pitted against a veteran criminal lawyer and the result was usually what it was intended to be—an acquittal.

As a result of this situation, cynicism had become rampant, and the average man felt that anyone could commit a crime and get away with it as long as he stood well in politics. If there ever was justification for invoking the powers vested by law in the Governor to investigate official crime with a view to eliminating its existence, the situation in New York City justified it as early as 1929.

There were times when it appeared that Roosevelt's conscience bothered him, particularly when civic leaders Holmes and Wise persisted in their demands for additional removals of Tammany officeholders by the Governor. On one such occasion Roosevelt made a grave political error when he unjustifiably denounced these two fighting clergymen as publicity seekers and insisted that if they "would serve their God as they seek to serve themselves, the people of the City of New York would be the gainers."[46]

It is true that Roosevelt did not forcefully interfere with Tammany, particularly with reference to Mayor Walker, until the disclosures by Seabury. However, the Governor was not completely inactive in this matter. The record shows that when the District Attorney of New York County failed to obtain an indictment in the Ewald case, Roosevelt ordered a special grand jury and superseded the district attorney with the State's Attorney General. When other disclosures involving magistrates and the adminstration of the Magistrates' Courts were brought to his attention, he called upon the Appellate Division to conduct a thorough investigation, which followed under the supervision of Seabury and Isador Kresel. When the City Club filed charges against District Attorney Crain, the Governor designated Seabury to investigate the validity of the claims. And, finally the Governor had consistently informed Republican legislative leaders that any thorough investigation of New York City should be undertaken by them and that he would approve an appropriation for such an investigation if adopted by the legislature.

When confronted by charges against Sheriff Farley, the Governor saw fit to remove him from office. During the hearings for Mayor Walker the Governor maintained a judicious, yet a vigorous search for the facts and placed Walker in a position where he had no recourse but to resign or, in all likelihood, be removed from office by the Governor.

Throughout his four years in Albany, however, Roosevelt made no attempt to initiate a crusade against Tammany. In this instance he followed public opinion instead of leading and educating it. Until 1932 he designated Tammany nominees to the judiciary in New York City. Even after his removal of Sheriff Farley, Roosevelt clearly indicated that patronage appointments would continue to be cleared through Tammany Hall when he ignored the recommendations of civic organizations and appointed, instead, John E. Sheehy as the new Sheriff of New York County. Sheehy, a close friend of Boss Curry, had recently been elected Tammany leader of the 15th Assembly District—the silk stocking district of Manhattan.[47]

Not until Tammany had retaliated against Walker's removal by denying Rosenman the judicial designation did Roosevelt, after his elevation to the presidency, attempt to subdue the Tammany Tiger by isolating it from patronage and by supporting opposition candidates for the mayoralty, including Joseph V. McKee and Fiorello H. La Guardia.

XIII

IN RETROSPECT

Despite the contentions of many historians, and of the great mass of America's citizenry, the seeds of the New Deal were first planted by a graduate of Tammany Hall and the Fulton fish market, the four-time Governor, Alfred E. Smith. It blossomed forth, however, under the affirmative and confident guidance of a Harvard product, a pragmatist who had devoted his political career to becoming President of the United States.

By his pragmatic tendencies, his willingness to experiment in times of crisis, and his belief that a nation must be prepared for changes in order to preserve and extend its finest features, Roosevelt clearly indicated his role as a liberal on the American political scene.

Viewing, in retrospect, the Smith adminstrations which preceded Roosevelt in Albany, one can readily see the foundations for Roosevelt's four years as Governor. In housing, education, budgeting, welfare legislation, parks, and water power, Roosevelt carried on the work initiated by the Happy Warrior.

Faced with the task of preserving and extending the gains of the Smith administrations, Roosevelt responded to the challenges of recalcitrant, obstructionist Republican majorites in the legislature by appealing directly to the citizenry for their support. Roosevelt's fireside chats, for example, were familiar to New Yorkers long before March 4, 1933.

The critical depression which began during Roosevelt's first year as Governor saw him respond with an open-minded, pragmatic approach to the many developing problems. This trait was particularly evident in the field of economics. Although

New Hampshire's John G. Winant was also sponsoring constructive, remedial legislation to ease the effects of the depression, Roosevelt's activities were in the forefront, for he was the Chief Executive of the Empire State and a leading aspirant for the Democratic presidential nomination. In addition, people were yearning for an inspiring and confident personality to replace the defaulting, bumbling leadership of the Hoover administration.

It is interesting to recall that Franklin D. Roosevelt was reared in an economic stratum which knew little of the struggles and heartaches of laboring men and women. He first acquired some knowledge of labor issues while State Senator and then as Assistant Secretary of the Navy. During his years of convalescence he gained considerable understanding of the American labor movement from many who had dedicated their lives to the nation's workers.

When drafted by the Democratic party in 1928, Roosevelt was pro-labor in the American sense of the term. On the European scene, however, he would have been viewed as a moderate liberal, not to be included within the fold of labor's spokesmen. He was a willing supporter of American labor's modest legislative requests, which earned him the official endorsement of organized labor. Although part of the vanguard of liberal Democrats, Roosevelt was yet to blaze new paths in the field of labor legislation.

During his four years in Albany, Roosevelt amassed an outstanding record for remedial farm legislation as a result of his political acumen, administrative ability, and understanding of rural problems and of the need for action. In contrast to the Republican administration in Washington, and to most state executives, Governor Roosevelt pushed through a dynamic farm program which, though not solving fundamental problems, captured the imagination of farmers and farm leaders throughout the nation. Roosevelt's objective was to raise the income and standard of living of farmers to match that of city workers. Before the conclusion of Roosevelt's New Deal, much of the nation's farm community experienced a tremendous increase in income and standard of living, a goal which Roosevelt had sought since 1929.

Although unable to attain his water power objectives because of Republican opposition in Albany and Washington, Roosevelt had opportunity to exhibit many of the leadership traits with which the nation became familiar during his presidency. He developed an educated public opinion and then activated it, when necessary, through organized campaigns.

Roosevelt was no Socialist. While business journals, utility lobbyists, and Republican spokesmen condemned Roosevelt for his "radicalism," Socialist spokesmen were vociferous in their criticism of the Governor for adopting watered-down versions of his original power proposals and for attempting to compete with, or outwit, the power trust instead of mastering it. Whereas the Socialists, led by Norman Thomas, demanded outright government ownership and operation of all utilities, Roosevelt felt that as a general rule the development of utilities should remain, with exceptions, a function for private initiative and private capital. In fact, Roosevelt's constructive water power policy, enunciated during a critical period in our nation's history, was instrumental in undermining the appeal of Socialists and contributing to their decline on the American scene.

By frustrating Roosevelt's attempts to secure cheap and plentiful electric power on the State level, utility spokesmen educated the Governor to seek far-reaching Federal, State, and local action and cooperation on the water power issue.

Franklin D. Roosevelt made many errors in judgment during his political career. On the other hand, when the American people yearned for positive and confident leadership to overcome the worsening economic crisis, Roosevelt filled the vacuum left by confused leaders of business, industry, and his political opposition. If the nation had continued unimpeded in its downward economic trend it might well have evolved into a totalitarian state of the right or left. Relying, to a great extent, on the positive program he had developed during his four years as Governor,

Roosevelt assumed the presidency and steered the nation in a democratic direction.

When faced with problems which had not confronted him while Governor, Roosevelt the pragmatist was willing to experiment in an attempt to revive the ailing economy and to liberate millions of men, women, and children from the tragic spectre of insecurity, impoverishment, and ill-health. In the process, Roosevelt helped preserve the free enterprise system and revitalized our democratic society. The radical movements, which normally flower during periods of economic crisis, were eventually stunted and frustrated by the constructive programs which Roosevelt directed on the State and national levels. Although not all New Deal legislation benefited the great mass of people, it was, on the whole, a sincere attempt to repel a challenging depression. Roosevelt was partially successful, for today our nation is strong and its wealth is distributed among a greater proportion of the population.

Because he was willing to meet this economic challenge with constructive proposals, because he benefited the great mass of our nation's citizenry, and because he helped retain our democratic system in the process, Franklin D. Roosevelt must be recognized as an outstanding liberal in American history.

NOTES

INTRODUCTION

1. *F.D.R., His Personal Letters, 1928-1945*, edited by Elliot Roosevelt (New York: Duell, Sloan and Pearce, 1950), p. 252.

Chapter I: *A NEW GOVERNOR*

1. Exactly thirty years earlier a fifth cousin, Theodore Roosevelt, who had successfully fought a crippling illness in his youth, had taken the oath of office as Governor of New York. Both Roosevelts had been Assistant Secretaries of the Navy prior to their respective elections to the Governor's seat in Albany.

2. For a definitive study—for our time—of Roosevelt's early years as State legislator and Assistant Secretary of the Navy, read the excellent work by Frank Freidel, *Franklin D. Roosevelt: The Apprenticeship* (Boston: Little, Brown and Co., 1952).

3. Group 11, Pol. Corres. "R-V," FDR to Mrs. S. Thompson, July 31, 1922. (Material hereafter cited with such references is in the Franklin D. Roosevelt Library at Hyde Park, New York.)

4. Group 11, Pol. Corres. "H," FDR to J. A. H. Hopkins, April 8, 1925.

5. *Ibid.*

6. For a definitive study—for our time—of Roosevelt as vice-presidential nominee, his bout with infantile paralysis, and as active party leader from 1921 to 1928, read Frank Freidel's *Franklin D. Roosevelt: The Ordeal* (Boston: Little, Brown and Co., 1954).

7. New York *World*, September 14, 1928.

8. *Ibid.*, September 28, 1928.

9. New York *Times*, September 30, 1928.

10. New York *Herald Tribune*, September 28, 1928.

11. New York *World*, October 2, 1928.

12. James A. Farley, *Behind the Ballots* (New York: Harcourt, Brace and Co., 1938), pp. 70-80.

13. 1928 Campaign Correspondence, New York State, Box 18, Folder D. FDR to Frederic A. Delano, October 8, 1928 (Franklin D. Roosevelt Library at Hyde Park).

14. New York *Times*, October 3, 1928.

15. James A. Farley, *Jim Farley's Story: The Roosevelt Years* (New York: McGraw-Hill, 1948), pp. 59-60; and John Gunther, *Roosevelt in Retrospect* (New York: Harper and Bros., 1950), p. 252.

16. 1928 Campaign Corres., New York State, Box 18, Folder D. FDR to Frederic A. Delano, October 8, 1928.

17. Farley, *Behind the Ballots*, pp. 79-80.

18. Machold, former speaker of the Assembly and newly designated State Chairman of the Republican party, had resigned only a few weeks before from various executive positions with private power trusts in New York State. New York *Times*, August 25, 1928.

19. New York *Times*, October 2, 1928.

20. Private Correspondence of FDR, 1928-32, Box 60, Ford Motor Company (Franklin D. Roosevelt Library at Hyde Park). Hereafter cited as Pr. Corres.

21. 1928 Campaign Corres., New York City, Box 16, 52.

22. 1928 Campaign Corres., New York City, Box 15, M-Q, Folder P-Q. Frances Perkins to FDR, October 11, 1928.

23. New York *World*, October 3, 1928.

24. New York *Herald Tribune*, October 3, 1928.

25. Pr. Corres., Box 92, "Jor," FDR to C. M. Jordan, July 21, 1931.

26. New York *Times*, October 3, 1928.

27. New York *Telegram*, October 3, 1928.

28. New York *Times*, October 11, 1928.

29. *Ibid.*, October 26, 1928.

30. *Ibid.*, October 27, 1928.

31. *New Leader*, February 4, 1928. The *New Leader* was a weekly Socialist newspaper published in New York City in the 1920's and 1930's. Since the defection of right wing elements of the Socialist party in the 1930's, it became the voice of American Social Democrats, until recent years.

32. *Ibid.*, February 11, 1928. The net profit of the Goodyear Tire and Rubber Company for 1927 mounted to $13,135,666 as against $8,799,148 in 1926. The Consolidated Gas Company of

New York and its affiliated gas and electric companies reported for 1927 a net income of $42,273,779, after all charges and taxes, compared with $25,666,893 in 1926. *New Leader*, February 25, 1928.

33. *Ibid.*, February 25, 1928.

34. James A. Hamilton, "Report to the Governor on Unemployment Conditions in the State by Industrial Commissioner," in *Public Papers of Alfred E. Smith, 1928* (Albany: J. B. Lyon Co., 1938), pp. 617-18.

35. New York *Times*, October 9, 1928.

36. New York *World*, October 5, 1928.

37. Harold F. Gosnell, *Champion Campaigner, Franklin D. Roosevelt* (New York: The Macmillan Co., 1952), p. 88.

38. New York *World*, October 16, 1928; and New York *Herald Tribune*, October 16, 1928.

39. New York *Times*, October 17, 1928.

40. 1928 Campaign Corres., New York State, Box 18.

41. New York *Times*, October 18, 1928.

42. Samuel I. Rosenman, *Working With Roosevelt* (New York: Harper and Bros., 1952), p. 16.

43. New York *Times*, October 18, 1928.

44. New York *World*, October 18, 1928.

45. Louis Howe Papers, Box 32, April-December, 1928. Belle Moskowitz had been a personal adviser to Al Smith. (Franklin D. Roosevelt Library at Hyde Park.)

46. Rosenman, *Working With Roosevelt*, p. 17.

47. For a very personal account of these developments read the able presentation by Samuel I. Rosenman in *Working With Roosevelt*.

48. New York *Times*, October 18, 1928.

49. New York *World*, October 19, 1928.

50. New York *Times*, October 20, 1928.

51. Albert Ottinger was an active leader of the Jewish community in New York City.

52. New York *Times*, October 21, 1928.

53. *Ibid.*, October 22, 1928.

54. *New Leader*, June 16, 1928.

55. New York *Herald Tribune*, October 23, 1928.

56. New York *Times*, October 24, 1928.

57. *Ibid.*, October 25, 1928.

58. *Ibid.*, October 26, 1928.

59. New York *Herald Tribune*, October 26, 1928.

60. *Ibid.*, October 27, 1928.

61. New York *Times*, October 28, 1928.

62. *Ibid.*, October 30, 1928.

63. "FDR 1928, Campaign Speech at Flushing High School, Flushing, L. I., Monday evening, October 29, 1928. FDR Gubernatorial Campaign, 1928. Addresses of Franklin D. Roosevelt. Stenographic copy. Bound." Unnumbered page. (Franklin D. Roosevelt Library at Hyde Park.)

64. "FDR Gubernatorial Campaign, 1928. Addresses of Franklin D. Roosevelt. Stenographic Copy. Bound." Unnumbered page. This volume contains stenographic copies of eleven of Roosevelt's major campaign addresses of 1928.

65. New York *World*, October 19, 1928.

66. Farley, *Behind the Ballots*, p. 53.

67. Some of these directives are available in "Private Correspondence of FDR, 1928-32, Box 42, Democratic State Committee."

68. Pr. Corres., Box 28, "Cas (cont.)," M. J. Cashel, Pres. of the Int'l. Brotherhood of Teamsters, Chauffeurs, Stablemen, and Helpers (AFL), to FDR, October 17, 1930.

69. Louis Howe Papers, August-December, 1931, Box 41. Louis Howe to Colonel House, August 17, 1931.

70. *Ibid.*

71. Pr. Corres., Box 38, "Cullman, Howard," Cullman to FDR, November 23, 1928.

72. New York *Herald Tribune*, November 7, 1928.

73. New York *Times*, November 10, 1928.

74. *Ibid.*, November 17, 1928.

75. Pr. Corres., Box 133, "Ot," Ottinger to Roosevelt, November 18, 1928.

76. Pr. Corres., Box 61, "Frankfurter, Felix," Frankfurter to FDR, November 8, 1928.

77. Henry F. Pringle, *Alfred E. Smith, A Critical Study* (New York: Macy-Masius, 1927), p. 218. This work remains the most competent of the biographical studies of Al Smith made to date, but is far from a definitive contribution.

78. For a description of Smith's actions on this issue read Pringle, *Alfred E. Smith*, pp. 236-46.

79. Alfred Lief, *Democracy's Norris: The Biography of a Lonely Crusade* (New York: Stackpole Sons, 1939), p. 319.

80. *Public Papers of Franklin D. Roosevelt, Forty-Eighth Governor of the State of New York, 1930* (Albany: J. B. Lyon Co., 1931), p. 759. Hereafter cited as *Public Papers, 1930*.

Chapter II: "UPSTAIRS IN ALBANY"

1. Leonard D. White, *Introduction to the Study of Public Administration* (New York: Macmillan Co., 1939), p. 51.

2. New York was one of nine states which adopted the Executive Budget in the nineteen twenties.

3. See F. G. Crawford, "The Executive Budget Decision in New York," *American Political Science Review*, XXIV (May, 1930), 403 ff; Lynton K. Caldwell, *The Government and Administration of New York* (New York: Thomas Y. Crowell Co., 1954), pp. 231-32.

4. White, *Introduction to the Study of Public Administration*, p. 212. Professor White cites the case in the Independent Office Appropriation Act of 1937-38 when the salary of the Executive Director of the Social Security Board was reduced $500 at the instance of a powerful senator who had been crossed in a patronage appointment by the director.

5. New York *Times*, February 12, 1929.

6. *Ibid.*, January 29, 1929.

7. *Ibid.*, February 28, 1929.

8. Robert Moses was prominently identified with the original drafting of the Executive Budget amendment.

9. New York *Times*, February 28, 1929.

10. *Ibid.*, March 10, 1929.

11. "Sec. 139. Segregation of Lump Sum Appropriations. When, by act of the legislature, a state department is created or reorganized, or state departments consolidated, or a board, commission, division or bureau within a department is created or reorganized, and a lump sum is appropriated for its maintenance and operation, or for personal service, during the first fiscal year thereafter, no moneys so appropriated shall be available for payments for personal service, except temporary service or day labor, until a schedule of positions and salaries shall have been approved by the governor, the chairman of the Finance Committee of the Senate and the chairman of the Ways and Means Committee of the Assembly, and a certificate of such approval filed with the comptroller." (Chapter 336, Laws of New York, 1921; Chapter 364, Laws of New York, 1927.)

12. *Public Papers of Franklin D. Roosevelt, Forty-Eighth Governor of the State of New York, 1929* (Albany: J. B. Lyon Co., 1930), p. 196. Hereafter cited as *Public Papers, 1929*.

13. Ibid.

14. New York *Times*, March 26, 1929.

15. *Ibid.*

16. Chapter 593, Laws of New York, 1929.

17. New York *Times*, March 28, 1929.

18. The legislature struck out 133 items for the Department of Law, aggregating $852,250, and 599 items for the Department of Labor, aggregating $2,700,000, and substituted lump items to the identical amounts.

19. The Governor has the right of item veto with relation to the budget.

20. New York *Times*, April 13, 1929.

21. *Ibid.*

22. William D. Guthrie, who had been chairman of the Executive Committee of the Judiciary Constitutional Convention of 1921, and former president of the Bar Association of New York City, was a Republican who some years previously had been prominently mentioned as a possible Republican candidate, first for United States Senator, and then for Governor. Griffin, as counsel to Roosevelt, was a holdover from the Smith administration.

23. New York *Times*, April 12, 1929.

24. Gubernatorial Papers, "Budget Suit Case," Lehman to Ward, April 21, 1929. "Gubernatorial Papers" are letters to, and from, Governor Roosevelt, which deal with matters concerning official State business and are the property of the State of New York. Hereafter cited as Gub. Papers.

25. *Ibid.*, joint statement of Lehman and Ward, April 29, 1929.

26. New York *Times*, May 24, 1929.

27. *Ibid.*

28. *Ibid.*

29. *Ibid.*

30. *Ibid.*, June 22, 1929.

31. People v. Tremaine, 235 N.Y.S. 555, 564 (1929).

32. Gub. Papers, "Budget Suit Case," Guthrie to FDR, July 8, 1929.

33. *Ibid.*, Griffin to FDR, September 25, 1929.

34. *Ibid.*, FDR to Guthrie, October 3, 1929.

35. *Ibid.*, Guthrie to FDR, October 7, 1929.

36. *Ibid.*, Griffin to FDR, October 7, 1929.

37. *Ibid.*, Griffin to FDR, October 9, 1929.

38. *Ibid.*, FDR to Guthrie, October 12, 1929.

39. *Ibid.*

40. New York *Times*, October 18, 1929.

41. *Ibid.*
42. *Ibid.*
43. New York *Times*, November 20, 1929.
44. People v. Tremaine, 252 N.Y. 27, 42 (1929).
45. *Ibid.*, pp. 44-45.
46. *Ibid.*, pp. 61-62.
47. *Ibid.*, p. 52.
48. New York *Times*, November 20, 1929.
49. Gub. Papers, "Budget Suit Case," Press release by FDR on November 18, 1929.
50. *Ibid.*, FDR to J. C. Martin, November 21, 1929.
51. New York *Times*, November 24, 1929.

Chapter III: REBELLION BEHIND BARS

1. New York *Times*, July 23, 1929.
2. *Ibid.*, July 29, 1929. New York State prisons handled 11,145 inmates in 1928-29.
3. New York *Times*, August 4, 1929.
4. *Ibid.*, July 29, 1929.
5. *Ibid.*, July 28, 1929.
6. *Ibid.*
7. *Ibid.*
8. *Ibid.*, August 4, 1929.
9. *Ibid.*
10. The average prison sentence in 1922 was three years, six and one-half months. Five years later it was six years, two and one-half months. New York *Times*, July 28, 1929.
11. New York *Times*, August 4, 1929.
12. *Ibid.*, July 30, 1929.
13. *Ibid.*, July 31, 1929.
14. *Ibid.*, August 22, 1929.
15. *Ibid.*, August 29, 1929.
16. New York *Times*, October 16, 1929. Dr. Thayer had just been appointed Superintendent of State Prisons in Maryland and was about to leave his post at Napanoch.
17. Pr. Corres., Box 113, "McG-McGo," McGinnies to FDR, July 31, 1929.
18. Gub. Papers, "Correction—Prison Riots," FDR to Frankfurter, August 5, 1929.

19. Gub. Papers, "Frankfurter, Felix," Frankfurter to FDR, August 10, 1929.

20. Those at the conference included Lehman; Dr. Kieb; the four wardens of the State prisons; the superintendents of the Elmira Reformatory and the Napanoch Institute for Defective Delinquents; John S. Kennedy, vice chairman, State Correction Commission; Caleb H. Baumes, chairman, New York State Crime Commission; B. Roger Wales, chairman, subcommittee of Crime Commission of Correctional Institutions; Milan E. Goodrich, chairman, Assembly Committee on Penal Institutions; T. C. Brown, chairman, Senate Committee on Penal Institutions; E. R. Cass, general secretary, American Prison Association; Charles D. Osborne, president, National Society of Penal Information; Louis Howe, secretary, National Crime Commission; Frederick A. Goetze, president, National Committee on Prisons and Prison Labor; Dr. Hastings Hart, Russell Sage Foundation; and Miss Jane Hoey, State Crime Commission.

21. New York *Times*, September 13, 1929.

22. *Ibid.*, November 13, 1929.

23. New York *Times*, December 5, 1929.

24. *Ibid.*, December 12, 1929.

25. *Ibid.*

26. Gub. Papers, "Auburn Prison Riots," Kieb to FDR, December 12, 1929.

27. *Ibid.*, Chandler to FDR, December 18, 1929.

28. New York *Times*, December 23, 1929.

29. *Ibid.*, December 21, 1929.

30. Ibid., December 30, 1929.

31. *Ibid.*, January 2, 1930.

32. *Ibid.*, January 3, 1930.

33. *Ibid.*

34. New York *Times*, January 7, 1930. The increased food allowance insured the addition of butter, sugar, and milk to the daily menus of 6,300 prisoners within a month. Infrequent desserts would also be possible.

35. *Public Papers, 1930*, pp. 40-41.

36. The other committee members included George W. Alger, Edwin J. Cooley, Jane M. Hoey, John S. Kennedy, and Raymond Moley.

37. *Public Papers, 1930*, pp. 491-504.

38. Chapter 283 and 824, Laws of New York, 1930.

39. Chapter 825, Laws of New York, 1930.

40. New York *Times*, February 15, 1930.

41. *Ibid.*, June 24, 1930.

42. *Ibid.*, June 15, 1930.

43. *Ibid.*, May 19, 1930.

44. New York *Telegram*, September 25, 1930.

45. Chapter 825, Laws of New York, 1930.

46. Besides Mr. Lewisohn the members of the Commission were: E. R. Cass, executive secretary of the Prison Associations of New York; Miss Julia K. Jaffray, secretary of the National Committee on Prisons and Prison Labor; Hastings H. Hart, consultant in delinquency and penology; Dr. Walter N. Thayer, Jr.; Thomas C. Brown, chairman of the Senate Committee on Penal Institutions; and Milan E. Goodrich, chairman of the Assembly Committee on Prisons.

47. New York *Times*, October 9, 1930.

48. *Ibid.*, October 14, 1930.

49. *Ibid.*, October 30, 1930.

50. New York *Times*, December 29, 1930, and February 17, 1931.

51. *Public Papers of Franklin D. Roosevelt, Forty-Eighth Governor of the State of New York, Second Term, 1931* (Albany: J. B. Lyon Co., 1937), pp. 95-96. Hereafter cited as *Public Papers, 1931.*

52. Chapter 348, Laws of New York, 1931; and New York *Times*, April 17, 1931.

53. Pr. Corres., Box 103, "Lewisohn," FDR to Adolph Lewisohn, April 13, 1931.

54. New York *Times*, May 1, 1931.

55. *Ibid.*, December 28, 1931.

56. *Ibid.*, February 15, 1932. Two years after the Governor appointed his advisory Committee on Prison Industries, headed by George Gordon Battle, the committee concluded that "the most desirable products of the prisons of New York in the final analysis is rehabilitated men and prison industries must be developed to that end." The committee recommended an apprenticeship plan similar to that employed in free industry, and the creation of a standing prison industries advisory board under the Commissioner of Correction. New York *Times*, February 29, 1932.

57. *Ibid.*, April 4, 1932.

58. Chapter 617, Laws of New York, 1932.

59. By July, 1932, the Department of Correction operated seven State prisons, two reformatories, two hospitals for the criminally insane, two institutions for defective delinquents, and one school

for juvenile delinquents. In 1931 this department spent $8,500,000, or 78 percent more than ten years previously. The number of inmates in the institutions had jumped 50 percent from 1922 and totaled 13,000. New York *Times,* July 29, 1932.

60. Pr. Corres., Box 169, "Ti-Til," FDR to M. B. Tillosson, February 14, 1931.

Chapter *IV*: PARITY FOR THE FARMER

1. Pr. Corres., Box 119, "Mit-Mis," FDR to editor of the Mitchell *Republican* of Mitchell, South Dakota, April 13, 1931.

2. Eleanor Roosevelt, *This I Remember* (New York: Harper and Bros., 1949), p. 72.

3. *Ibid.*

4. Gub. Papers, "Dairymen's League, June 20, 1929."

5. Pr. Corres., Box 103, "Levinsky-Levitt," Levitan to FDR, November 19, 1931.

6. *American Agriculturist,* October 13, 1928. This weekly farm journal was published in New York State primarily for the Middle Atlantic and New England region.

7. *American Agriculturist,* November 17, 1928. The index was based on the average of 100 for the years 1909 to 1914.

8. New York *Times,* November 22, 1928.

9. *Public Papers, 1929,* p. 689.

10. Eleanor Roosevelt, *This I Remember,* p. 170.

11. Pr. Corres., Box 121, "Morgenthau, Henry Jr., -2-," FDR to E. R. Eastman, May 22, 1930.

12. Fifty cents tax on each thousand dollars of property valuation.

13. Pr. Corres., Box 121, "Morgenthau, Henry Jr., -2-," Morgenthau to FDR, November 25, 1928.

14. *Ibid.*

15. *Public Papers, 1929,* pp. 477-78.

16. New York *Times,* January 17, 1929.

17. *Ibid.*

18. *American Agriculturist,* February 2, 1929.

19. *Public Papers, 1929,* p. 482. The Webb-Rice bills provided for a uniform tax in the one-room district of four mills—$4.00 per thousand of actual valuation—and guaranteed to such districts a school of acceptable standard, with the assurance that the State would pay the difference between the sum of the four-mill tax and

the standard of $1,500—later amended to $1,300—as stated in the bill.

20. Pr. Corres., Box 121, "Morgenthau, H. Jr.," FDR to Morgenthau, May 13, 1929.

21. New York *Times*, March 5, 1929.

22. *Public Papers, 1929*, pp. 486-87.

23. *Ibid.*, pp. 496-97.

24. *Ibid.*, p. 498.

25. *Rural New Yorker*, January 18, 1930.

26. Chapter 459, Laws of New York, 1929.

27. Chapter 461, Laws of New York, 1929.

28. Chapter 458, Laws of New York, 1929.

29. Chapter 358, Laws of New York, 1929.

30. Chapter 357, Laws of New York, 1929.

31. Chapter 364, Laws of New York, 1929.

32. *American Agriculturist*, April 13, 1929.

33. *Ibid.*, April 20, 1929.

34. Pr. Corres., Box 156, "Sg-Shap," an undated letter from Roosevelt addressed to the editor of the *Cold Spring Recorder*, of Cold Spring, N. Y. A copy was attached to a letter from Francis Shackel, dated February 17, 1930.

35. *Ibid.*

36. *Rural New Yorker*, April 20, 1929; and subsequent issues.

37. *American Agriculturist*, April 13, 1929; and subsequent issues.

38. Louis Howe Papers, Box 84, "Howe, L. M.," June 26, 1930. The Governor appears to have been too liberal with his percentages, for the November 21, 1931, issue of the *American Agriculturist* claimed a circulation of 164,610, whereas its circulation three years previous had been a little more than 150,000.

39. Pr. Corres., Box 121, "Morgenthau, Henry Jr.," Morgenthau to FDR, April 19, 1929.

40. Pr. Corres., Box 127, "Newspaper Articles," FDR to Hugh Parker of the Oneida *Post*.

41. Pr. Corres., Box 107, "Lyo," FDR to Lyon, March 3, 1931.

42. The members of the commission in 1930 included Henry Morgenthau, Jr.; Jared Van Wagenen, Jr., Farmers' Institute Worker; John Fallon, Master Farmer; Commissioner A. W. Brandt, Division of Highways; Paul Judson, former president, New York State Farm Bureau Federation; Isaiah D. Karr, Master Farmer; Assemblyman W. L. Pratt, Chairman, Assembly Committee on Taxation and Retrenchment; E. R. Eastman, editor, *American Agriculturist*; Dr. George F. Warren, Department of Agricultural

Economics, New York State College of Agriculture; Dr. C. E. Ladd, Director of Extension, College of Agriculture; Dr. Martha Van Rensselaer, director, College of Home Economics; Mrs. Edward Young, former president, Home Bureau Federation; M. C. Burritt, Master Farmer; Elizabeth MacDonald, president, Home Bureau Federation; Deputy Commissioner B. C. Brooks, Department of Health; Fred Freestone, Master, New York State Grange; Berne A. Pyrke, Commissioner of Agriculture; Dr. Thomas J. Parran, State Commissioner of Health; and Dr. Livingston Farrand, president, Cornell University.

43. *Public Papers, 1930,* pp. 411-12.

44. *Ibid.,* pp. 412-14. The eighth report of the commission was given to the Governor on December 19, 1930, and is found in *Public Papers, 1930,* pp. 418-19.

45. Chapter 772, Laws of New York, 1930.

46. Chapter 771, Laws of New York, 1930.

47. Chapter 763, Laws of New York, 1930.

48. Chapter 765, Laws of New York, 1930.

49. Chapter 764, Laws of New York, 1930.

50. Chapters 767, 768, Laws of New York, 1930.

51. Chapter 766, Laws of New York, 1930.

52. *American Agriculturist,* May 3, 1930.

53. *Rural New Yorker,* September 20, 1930.

54. *American Agriculturist,* May 9, 1931.

55. Chapter 581, Laws of New York, 1931.

56. Chapter 96, Laws of New York, 1931.

57. Chapter 95, Laws of New York, 1931.

58. Pr. Corres., Box 161, "Smith, L.—Smith, R.," FDR to Moses Smith, May 20, 1929.

59. Eleanor Roosevelt, *This I Remember,* p. 55.

60. More on this subject is in Chapter VII.

61. Russell Lord, *The Wallaces of Iowa* (Boston: Houghton Mifflin Co., 1947), p. 294.

62. *Ibid.,* p. 295.

63. *American Agriculturist,* May 30, 1931; and *Statistical Abstract of the United States* (Washington: U. S. Government Printing Office, 1933), p. 568.

64. Pr. Corres., Box 112, "Mat," A. N. Mathers to FDR, March 3, 1930.

65. *Ibid.,* FDR to A. N. Mathers, March 11, 1930.

66. *Public Papers, 1929,* p. 40.

67. The domestic allotment plan appears to have been first

initiated by W. J. Spillman— W. J. Spillman, *Use of the Exponential Yield Curve in Fertilizer*, U. S. Department of Agriculture Technical Bulletin No. 348, April, 1938—and then by Dr. John D. Black in his *Agricultural Reform in the United States*, published in 1929.

68. Pr. Corres., Box 112, "Mat," FDR to A. N. Mathers, March 11, 1930.

69. Lord, *The Wallaces*, p. 323.

70. *Public Papers and Addresses of Franklin D. Roosevelt*, Vol. I (New York: Random House, 1938), p. 704. Hereafter cited as *Public Papers and Addresses*, Vol. I.

71. *Ibid.*, p. 705.

72. Pr. Corres., Box 119, "Mit-Miz," April 1, 1931.

73. *Public Papers, 1931*, p. 679; and Gub. Papers, "Conservation-Reforestation."

74. Gub. Papers, "Conservation-Reforestation."

75. *Rural New Yorker*, October 31, 1931.

76. New York *Times*, October 22, 1931.

77. *Ibid.*, October 27, 1931.

78. *Ibid.*

79. Pr. Corres., Box 121, "Morgan, Keith -2-," K. Morgan to FDR, November 4, 1931.

80. Pr. Corres., Box 153, "Saxe, John G.," FDR to Saxe, "Election Day, 1931."

81. Pr. Corres., Box 53, "Edm-Ef," October 30, 1931, issue of *The Sentinel* of Shenandoah, Iowa.

82. Pr. Corres., Box 43, "Dern, George H.," Dern to FDR, November 10, 1931.

83. *Public Papers and Addresses*, Vol. I, pp. 699-700.

84. Chapters 237, 238, and 239, Laws of New York, 1932.

85. *Public Papers of Franklin D. Roosevelt, Forty-Eighth Governor of the State of New York, Second Term, 1932* (Albany: J. B. Lyon Co., 1939), pp. 552-56. Hereafter cited as *Public Papers, 1932*.

86. *Ibid.*, p. 555. A table of figures, showing the amount of additional State help given the 57 counties in 1930, over 1928, the increase and decrease in general property tax in 1930 over 1928, and the actual rise in the cost of local government for the respective 57 counties is shown in the February 20, 1932, issue of the *American Agriculturist*, and on p. 557 of *Public Papers, 1932*.

87. Pr. Corres., Box 122, "Morell-Morrison," A. N. Morrier to FDR, December 8, 1932. Written in longhand.

Chapter V: "SECURE OUR SAVINGS"

1. *Public Papers, 1931*, p. 124.

2. Robert Moses, *Report to Governor Franklin D. Roosevelt on the Investigation of the Department of Banking in Relation to the City Trust Company* (Albany: J. B. Lyon Co., 1929), pp. 10-27. Hereafter cited as Moses, *Report to FDR*.

3. See *Brooklyn Daily Eagle*, April 11, 1929.

4. New York *Times*, March 24, 1929.

5. Gub. Papers, "Banking Commission, City Trust Company, Banking Department," F. H. Warder to FDR, April 19, 1929.

6. *Ibid.* Leon Leighton to Lehman, undated telegram which appears to have been sent between the 22nd of April, Warder's official date of resignation, and the 25th of April, the day Robert Moses was appointed Moreland Act Commissioner.

7. The Moreland Act is an amendment to the executive law which gives the Governor, through himself or any person designated by him, the right to inquire into the affairs of any board, bureau or commission of the State government and to require people to testify under oath and to issue subpoenas for their attendance.

8. Pr. Corres., Box 102, "Herbert Lehman," Lehman to FDR, April 30, 1929.

9. Gub. Papers, "Banking Commission. Investigation—City Trust Company—Banking Department," W. K. Macy to FDR, May 16, 1929.

10. *Ibid.*, FDR to Macy, May 20, 1929.

11. Files of Lieutenant Governor Herbert H. Lehman, "City Trust Company," Macy to Lehman, June 7, 1929. These files are the property of the State of New York, on loan to the Franklin D. Roosevelt Library. In contrast to the Gubernatorial Papers of Roosevelt, they are in excellent condition and logically arranged. Hereafter cited as Lehman file.

12. New York *Times*, June 14, 1929.

13. *Ibid.*, June 26, 1929.

14. *New Leader*, July 13, 1929.

15. Lehman file, "City Trust Company," Moses to Basil O'Connor, July 17, 1929.

16. *New Leader*, July 13, 1929. Governor Roosevelt had been the principal speaker at the dedication of the new headquarters of Tammany Hall, facing Union Square, on July 4, 1929. The Tam-

many Sachems have since sold that building to the International Ladies' Garment Workers' Union.

17. The official transcripts of the hearings before Commissioner Robert Moses are available in the files of the Gubernatorial Papers of Franklin D. Roosevelt, of which there are more than a dozen huge volumes totaling some 5,575 pages.

18. Moses, *Report to FDR*. The most damaging evidence against Ferrari and Warder is found on pp. 10, 17, 20, 24, and 27.

19. Lehman file, "Banking Department, 1929-32," Lehman to J. A. Broderick, June 3, 1929.

20. Moses, *Report to FDR*, pp. 64-65.

21. *Ibid.*

22. *Ibid.*, p. 67.

23. *Ibid.*, p. 50.

24. Gub. Papers, "Banking Commission, City Trust Company, Banking Department," Moses to FDR, undated.

25. Lehman file, "City Trust Company," Moses to FDR, attached to a letter of July 17, 1929, from Moses to Lehman. The Governor's invitation to the law associations had been prepared by Moses.

26. New York *Times*, October 10, 1929.

27. *Ibid.*, November 6, 9, 15, and 27, 1929.

28. Gub. Papers, "Banking Commission" FDR to N. W. Cheney, July 20, 1929.

29. The members of the Banking Commission were Messrs. George W. Davison, chairman, president of the Central Hanover Bank and Trust Company; Howard Bissell, president of the M. & T. People's Trust Company of Buffalo; James Byrne, lawyer and former president of the State Banking Association; Darwin R. James, Jr., president of the East River Savings Bank; Russell C. Leffingwell, a Morgan partner; Ray Morris; William H. Woodin, president of the American Car and Foundry Company and later to become Secretary of the Treasury under President Roosevelt; Henry W. Pollock, counsel to the Bank of United States; Jesse Isador Straus, of R. H. Macy and Company; State Senator W. W. Campbell; and Assemblyman Nelson W. Cheney.

30. Lehman file, "City Trust Company," Moses to Lehman, July 17, 1929.

31. *Public Papers, 1930*, p. 29.

32. *Ibid.*, p. 472.

33. *Ibid.*

34. *Ibid.*

35. *Ibid.*, p. 476.

36. *Ibid.*, p. 479.

37. *Ibid.*, p. 483.

38. Chapters 678 and 679, Laws of New York, 1930.

39. *Public Papers, 1930*, p. 534.

40. Gub. Papers, "Broderick, Joseph A.," Broderick to FDR, May 21, 1930.

41. *Public Papers, 1930*, p. 536.

42. New York *Times*, December 12, 1930.

43. Gub. Papers, "Banking Commission—Bank of United States Failure," Broderick to I. M. Freidman, January 7, 1931.

44. When the Bank of United States closed its doors 300,000 of its 440,000 depositors had thrift accounts in its 57 branches in Manhattan, The Bronx, Brooklyn, and Queens counties.

45. Pr. Corres., Box 30, "Clarkson, Grosvenor," FDR to G. Clarkson, July 15, 1929.

46. M. R. Werner, *Little Napoleons and Dummy Directors* (New York: Harper and Bros., 1933), p. 6.

47. *Ibid.*, p. 143.

48. *Ibid.*, pp. 179, 195-96 and 183-87.

49. New York *Times*, December 28, 1930.

50. Gub. Papers, "Banking Commission—Bank of United States Failure," FDR to Norman Thomas, January 5, 1931.

51. *Ibid.*, FDR to Crain, January 5, 1931.

52. Due to his illness, Kresel's trial was temporarily postponed.

53. Lehman file, David Shapiro, publisher of *The Day*, to Lehman, undated telegram. Mrs. Roosevelt related to this writer the incident of the worried Lieutenant Governor excitedly pacing the floor of the Roosevelt house in New York City as he spoke with an unruffled Governor just returned from Warm Springs, Georgia. Lehman was verbally expressing his worries concerning the depositors of the defunct bank.

54. Gub. Papers, "Broderick, Joseph," Macy to FDR, June 24, 1931.

55. New York *Times*, June 27, 1931.

56. Pr. Corres., Box 172, "Van Schaick, George," FDR to Van Schaick, May 9, 1932.

57. Pr. Corres., Box 19, "Brod-Bronx," FDR to Broderick, December 8, 1931.

58. New York *Times*, April 15, 1932.

59. *Ibid.*, April 30, 1932.

60. *Ibid.*

61. *Ibid.*, May 28, 1932.

62. *Public Papers, 1931*, pp. 124-25.

63. *Ibid.*, p. 128.

64. *Ibid.*

65. Pr. Corres., Box 138, "Platt, C. E.," FDR to Edmund Platt, March 24, 1931.

66. *Public Papers, 1931*, p. 129.

67. *Ibid.*, p. 210.

68. *Public Papers, 1931*, p. 606.

69. New York *Times*, June 17, 1933.

70. The only banking law of consequence adopted by the 1932 legislature redefined the terminology which referred to Banking Department examinations of financial institutions "at least twice in each year." At the Governor's request the lawmakers amended the original statute to require the Banking Superintendent to conduct examinations "at least twice in each calendar year, upon such dates as in his discretion he deemed proper." Chapter 170, Laws of New York, 1932.

71. *Public Papers, 1932*, p. 31.

72. *Public Papers and Addresses*, Vol. I, p. 653.

73. *Ibid.*, p. 682.

74. *Ibid.*

75. "An Act to provide full and fair disclosure of the character of securities sold in interstate and foreign commerce and through the mails, and to prevent frauds in the sale thereof, and for other purposes." (Public Law No. 22, 73rd Congress.)

Chapter VI: *"TO PREVENT STARVATION AND DISTRESS"*

1. With 1925-27 as the base for 100, the index of factory employment in New York State, in September, 1929, was 97.9—New York State Department of Labor, *Trend of Employment in New York State Factories from 1914 to 1939* (Special Bulletin No. 206 [Albany, 1940]), p. 188.

2. *New Leader*, March 2, 1929. Old-law tenements were those built prior to the housing Law of 1901, and which housed approximately one-third of the city's population.

3. New York *Times*, January 4, 1929.

4. *Ibid.*, February 8, 1929.

5. Pr. Corres., Box 127, "Newspapers: New York American," Victor Watson to FDR, October 24, 1929; and FDR to Victor Watson, October 25, 1929.

6. *New Leader*, November 23, 1929.

7. Pr. Corres., Box 84, "Howe, Louis M.," FDR to Howe, December 1, 1929.

8. Chapter 713, Laws of New York, 1929.

9. *Public Papers, 1930*, p. 505.

10. *Ibid.*, p. 506.

11. *Ibid.*, p. 537.

12. The members of this committee were Henry Bruere, vice-president, Bowery Savings Bank, New York City; Maxwell Wheeler, vice-president, Larkin Co., Buffalo; Ernest Draper, vice-president, Hills Brothers, Brooklyn; and John Sullivan, president, New York State Federation of Labor. Professor Paul H. Douglas was its technical adviser.

13. *Public Papers, 1930*, p. 670.

14. *Ibid.*, p. 507.

15. Pr. Corres., Box 114, "McCarthy, C. H.," C. H. McCarthy to FDR, July 31, 1930.

16. Gub. Papers, "Unemployment-2-General," Frankfurter to FDR, April 18, 1930.

17. *Ibid.*, FDR to A. Hitch, May 7, 1930.

18. *Ibid.*, FDR to Lamont, April 30, 1930.

19. David M. Schneider and Albert Deutsch, *The History of Public Welfare in New York State, 1867 to 1940* (Chicago: University of Chicago, 1941), p. 295.

20. *Public Papers, 1930*, p. 601. The committee's lengthy report is available on pp. 591-670.

21. Gub. Papers, "Unemployment Commission," November 15, 1930, press release by FDR.

22. Schneider and Deutsch, *Public Welfare in New York*, p. 302.

23. *Public Papers, 1931*, p. 721.

24. Pr. Corres., Box 104, "Lin-Lind," W. A. White to FDR, December 17, 1930.

25. Pr. Corres., Box 217, "Young, Owen D.," June 22, 1931.

26. Pr. Corres., Box 88, "Jacobs, Dr. Thornwell," address by FDR, May 24, 1932.

27. "A Report on Unemployment and Emergency Relief in the 59 New York Cities Exclusive of New York City. To Franklin D. Roosevelt, Governor of the State of New York, by the Governor's Commission on Unemployment Problems for the State of New York, January, 1931," p. 1. This confidential report is on twenty-two legal-size pages.

28. *Ibid.*, p. 2.

29. *Ibid.*, pp. 6-7.
30. *Ibid.*, pp. 8-9.
31. *Ibid.*, p. 21.
32. Pr. Corres., Box 128, "N.Y. State," William Haugaard to FDR, October 16, 1930.
33. Gub. Papers, "Public Works Department, Greene, Frederick Stuart," memo to FDR, July 1, 1931.
34. *Ibid.*, Greene to FDR, July 26, 1932.
35. Pr. Corres., Box 173, "Wal-Walk," Waldman to FDR, August 26, 1930.
36. *Ibid.*
37. *Public Papers, 1931*, p. 39.
38. *Ibid.*, pp. 40 and 723.
39. Pr. Corres., Box 104, "Lin-Lind," FDR to C. A. Lindley, August 20, 1931.
40. Lewis E. Talbert and Herman B. Byer, *Employment and Payrolls, December, 1940* (U.S. Bureau of Labor Statistics Serial No. R 1250 [Washington, D. C., 1941]), p. 28. The base used for 100 was 1923 to 1925.
41. Joint Committee on Unemployment Relief of the State Board of Social Welfare and the State Charities Aid Association, *Prospects for Unemployment Relief in 1931-32 in 45 cities of New York State* (Mimeographed: New York, August, 1932).
42. Schneider and Deutsch, *Public Welfare in New York*, p. 306.
43. Gub. Papers, "Extra Session," William Hodson to FDR, August 19, 1931.
44. *Public Papers, 1931*, p. 173.
45. Pr. Corres., Box 118, "Milbank Memorial Fund," FDR to John A. Kingsbury, May 12, 1930.
46. *Public Papers, 1931*, p. 178.
47. New York *Times*, September 9, 1931.
48. Chapter 798, Laws of New York, 1931.
49. In 1932 the residence proviso was amended so that the two years of residence were to precede immediately the date of application.
50. *Public Papers, 1932*, p. 441.
51. *Ibid.*, p. 29.
52. *Ibid.*, p. 32.
53. *Ibid.*, p. 96.
54. Gub. Papers, "T.E.R.A., R-Z," and *Public Papers, 1932*, p. 474.
55. This became Chapter 567 of the Laws of New York, 1932. The legislature also placed State grants to localities for work relief

on the same 40 percent basis of reimbursement as grants for home relief.

56. Chapter 566, Laws of New York, 1932.

57. Gub. Papers, "Bureau," Hart to FDR, January 18, 1932.

58. *Ibid.*, FDR to Hart, January 14, 1932.

59. Gub. Papers, "Committee of 25," Moses to FDR, October 30, 1929.

60. Gub. Papers, "Budget Bureau," Hart to FDR, January 21, 1932.

61. *Ibid.*, FDR to J. W. Stoddard, March 31, 1932.

62. Pr. Corres., Box 38, "Cullman, Howard-I," Cullman to FDR, May 24, 1932.

63. New York State Department of Labor, *Trend of Employment in New York State Factories from 1914 to 1939*, p. 188.

64. From November 1, 1931, to August 31, 1932, $48,696,595 of State and local funds was expended under supervision of the T.E.R.A. in home relief and work relief for 379,070 families comprising about 1,500,000 people. New York State T.E.R.A., "Report, October 15, 1932" (not published, 1932), p. 9.

65. Gub. Papers, "Temporary Emergency Relief Administration-3-Misc.—Reference Letters—Reports," July 7, 1932. During August, 1932, less than 32,000 persons were employed on work relief projects in upstate districts. Owing to a lack of funds the number of approved applicants waiting for work at the end of August was more than 88,000. New York State T.E.R.A., "Report, October 15, 1932," p. 9.

66. In August, 1931, Paul Blanshard informed Roosevelt that whereas New York levied only a 2 percent tax on net incomes of $10,000 to $50,000, Wisconsin levied 5 percent on all incomes of $25,000 to $50,000. Wisconsin levied about a 7 percent tax on incomes over one million dollars, whereas New York levied less than 3 percent. Gub. Papers, "Blanshard, Paul," Blanshard to FDR, August 26, 1931.

67. Gub. Papers, "Washington—Washington Legislation," FDR to R. M. LaFollette, February 10, 1932.

68. *Public Papers and Addresses*, Vol. I, pp. 788-89.

69. Outstanding as a human being, and as the Governor of a small, neighboring state, was John G. Winant of New Hampshire. Here was a man who initiated, in a rock-ribbed Republican state, a social welfare program startlingly similar to the New Deal of Franklin D. Roosevelt.

Chapter VII: *A BATTLE ON TWO FRONTS*

1. Pr. Corres., Box 61, "Frankfurter, Felix," Frankfurter to FDR, September 14, 1931.

2. Pr. Corres., Box 121, "Morg-Morgan," F. B. Morgan to FDR, January 9, 1929 .

3. Pr. Corres., Box 102, "Lehman, Herbert," FDR to Lehman, May 14, 1930.

4. *New Leader*, March 23, 1929.

5. See Robert Bendiner, "Racketeers and Reformers in City Hall," *Park East*, October, 1951, pp. 43-50; Henry F. Pringle, "Tammany Hall, Inc.," *Atlantic Monthly*, pp. 425-34, October, 1932; and Alva Johnston, "The Scandals of New York," *Harpers*, March, 1931, pp. 409-18.

6. Pr. Corres., Box 28, "Cas-Cont," FDR to K. J. Casey, July 8, 1929.

7. New York *Times*, March 3, 1931.

8. New York *Enquirer*, March 30, 1930.

9. New York *Times*, April 9, 1930.

10. New York *Times*, September 17, 1930.

11. Pr. Corres., Box 27, "Newspapers; New York *Evening Post*," Julian Mason to FDR, July 1, 1930.

12. New York *Times*, May 11 and 19, 1930. Decisions for or against, by the Board, could mean fortunes for those involved. Over the years two men seemed to have had phenomenal success with the Board. Dr. William F. Doyle, a Tammany favorite, had influenced the Board to reverse itself in at least 49 cases, after dozens of lawyers had failed. In seven years, this practice netted Doyle some $2,000,000. Former Tammany Leader George Olvany, the other successful individual, intimately knew the Tammany-appointed chairman, William E. Walsh, with whom he conferred privately while cases were pending. Walsh later resigned under fire and was indicted, but the Tammany prosecutor failed to secure a conviction.

13. New York *Times*, October 1, 1930.

14. Pr. Corres., Box 37, "Cullman, Howard S.," Cullman to FDR, September 17, 1930.

15. Howe Papers, Box 37, "Campaign Strategy," Howe to FDR, undated memo.

16. Gub. Papers, "Port Authority, Howard S. Cullman," Cullman to FDR, June 4, 1930.

17. *Ibid.*, FDR to Cullman, June 16, 1930.

18. Howe Papers, "Radio and Theatre Material," 1930 campaign, Box 40.

19. See Howe Papers, Box 34, "September 1930," Cullman to Howe, September 25, 1930; and Cullman to FDR, September 13, 1930.

20. The issues of water power and public utility regulation will be discussed in subsequent chapters.

21. Pr. Corres., Box 114, "McCarthy, C. H." Mark Sullivan in the Washington *Star*, March 23, 1930.

22. New York *Herald Tribune*, September 26, 1930. Primary contests throughout the nation had already revealed that the pendulum of public opinion had swung toward repeal of prohibition.

23. Syracuse *Herald*, September 18, 1930.

24. New York *Herald Tribune*, September 27, 1930.

25. New York *World*, September 18, 1930.

26. Gub. Papers, "New York County Special Term Court (Ewald Case) (3)," Tuttle to T.C.T. Crain, August 4, 1930.

27. New York *Times*, August 16 and 20, 1930.

28. Alva Johnston, "The Scandals of New York," *Harper's*, March, 1931, p. 410.

29. New York *Times*, September 29, 1930.

30. *Ibid.*, September 30, 1930.

31. *Public Papers, 1930*, p. 577.

32. New York *World*, October 4, 1930.

33. New York *Herald Tribune*, September 29, 1930.

34. Pr. Corres., Box 37, "Cullman, Howard S.," Perkins to FDR, July 15, 1930. Perkins had suggested to Roosevelt that he "go cautiously when talking about unemployment insurance by that name. Unemployment reserves is safer and more educative for the present."

35. "Platform of the Democratic Party. Syracuse, New York, September 29, 1930." Mimeographed press release.

36. *Ibid.*

37. New York *Times*, October 1, 1930.

38. The complete Democratic slate included Morris S. Tremaine for Controller and John J. Bennett, Jr., of Brooklyn, for Attorney General.

39. New York *Herald Tribune*, October 1, 1930.

40. In the midst of the campaign Governor Roosevelt ignored the requests of civic leaders to extend the scope of the judicial investigation of the Ewald case to include that of Judge Bertini. The Governor had based his decision on the interpretation of the Executive Law by former presidential candidate John W. Davis, who

contended that Roosevelt lacked the power to do so without concrete evidence. New York *Times*, October 7, 1930.

41. New York *Herald Tribune*, October 1, 1930.

42. *Ibid.* Roosevelt vetoed the Republican-sponsored New York City inquiry bill, contending that it sought to set a precedent which would add "unheard of duties" to the functions of a Governor. The bill, if approved, would have made it mandatory for Roosevelt to appoint a temporary commission to investigate "the administration and certain local authorities in the City of New York." New York *Times*, March 30, 1930. In an earlier reply to similar charges, Roosevelt contended that he had ordered only four upstate inquiries while rejecting hundreds of others.

43. Judge Bertini was cleared of these charges shortly before he died in March, 1931.

44. New York *Herald Tribune*, October 5, 1930.

45. *Ibid.*, October 9, 1930.

46. *Ibid.*, October 11, 1930.

47. *Ibid.*, October 12, 1930. The old age pension will be discussed in a subsequent chapter.

48. New York *Herald Tribune*, October 19, 1930.

49. *Ibid.*, October 19, 1930.

50. *Ibid.*, October 20, 1930.

51. New York *World*, October 21, 1930.

52. In contrast to the 17 percent increase in New York City registration, 42 upstate cities showed an increase of only 5 percent over their 1926 registration figures. New York *Times*, October 20, 1930.

53. New York *Herald Tribune*, October 20, 1930.

54. *Ibid.*, October 22, 1930

55. New York *World*, September 27, 1930.

56. Pr. Corres., Box 37, "Cullman, Howard S.," Cullman to FDR, October 8, 1930. Morris Hillquit was an outstanding Socialist lawyer.

57. New York *Times*, October 28, 1930.

58. New York *Times*, October 29, 1930.

59. New York *World*, October 29, 1930. Although the *World* refused to support Roosevelt for re-election, it appealed to its readers to elect Democratic congressmen, "for a Democratic Congress alone can now give the country unified legislative authority." New York *World*, October 31, 1930.

60. Pr. Corres., Box 68, "Green," Green to FDR, August 22, 1930. Green referred to the regulation of the issuance of injunc-

tions in labor controversies; old age relief for the needy; the extension and more practical application of the eight-hour day on public works and in public enterprises; the extension of half holiday on Saturdays to women and minors employed in factories and stores; and the improvement of the workmen's compensation and factory inspection laws. Green also cited the legislature for prohibiting the importation and sale in New York of goods manufactured by convicts in other states.

61. New York *Herald Tribune,* October 26, 1930.

62. New York *Times,* October 29, 1930. In a critical period in our nation's history, Henry L. Stimson would accept the post of Secretary of War from this "unfit" man who had since become President of the United States.

63. New York *World,* October 28, 1931.

64. New York *Times,* November 2, 1930.

65. *Ibid.*

66. New York *World,* October 2, 1930.

67. James A. Farley, *Behind the Ballots* (New York: Harcourt, Brace and Co., 1938), p. 63. In 1922, Smith set the record figure of 386,000 plurality when he defeated Nathan L. Miller for the same post.

68. The town of Potsdam went Democrat for the first time in 70 years. Pr. Corres., Box 44, "Dil-Dj," Dineen to FDR, November 19, 1930. Chatauqua County went Democrat for the first time since the Civil War, except when Grover Cleveland won in 1882. Pr. Corres., Box 123, "Mot," Mott to FDR, November 6, 1930.

69. James Malcolm, *The New York Red Book* (Albany: J. B. Lyon Co., 1931), pp. 394-95. The Republicans had a narrow escape in the State Senate, retaining control of that body by only one vote. The new Assembly contained 80 Republicans and 70 Democrats.

70. Pr. Corres., Box 91, "Johnson-contd-," L. C. Johnson to FDR, November 5, 1930. To this Paris correspondent the Governor replied, "Two years ago one of the papers announced that I was the brother of Theodore Roosevelt and had been defeated for Governor in 1924 and had just been elected Mayor of New York City. Why don't you drop around the office of *L'Intransigeant* and tell them that I am a Bolshevist and have just been elected Governor of Puerto Rico. Some of the foreign news which American papers print is almost equally good." Pr. Corres., Box 91, "Johnson-contd-," FDR to L. C. Johnson, November 26, 1930.

71. Pr. Corres., Box 147, "Roosevelt, Kermit," Kermit Roosevelt to FDR, December 12, 1930.

72. Pr. Corres., Box 61, "Frankfurter, F.," Frankfurter to FDR, November 11, 1930.

Chapter VIII: *"IN QUEST OF SECURITY"*

1. *Public Papers and Addresses*, Vol. I, p. 43.
2. *Public Papers, 1929*, p. 148.
3. *Ibid.*, p. 149.
4. New York *Times*, March 1, 1929.
5. Chapter 664, Laws of New York, 1929.
6. New York State Commission on Old Age Security, *Old Age Security*, *Report* (Leg. Doc. [1930] No. 67 [Albany, 1930]), pp. 1-20.
7. Chapter 388, Laws of New York, 1930.
8. New York *Sun*, February 19, 1930.
9. New York *Times*, February 21, 1930.
10. *Public Papers, 1930*, p. 522.
11. *Ibid.*, pp. 522-23.
12. *Ibid.*, p. 523.
13. Chapter 565, Laws of New York, 1929.
14. *Laws of the State of New York. Passed at the 152nd Session of the Legislature*, Vols. I-II (Albany: J. B. Lyon Co., 1929), p. 1170.
15. Sec. 122, Chapter 387, Laws of New York, 1930.
16. Sec. 124, Chapter 387, Laws of New York, 1930.
17. Sec. 77, Article 9, Chapter 565, Laws of New York, 1929.
18. *Public Papers and Addresses*, Vol. I, p. 417.
19. *Public Papers, 1931*, p. 39.
20. In June, 1931, an average grant of $27.16 per month was made to 38,856 recipients of the new law. David M. Schneider and Albert Deutsch, *The History of Public Welfare in New York* (Chicago: University of Chicago, 1941), Vol. II, pp. 348-49.
21. *Public Papers and Addresses*, Vol. I, p. 668.
22. Pr. Corres., Box 59, "-Grig-," Rev. T. B. Griswold to FDR, October 7, 1930.
23. *New Leader*, October 18, 1930.
24. Gub. Papers, "Governors' Conference—1930," Cary A. Hardee to FDR, June 18, 1930.
25. New York *Times*, July 1, 1930.
26. *Ibid.*

27. Cleveland *Plain Dealer*, September 13, 1930.

28. *Public Papers, 1930*, p. 577.

29. New York *Herald Tribune*, September 27, 1930.

30. *Public Papers, 1931*, p. 40.

31. Gub. Papers, "Governors' Conference on Unemployment, January 23, 1931. A report prepared by the New York State Department of Labor," F. H. La Guardia to FDR, January 26, 1931.

32. *Ibid.*

33. Governors Joseph B. Ely of Massachusetts, Norman S. Case of Rhode Island, Morgan F. Larson of New Jersey, Wilbur L. Cross of Connecticut, George White of Ohio, and Franklin D. Roosevelt of New York. Dr. Charles Reitell represented Governor Gifford Pinchot of Pennsylvania.

34. By January, 1931, Governor Roosevelt had laid the groundwork for his future "Brain Trust," for we witness here his receptiveness to the use of college faculty and experts. Professor Leiserson, for example, was to hold important administrative posts with the New Deal in Washington. Professor Chamberlain was to be consulted frequently by leading New Deal personalities, including John G. Winant, and Professor Douglas was to leave the academic field to become a leading advocate of the New Deal in the United States Senate.

35. The speeches, and part of the discussions, are available in *Public Papers, 1931*, pp. 531-82. There were also brief talks by Bryce M. Stewart of the President's Emergency Committee on Unemployment, John H. Fahey of the New England Council, Henry Bruere of New York's Stabilization Committee, Mary B. Gilson of the University of Chicago, and James D. Currie of the Metropolitan Life Insurance Company.

36. New York *Times*, March 19, 1931.

37. *Ibid.*

38. *Public Papers, 1931*, p. 130; and New York *Times*, March 26, 1931.

39. Gub. Papers, "Unemployment-2-General," FDR to G. Hall Roosevelt, February 24, 1931.

40. *Public Papers, 1931*, p. 238.

41. The commission members included Leo Wolman, representing Governor Roosevelt; A. Lincoln Filene, representing Governor Ely of Massachusetts; Professor W. M. Leiserson, representing Governor White of Ohio; Col. Charles R. Blunt, representing Governor Larson of New Jersey; Professor C. A. Kulp, representing Governor Pinchot of Pennsylvania; Professor Elliot D. Smith,

representing Governor Cross of Connecticut; and Commissioner Daniel McLaughlin, representing Governor Case of Rhode Island.

42. *Public Papers, 1932*, pp. 69-74.

43. *Ibid.*, p. 467.

44. New York State Joint Legislative Committee on Unemployment, "Preliminary Report, February 15, 1932" (Leg. Doc. [1932] No. 69 [Albany, 1932]), pp. 4-5; and the New York *Times*, March 4, 1932. In 1933, this committee again recommended postponement of legislation pending further study, with the minority still opposed to delay.

Chapter IX: *"I STAND FAIRLY WELL WITH LABOR"*

1. Frank Freidel, *Franklin D. Roosevelt: The Apprenticeship* (Boston: Little, Brown and Company, 1952), pp. 121-22.

2. New York *Times*, October 31, 1928.

3. *Public Papers and Addresses*, Vol. I, p. 36.

4. To a great extent Al Smith's Industrial Commissioner, James Hamilton, had been carried along by Frances Perkins, who was chairman of the Industrial Board of the Department. Perhaps no part of the work of the Department of Labor was so difficult and so complicated as the administration of the Workmen's Compensation Law. Yet, by the following figures, we see a decided improvement within one year after Frances Perkins was appointed Industrial Commissioner.

INDUSTRIAL ACCIDENTS REPORTED			COMPENSATION CASES INDEXED		
1927	1928	1929	1927	1928	1929
521,624	507,980	523,604	170,556	175,842	199,035

COMPENSATION CASES ADJUDICATED		
1927	1928	1929
171,411	171,704	197,970

There was an increase of 26,000 compensation cases adjudicated in the year 1929 over 1928 and 1927. This work was accomplished without additions to the personnel of the Bureau of Workmen's Compensation. Gub. Papers, "Labor-Perkins," Perkins to FDR, August 27, 1930.

5. *Public Papers and Addresses*, Vol. I, p. 83.

6. Pr. Corres., Box 61, "Fox," H. W. Fox to FDR, January 20, 1929.

7. New York *Herald Tribune*, September 30, 1928.

8. *Ibid.*

9. New York *Times*, March 20, 1929.

10. *Ibid.*, April 7, 1929.

11. *Public Papers and Addresses*, Vol. I, p. 547.

12. B. Levy to FDR, April 8, 1929.

13. FDR to B. Levy, April 9, 1929.

14. Wilford I. King, *The National Income and Its Purchasing Power* (New York: National Bureau of Economic Research, 1930), pp. 141-51; and *New Leader*, October 11, 1930.

15. U. S. Department of Labor, Women's Bureau, *Eleventh Annual Report of the Director of the Women's Bureau* (Washington: U. S. Government Printing Office, 1929), p. 2.

16. Benjamin Stolberg, *Tailor's Progress* (New York: Doubleday, Doran and Co., 1944), p. 152.

17. Gub. Papers, "Cloak and Suit Conference at Hotel Roosevelt, December 12, 1929," R. Ingersoll to FDR, December 4, 1929.

18. New York *Times*, February 5, 1930.

19. New York *Times*, February 12 and 13, 1930.

20. *New Leader*, August 17, September 7, and October 12, 1929.

21. *Ibid.*, March 15, 1930.

22. *Ibid.*, December 13, 1930. Twenty-two years later the Danville mill owners and city authorities were more effective in breaking strikes.

23. *Ibid.*, February 28, 1931.

24. *Ibid.*, June 6, 1931.

25. Gub. Papers, "Endicott-Johnson Strike," L. E. Youngs to Lehman, May 15, 1932.

26. *Ibid.*, Lehman to L. E. Youngs, May 15, 1932.

27. Lehman file, "Battle, George Gordon," undated reply by Lehman to Battle's letter of February 19, 1929. When the union requested a loan of $10,000 in January, 1932, Lehman replied that he was unable to comply because he was no longer active in the business world and couldn't afford such a loan.

28. Senators Wheeler, Nye, Schall, LaFollette, Norris, Costigan, Shipstead, and Walsh (of Massachusetts); Governors Hunt of Arizona, LaFollette of Wisconsin, and Olson of Minnesota; and Mayors Hoan of Milwaukee, Anderson of Minneapolis, and Walker of New York. Walker felt so convinced of Mooney's innocence

that he journeyed to California to plead personally Mooney's case before Governor Rolph on December 1, 1931.

29. Gub. Papers, "Mooney, Thomas J.," FDR to Mooney, January 21, 1932.

30. Pr. Corres., Box 65, "Cil-Cly," A. Hurff to FDR, October 23, 1929.

31. Pr. Corres., Box 162, "Son-Spa," FDR to D. Clark, December 17, 1929.

32. *Public Papers, 1930*, p. 32.

33. Chapters 867 and 868, Laws of New York, 1930.

34. Pr. Corres., Box 154, "Schn," R. Schneiderman to FDR, May 7, 1930.

35. *Ibid.*, FDR to R. Schneiderman, May 12, 1930.

36. Chapter 60, Laws of New York, 1930.

37. Chapter 378, Laws of New York, 1930. Excluded, however, was provision for trial before a jury for persons accused of violating such injunctions. Despite Roosevelt's pleas, the 1931 and 1932 legislatures would not adopt this proposal.

38. Pr. Corres., Box 22, "Bud-Bug," G. M. Bugniazet, International Secretary, International Brotherhood of Electrical Workers, to FDR, May 13, 1930.

39. New York *Times*, January 22, 1929.

40. Gub. Papers, "Prison Labor Committee, Meeting 8/13/30, Executive Chambers," Green to FDR, August 5, 1930.

41. *Ibid.*

42. *Ibid.*, FDR to Green, August 12, 1930.

43. *Public Papers, 1930*, p. 752.

44. Pr. Corres., Box 2, "Alli-Alt," FDR to International Association of Garment Manufacturers, October 8, 1930.

45. *Public Papers, 1931*, p. 40.

46. Chapter 509, Laws of New York, 1931.

47. Chapters 785 and 786, Laws of New York, 1931.

48. Pr. Corres., Box 73, "Hart, Merwin K.," Hart to FDR, September 19, 1931.

49. *Ibid.*, FDR to Hart, September 23, 1931.

50. *Public Papers, 1931*, p. 674.

51. Lehman file, "Cloth, Hat, Cap, and Millinery Workers," Zaritsky to Lehman, May 13, 1932. This letter is also available in *Public Papers, 1931*, with the incorrect date of October 8, 1931.

52. *Public Papers and Addresses*, Vol. I, p. 123.

53. Irving Bernstein, *The New Deal Collective Bargaining Policy* (Berkeley: University of California, 1950), p. 129. This able mono-

graph recounts the development of collective bargaining during its formative period under Roosevelt's New Deal.

Chapter X: "POWER BELONGS TO THE PEOPLE"

1. *Public Papers and Addresses*, Vol. I, p. 45; and Pr. Corres., Box 152, "Sal-Sam," FDR to H. Salant, April 13, 1931. Roosevelt, as State Senator, played a role in the repeal of the charter which had been granted to the utility.

2. This act created a body called the Water Power Commission, consisting of the Speaker of the Assembly, the majority leader of the Senate, the Conservation Commissioner, the State Engineer, and the Attorney General. This Commission had the power to grant licenses to private persons or corporations authorizing the diversion and use for power or other purposes of the water resources of the State. The Water Power Commission went out of existence with the reorganization of the State government on January 1, 1927.

3. *Public Papers, 1930*, p. 694.

4. *Public Papers and Addresses*, Vol. I, pp. 77-78.

5. Gub. Papers, "Water Power, D-L," F. Frankfurter to FDR, January 5, 1929.

6. New York *Times*, January 28, 1929.

7. *Ibid.*, January 2, 1929.

8. *Ibid.*, March 13, 1929.

9. *New Republic*, March 20, 1929.

10. New York *Times*, March 27, 1929. The close affinity of the Republican party to the utility interests is observable in the case of H. Edmund Machold. During the nineteen-twenties Machold had been one of the Republican legislative leaders in Albany. In 1924, he retired as Speaker of the Assembly to become president of the Northeastern Power Company. In 1930, he became chairman of the State Republican Committee, only to resign shortly after the disastrous defeat suffered by the Republicans in the gubernatorial election.

11. Gub. Papers, "Attorney General: Power Investigation," FDR to Hamilton Ward, June 29, 1929.

12. *Ibid.*, Ward to FDR, July 29, 1929.

13. New York *Times*, July 5, 1929.

14. *New Leader*, July 13, 1929.

15. *Ibid.*

16. Pr. Corres., Box 96, "King, W.L.M.," FDR to Mackenzie King, June 17, 1929.
17. *Ibid.*
18. *Ibid.*, King to FDR, July 3, 1929.
19. *Ibid.*
20. *Ibid.*, FDR to MacKenzie King, July 20, 1929.
21. Pr. Corres., Box 24, "Calwell, Robert J.," R. Albertson to FDR, September 27, 1929.
22. Pr. Corres., Box 40, "Davis-Davison," J. L. Davis to FDR, September 23, 1929.
23. Pr. Corres., Box 24, "Calwell, Robert J.," R. Albertson to FDR, September 27, 1929.
24. *Ibid.*, FDR to R. Albertson, October 3, 1929.
25. Pr. Corres., Box 84, "Howe, L. M.," FDR to Howe, October 7, 1929.
26. *Public Papers, 1930*, p. 33.
27. New York *Times*, January 2, 1930.
28. *Public Papers, 1930*, p. 738.
29. New York *Times*, January 2, 1930.
30. Gub. Papers, "Water Power Bill," Carlisle to FDR, January 10, 1930.
31. New York *Times*, January 14, 1930.
32. *Ibid.*, January 15, 1930.
33. Gub. Papers, "Water Power Bill," FDR to Smith, January 14, 1930.
34. *Ibid.*, Smith to FDR, January 15, 1930.
35. *Ibid.*, Lippmann to FDR, January 14, 1930.
36. *Ibid.*, Frankfurter to FDR, January 17, 1930.
37. *New Leader*, January 18, 1930.
38. Gub. Papers, "Water Power Bill," FDR to N. Thomas, January 24, 1930.
39. Pr. Corres., Box 257, "Interviews T," Thomas to FDR, January 28, 1930.
40. Chapter 207, Laws of New York, 1930. The entire act is found in *Public Papers, 1930*, pp. 442-43. Roosevelt's comments, as he signed the bill, are on pp. 438-41, with the incorrect date of 1931.
41. Those appointed to the St. Lawrence Power Development Commission were Robert Murray Haig, chairman, Julius Henry Cohen, vice-chairman and counsel, former Lieutenant Governor Thomas F. Conway, Congressman Frederick M. Davenport, Samuel L. Fuller, and S. Burton Heath, secretary. The "Marketing Board" was composed of John Bauer and John P. Hogan. The legal staff

included W. Charles Poletti, Kenneth Dayton, and A. Mackay Smith.

42. *Public Papers and Addresses*, Vol. I, p. 161.

43. *Public Papers, 1931*, p. 81. In 1929 the electrical utilities throughout the United States received for all classes of services the total sum of $2,017,000,000. The power customers, using 74 percent of the current, paid 42 percent of the receipts. The so-called lighting customers, of whom some 85 percent were domestic, used 26 percent of the current and paid 58 percent of the receipts. Gub. Papers, "Water Power Correspondence, A-C," M. L. Cooke to FDR, January 26, 1931.

44. *Public Papers, 1931*, pp. 84-85.

45. *Ibid.*, pp. 80-85.

46. Gub. Papers, "St. Lawrence Power Development Commission," J. C. Bonbright to FDR, January 20, 1931.

47. *Ibid.*, Bonbright to Frankfurter, January 21, 1931.

48. *Ibid.*, Frankfurter to Bonbright, January 23, 1931.

49. *Ibid.*, FDR to Frankfurter, January 28, 1931.

50. Gub. Papers, "Water Power D-L," E. Keating to FDR, January 23, 1931.

51. *Rural New Yorker*, January 31, 1931.

52. In a message to Senator John Knight, later that month, Roosevelt suggested seven amendments to improve, though not alter, the fundamental principles of the Cornaire bill. The proposed amendments were rejected.

53. New York *Times*, April 3, 1931. Aware that none of the members of the St. Lawrence Commission were experts on rate regulations, a deficiency which would have become serious if the commission's personnel were continued in the proposed power authority, Roosevelt had planned to name five new men to the authority. Gub. Papers, "St. Lawrence," Bonbright to Frankfurter, January 21, 1931.

54. *Public Papers, 1931*, pp. 604-6.

55. Gub. Papers, "Water Power, S-Z," Rosenman to F. J. Shaughnessy, April 3, 1931.

56. New York *Times*, April 4, 1931. The five cities were Ogdensburg, Canton, Potsdam, Gouvernor, and Massena.

57. Gub. Papers, "Water Power Bill," E. B. Crosby to FDR, April 14, 1931.

58. New York *Times*, April 8, 1931.

59. *Public Papers and Addresses*, Vol. I, pp. 201-2.

60. Chapter 772, Laws of New York, 1931.

61. Pr. Corres., Box 174, "Walsh, Thomas J.," Walsh to FDR,

April 15, 1931.

62. Chicago *Journal of Commerce*, May 10, 1931.

63. *Public Papers and Addresses*, Vol. I, p. 164.

64. Gub. Papers, "Power Authority, Walsh, Frank P.," Walsh to Hoover, October 3, 1931.

65. *Ibid.*

66. *Ibid.*

67. *Ibid.*, Hoover to Walsh, July 29, 1931.

68. Gub. Papers, "Power Authority, D-M," FDR to Hoover, August 11, 1931.

69. *Ibid.*, W. R. Castle to FDR, August 13, 1931.

70. New York *Times*, August 19, 1931.

71. Gub. Papers, "Power Authority, Walsh," Walsh to Hoover, October 14, 1931.

72. New York *Times*, October 28 and 29, 1931.

73. Gub. Papers, "Power Authority, Walsh," Walsh to FDR, November 2, 1931; New York *Times*, October 29, 1931; and *United States Daily*, October 29, 1931.

74. New York *Times*, November 5, 1931. The full text of Stimson's letter is available in *United States Daily*, November 5, 1931.

75. Gub. Papers, "Power Authority, Walsh," Walsh to Stimson, November 10, 1931.

76. Typical of State Department tactics was one proposal that the Federal government construct all the works for both navigation and power on the American side, and that New York pay $150,000,000 as its share of the cost. After it was pointed out by Power Authority conferees that payment of such an amount exceeded the costs of all the works both for navigation and power on the American side, that it would defeat State plans for the production and distribution of cheap electricity for the industries and homes of the people, and that, in addition, it would drive industry and American capital across the river, the proposal was dropped. No alternative cost, however, was offered by the Federal government in the remaining conferences. Gub. Papers, "Power Authority, A-C," Walsh to FDR, March 10, 1932.

77. The oral agreements included: (1) The project was to be regarded as a joint enterprise of the Federal government and the State of New York. (2) The Federal government was to be responsible for the general project on the American side. (3) New York would construct the power house superstructures and install the machinery and equipment. (4) New York would have representation on all of the agencies created to plan and construct the

works. (5) New York would pay for its superstructures and their equipment and reimburse the Federal government over a period of years for full cost of the power house substructures, head and tail races, and for an agreed share of the cost of works common to navigation and power. (6) New York would have title to the power houses and own and control all of the power produced on the American side in perpetuity. Gub. Papers, "Power Authority."

78. Gub. Papers, "Power Authority, A-C," Walsh to FDR, March 30, 1932.

79. *Ibid.*

80. *Public Papers and Addresses,* Vol. I, pp. 203-5.

81. *Ibid.,* pp. 205-6; and New York *Times,* July 11, 1932.

82. In Volumes II and III of his memoirs, Herbert Hoover makes no significant reference to this strugggle between the New York Power Authority and himself as he discusses national water resources and the St. Lawrence waterway.

83. *Public Papers and Addresses,* Vol. I, p. 206.

84. Herbert Hoover, *The Memoirs of Herbert Hoover, The Cabinet and The Presidency, 1920-1933* (New York: Macmillan Co., 1952), p. 122.

85. Gub. Papers, "Power Authority, Walsh," memorandum to Walsh following a telephone call from Basil Manly in Washington, on July 11, 1932. Between meetings of State Department and New York Power Authority representatives, Basil Manly represented the Power Authority in Washington in all matters relating to the St. Lawrence waterway development.

86. Lehman file, "Brooklyn Edison," F. H. LaGuardia to Lehman, June 1, 1931.

87. *Public Papers, 1932,* pp. 39 and 74.

88. See William E. Mosher, "Public Utility Regulation," in G. A. Graham and H. Reining, Jr., *Regulatory Administration* (New York: John Wiley and Sons, Inc., 1943), p. 152; C. Herman Pritchett, *The TVA, a Study in Public Administration* (Chapel Hill: University of North Carolina, 1943); and Philip Selznick, *TVA and the Grass Roots: A Study in the Sociology of Formal Organization* (Berkeley: University of California, 1949).

89. *Public Papers and Addresses,* Vol. I, pp. 738-39.

Chapter XI: *"A REASONABLE RETURN"*

1. The Public Service Commission was composed of five mem-

bers appointed by the Governor for ten-year terms. The commission regulated common carriers and had jurisdiction over light, heat, and power corporations, telephone and telegraph corporations, steam, stockyard, and freight terminal corporations, bus lines, and motor vehicle lines. The commission could regulate rates, fix the standards of illuminating power of gas, prescribe the efficiency of electric supply systems, and prescribe uniform methods of keeping accounts.

2. New York *World*, January 21 and 24, 1929.

3. During this period financial interests were issuing more and more securities against the existing property of utility operating companies, which was a symptom of excessive earnings or expected earnings. The danger from this development lay in the possibility that increased fixed charges and dividend requirements would make it difficult, if not impossible, to secure the low rates which Roosevelt desired. Under the existing system the operating companies were not permitted to recapitalize, but overcapitalization of holding companies had, indirectly, much the same effect.

4. Gub. Papers, "Public Utilities Bureau," E. G. Griffin to FDR, February 4, 1929.

5. New York *World*, January 21, 1929.

6. Pr. Corres., Box 257, "Interviews V," Van Namee to FDR, January 25, 1929. Less than a month after writing this letter, Van Namee joined the other commission members in requesting the legislature to grant the P.S.C. control over holding companies and authority to establish a uniform electric rate. New York *Times*, February 15, 1929.

7. *Public Papers and Addresses*, Vol. I, p. 78.

8. *Ibid.*, p. 233.

9. Chapter 673, Laws of New York, 1929.

10. *Public Papers, 1929*, p. 282.

11. Albany *Evening News*, May 9, 1929.

12. New York *Times*, September 17, 1933.

13. Pr. Corres., Box 40, "Davis-Davison," FDR to J. L. Davis, October 5, 1929.

14. New York *Times*, March 30, 1934.

15. The Republican members of the commission, who later endorsed the majority report, were Senators John Knight, chairman, Warren T. Thayer, and William J. Hickey, and Assemblyman Horace M. Stone, vice-chairman, Joseph A. McGinnies, and Russell G. Dunmore. The three Roosevelt appointees, who later offered a minority report, were Frank P. Walsh, Professor James C. Bon-

bright, and David C. Adie. The counsel for the commission was William J. Donovan, and the director of research, Dr. W. E. Mosher.

16. Gub. Papers, "Public Service Survey Commission," FDR to J. C. Bonbright, October 12, 1929.

17. *Ibid.*, FDR to F. P. Walsh, November 30, 1929.

18. *Ibid.*, Bonbright to FDR, November 21, 1929.

19. *Ibid.*, Bonbright to FDR, December 21, 1929.

20. New York State, Commission on Revision of the Public Service Commission Laws, *Report* (1930), Vol. III, pp. 1729 and 1855.

21. Gub. Papers, "Public Service Survey Commission," Bonbright to FDR, December 21, 1929.

22. New York *Times*, February 5, 1930.

23. New York *Times*, March 1, 1930. The other members of the P.S.C. at this time were Lunn, a Democrat regarded as a progressive, Van Namee and Brewster, conservative Democrats, and Pooley, the lone Republican holdover.

24. New York *Times*, February 25 and March 4, 1930.

25. *Ibid.*, March 4, 1930. The other majority recommendations were: to authorize the P.S.C. to secure complete information regarding the identity of stockholders of utility corporations and transactions and agreements between such corporations and holding companies, service agencies, and other affiliated interests; extension of the powers of the P.S.C. with respect to accounting control, the issuing of securities, mergers, transfer of franchises or property, and acquisition of stock by utility corporations; and legislation to enable the State to take advantage of a provision in the Federal law for interlocutory injunctions staying the proceedings in the Federal courts when litigation had begun in a state court to enforce an order in issue in Federal court proceedings.

26. New York *Times*, February 25, 1930.

27. New York State, Commission on Revision of the Public Service Commission Laws, *Report* (1930), Vol. I, p. 53.

28. Gub. Papers, "Public Service Survey Commission," Bonbright to FDR, December 21, 1929.

29. *Ibid.*

30. Southwestern Bell Tel. Co. v. Public Service Commission, 262 U. S. 276 (1923), p. 306.

31. Alpheus T. Mason, *Brandeis: A Free Man's Life* (New York: The Viking Press, 1946), p. 551.

32. New York *Times*, February 25, 1930. A people's counsel

would have inherited the prosecutor-type functions of the utilities commission.

33. Gub. Papers, "Power Authority, Misc. File," Frankfurter to FDR, February 28, 1930. Frankfurter was quite correct concerning the attitude of utilities, for by December, 1937, the president of the Philadelphia Electric Company was publicly endorsing the Brandeis viewpoint on "prudent investment." New York *Times*, December 22, 1937.

34. Gub. Papers, "Power Authority, Misc. File," Frankfurter to FDR, March 18, 1930.

35. *Public Papers, 1930*, pp. 734-39.

36. *Ibid.*, p. 739.

37. The Governor contended that the P.S.C. itself should act as the People's Counsel and should be given all the legal, engineering, and accounting assistance possible. In addition, he feared there would be a division of responsibility if both the Attorney General's office and the P.S.C. were charged with the people's protection in utility matters.

38. Chapters 760, 850, and 865, Laws of New York, 1930.

39. Senate Bill, Int. No. 1433, Pr. No. 2501, 1930 legislative session.

40. New York *Times*, April 1, 1930.

41. *Public Papers, 1930*, pp. 234-37.

42. *Ibid.*, pp. 240-42.

43. *Ibid.*, p. 736.

44. Pr. Corres., Box 148, "Rosenman, Samuel I.," Rosenman to FDR, May 23, 1930.

45. See reference to Tom Mooney in Chapter IX.

46. Gub. Papers, "Public Utilities Bureau," FDR to C. C. Dill, May 29, 1930.

47. Pr. Corres., Box 67, "Grav," H. N. Graven to FDR, June 30, 1930.

48. Pr. Corres., Box 121, "More-Morf," F. H. Morehead to FDR, September 29, 1930.

49. Pr. Corres., Box 7, "Baker," J. G. Baker to FDR, June 30, 1930.

50. Pr. Corres., Box 8, "Bal," Mrs. Ed. Ballman to FDR, August 18, 1930.

51. New York *Times*, May 2, 1930.

52. Gub. Papers, "Public Service Commission, Maltbie, Milo R.," Maltbie to FDR, October 14, 1930. An "informal complaint" was any communication received by the commission regarding anything done or omitted to be done by a public service corporation which was not satisfactory to a customer, the remedy for which did not

involve an order by the commission changing the existing practices of the utility which were of general application.

53. Gub. Papers, "Public Service Commission, Maltbie, Milo R.," Maltbie to FDR, January 27, 1932.

54. Lehman file, "Brooklyn Edison," Maltbie to Lehman, June 5, 1931.

55. The Long Island Lighting Company, which reported an investment in common capital stock of $3,000,000, had in the seven-year period from 1925 to 1931, paid a total of 307½ percent in dividends to its stockholders. This meant that the company had paid back to its stockholders over three times the book investment. In 1931, despite the economic depression, the company paid 60 percent dividends. Gub. Papers, "Public Service Commission, Maltbie, Milo R.," Maltbie to FDR, December 19, 1931.

56. Pr. Corres., Box 159, "Sin-Sir," undated editorial from Chicago *Journal of Commerce*, attached to letter from H. Sites to FDR, November 26, 1930.

57. Personal Papers of Louis Howe, 1928-32, Box 85, FDR to S. R. Bertron, October 1, 1930.

58. *Public Papers and Addresses*, Vol. I, p. 261.

59. *Wall Street Journal*, July 1, 1931.

60. Pr. Corres., Box 175, "Warren," F. Welch to Editor, *Wall Street Journal*, July 2, 1931. A week after his attack on Roosevelt, Thomas Woodlock proposed to Colonel Edward M. House a personal discussion of the utility issue with Roosevelt. Colonel House conveyed the proposal to the Governor, who thereupon advised the journalist that he could not see where both could have a dispassionate discussion on utilities when he, Woodlock, in his letter to Colonel House, had attributed to the Governor "in five numbered paragraphs, opinions which are so stated as to be wholly incorrect." Pr. Corres., Box 182, "Wooda-Woods," FDR to Woodlock, July 15, 1931.

61. Pr. Corres., Box 175, FDR to S. Warren, Jr., July 14, 1931.

62. Los Angeles G. & E. Corp. v. Railroad Co., 289 U. S. 237 (1933).

63. New York *Times*, December 22, 1937.

64. *Public Papers, 1932*, p. 39.

65. *Ibid.*, p. 97.

66. William E. Mosher, "Public Utility Regulation," in G. A. Graham and H. Reining, Jr., *Regulatory Administration* (New York: John Wiley and Sons, 1943), p. 163.

67. *Public Papers and Addresses*, Vol. I, p. 727.

68. *Ibid.,* p. 731.

69. James W. Fesler, *The Independence of State Regulatory Agencies* (Chicago: Public Administration Service, 1942), p. 61.

Chapter XII: *"HONEST GRAFT"*

1. New York *Times,* March 24, 1931. The other members of the committee included Republican Senator Leon F. Wheatley of Steuben County and Democratic Senator John J. McNaboe of New York City; Assemblyman Abbot Low Moffat of New York City, Hamilton F. Potter of Suffolk County, and William Lamont of Orange County, all Republicans, and Louis A. Cuvillier of New York City, a Democrat.

2. See New York *Times,* January 16 and 17, February 14 and 20, June 26 and July 3, 1931; and Robert Bendiner, "Racketeers and Reformers in City Hall," *Park East,* October, 1951, pp. 43-50.

3. See New York *Times,* March 10, 1931; and *Public Papers, 1931,* pp. 413-14.

4. Gub. Papers, "Crain, Thomas T. C.," FDR to Seabury, March 8, 1931.

5. See New York *Times,* April 19, 1931; and *Public Papers, 1931,* pp. 416-48.

6. Gub. Papers, "New York City Investigation (Folder 3)," press release by FDR, March 18, 1931. Under the State Constitution, or under city charters, the Governor has the power to remove specified county or city officials. On receipt of charges seeking removal of public officers, the Governor can do one of three things: take no action on the charges; invite the official complained against to submit his version of the facts complained about; or take evidence concerning the charges either in person or by a commissioner appointed by him.

7. *Public Papers, 1931,* pp. 455-84.

8. *Ibid.,* pp. 485-86.

9. Pr. Corres., Box 85, "Howell, Clark," FDR to Howell, March 31, 1931.

10. Tammany was fully aware of the type of investigation they might expect from Seabury. During the latter's inquiry into the Magistrates' Courts, the average amount of one day's hearing was 80 pages of transcript totaling some 15,000 words, the equivalent of four months of work by the September grand jury investigating

racketeering in New York County under District Attorney Crain. New York *Times*, April 15, 1931.

11. New York *Times*, March 31, 1931.

12. *Ibid.*, April 12, 1931.

13. *Ibid.*, May 15, 1931.

14. *Ibid.*, July 22, 1931.

15. *Ibid.*, July 23, 1931.

16. *Ibid.*, August 15, 1931.

17. Chapter 773, Laws of New York, 1931.

18. New York *Times*, September 24, 1931.

19. *Ibid.*, October 5, 1931.

20. *Ibid.*, November 10, 1931.

21. *Ibid.*, October 22, 1931.

22. *Ibid.*, October 7, 1931.

23. See New York *Times*, February 25, 1932; and *Public Papers*, *1932*, pp. 247-87.

24. New York *Times*, April 13, 1932.

25. See New York *Times*, April 27 and 30, May 3, 5, 19, and 21, 1932; and *Public Papers*, *1932*, p. 298.

26. New York *Times*, May 13 and 26, 1932.

27. *Public Papers*, *1932*, pp. 300 and 373-74.

28. See New York *Times*, May 27, 1932; and *Public Papers*, *1932*, p. 299.

29. New York *Times*, May 26 and 27, 1932.

30. *Ibid.*, May 27, 1932.

31. New York *Post*, May 26, 1932.

32. Some 600,000 words were contained in the eight volumes of the Hofstadter hearings, although not all of them dealt with Mayor Walker.

33. See New York *Times*, June 9, 1932; and *Public Papers*, *1932*, pp. 297-300.

34. See New York *Times*, July 29, 1932; and *Public Papers*, *1932*, pp. 310-52.

35. See New York *Times*, August 4, 1932; and *Public Papers*, *1932*, pp. 353-83.

36. New York *Times*, August 7, 1932. Governor Roosevelt selected lawyers Martin Conboy of New York, and John E. Mack of Poughkeepsie, to assist him at the hearings. When Mack became ill, the work evolved upon Conboy and Roosevelt's new counsel, M. Maldwin Fertig.

37. New York *Times*, August 12, 1932.

38. *Ibid.*, August 16, 1932.

39. *Ibid.*, August 20, 1932.

40. *Ibid.*, August 22, 1932.

41. See *Public Papers, 1932*, pp. 404-5; and Matter of Donnelly v. Roosevelt (In re Walker), 144 Misc. 523.

42. New York *Times*, September 2, 1932.

43. *Ibid.*, September 5, 1932.

44. *Ibid.*, October 5, 1932.

45. Gub. Papers, "Walbone-Walsey," L. Waldman to FDR, June 19, 1930. Quotation from FDR is referred to by Waldman as having been sent by FDR on June 13, 1930.

46. See Boston *Globe*, April 3, 1932; Gub. Papers, "Theofel, John," Holmes and Wise to FDR, March 17, 1932; FDR to Holmes and Wise, March 30, 1932; Holmes and Wise to FDR, April 1, 1932.

47. Only the previous August, Sheehy had entered a primary contest for the district leadership at the personal request of Tammany Boss Curry.

INDEX